A Waste of Good Weather

Janice Russell

Janice Russell, PhD, was born in Birmingham. She left home at seventeen to study for her first degree in Sociology. She subsequently acquired three postgraduate degrees, including her MA in Creative Writing, while being a full-time mum. Janice has worked extensively across many cultures, coaching, teaching, developing and writing. She has been a Birmingham Roller widow for twenty years.

More books from Janice Russell:

Fiction

Keeping Abreast (1998) Insight Press
An Algarve Affair (2013) Insight Press

Non Fiction

Out of Bounds (1994) London: Sage
Blank Minds and Sticky Moments in Counselling (1998, 2008) London: Sage
An Introduction to Coaching (2011) London: Sage

This book is dedicated with love and affection to the memory of George Kitson, the Big Man, whose odyssey was full of mischief and adventure, and who was always surrounded by friends and family.
We miss you George, and wish that you were here to read this tale.

It is also for Graham Dexter. My rock when the waves get high.

Acknowledgements

When I write, my aim is to write an intelligent thumping good read that appeals to the universal in us all, while offering a unique and entertaining angle on life. I have been helped in achieving this for this book by several people. Heather Beck encouraged me, and gave me invaluable feedback, as did Liz Richards, Keziah Gibbons, Dave Napthine, Sue Russell-Taylor, Rodger Holcombe, Graham Dexter, and Lisa Selvidge. Some of these people read parts or all of the manuscript over and over, with specific and challenging remarks all of which have improved the book.

My knowledge of the world of the Birmingham Roller fancier came from the privilege and pleasure of going around some national flies in the UK, and from visitors to our house from all over the world. The old Middlesbrough bunch was particularly distinctive, especially DFD, George, Fadgey, and Lez. I had a lot of fun and gained a great deal of knowledge with them, me a feminist amongst rough diamonds who were truly salt of the earth. Wonderful.

Graham Dexter has been chief research man on the Birmingham Roller, and helped with innumerable points of specific knowledge pertinent to the plot. His is the only character in the book that is real, and he has a distinctive place in my life.

My research in Amsterdam was undertaken on various trips with my friend Sara, and one with my big kids Kez and Sam. It was a dirty job, but someone had to do it.

Very big thanks and love to all.

Table of Contents

One
Death Has Reared its Ugly Head

Card XIII - Death

In the Tarots, Death signifies an important ending, while opening the doors for a change of direction. While there may be sadness, there may also be relief and a sense of completion.

Death brings also a verve for life, inviting the Querent to explore the value of their chosen path, perhaps to diversify and listen for the spaces where fate may enter in.

Evie Cutler couldn't say for sure when she realised beyond reasonable doubt that Stan had metamorphosed into a man with the sexual finesse of a doorstop. She could however name the day that she knew something had to be *done* about it, the day of the palm reading.

A Thursday.

She woke reluctantly that morning, aware of Stan's early morning erection heading hopefully in the general direction of her crotch, stopping off en route around her backside.

Which was having none of it.

`For Christ's sake, man, not now, bugger off!'

Her indignance sliced the air. There she was, not even awake, and there was Stan all fired up and ready for docking. No ifs and buts, no warm up, just straight in.

Or not, as the case may be.

Evie sighed, the desire for desire almost overwhelming. She squeezed her eyes tight shut, conjuring memories of when they first met, the days when Stan actually thought it might be good if she was awake, too. She'd fancied him something rotten.

Still did fancy him – he was a good looking bloke.

Yet so much had changed. `Fancy a shag' constituted foreplay these days, often accompanied by a kind of desperate clutching of her body parts, usually, funnily enough, when her back was turned: often when she was washing up, peeling potatoes, or cooking.

So by that fateful Thursday, Evie was at the point that she just had to say no to Stan's clumsy sexual overtures, lacking the energy or inclination to go through the motions, even though she loved him dearly.

Or at least, she thought she did.

The spring of the bed as Stan got out jolted her, and she surreptitiously opened one eye to see him covering himself with his Primark dressing gown, saw him look out of the window. He came across and bent towards her.

`Cup of tea?'

She grunted acceptance.

9

Heard him fart.

Knew that something had to be done. Something more than opening the window to freshen the air.

When Stan brought her the tea, Evie mumbled her gratitude, felt him nudge her face awkwardly with his nose.

`I'll get down to the pigeon shed, then', he said, and with that, another day full of inevitability began.

Pigeon shed.

Very bloody exciting. He spent so much time with those daft birds, Stan. No quick *fancy a fly* attitude there. On the contrary, he had loads of time for gazing at *them*. Evie even caught him talking to his pigeons in a cooing kind of voice, all gentle, soft, and inquisitive.

The kind of voice he used to be in the habit of using for her.

Evie sat up, took a sip of sweet tea from her cup, felt a bitter aftertaste in her throat. She heard their son Damien clodding about, getting ready for work. He'd be out for the weekend now, straight to Susannah's from work, back on Sunday. He wouldn't say goodbye.

Leaving just Evie and Stan, house to themselves.

Evie felt a lump in her throat: tears threatened. She sniffed, and finished her tea.

Once dressed, Evie went downstairs and began cooking the usual greasy breakfast. Clearly, her real life awaited somewhere beyond the confines of domestic bliss. She imagined that when she found it, the claustrophobic feeling that squeezed at her chest would go. She stabbed the sausages with just a hint of violence – *wham!* – cracked the eggs with a touch more force than was necessary – *splat!* She gave the pan a brisk shake, then picked up the phone and rang her best friend Jeannie.

Jeannie answered after two rings.

`Morning, welcome to the madhouse. What can I do for you?'

`Morning. I'd like to order a pigeon outfit please, complete with black stockings and suspenders, so that when I put it on, Bob's your uncle, Fanny's your aunt, me and our Stan can have great sex and enjoy mutual orgasms as we fly off into the sunset.'

`Evie! Everything alright, love?'

Evie could hear the sounds of kids in the background.

`Same old, same old. Listen, Jeannie, d'you fancy a bit of a drink after work, just a half or two? Be great to see you.'

`Love to. I'll come and meet you after your shift. Oi!' Jeannie shouted, but Evie knew it wasn't at her. `Listen, got to go, our Marnie's got Steve's underpants on her head, and they're straight out the dirty wash. See you later!'

Evie hung up. She finished the breakfast, set it on the table, and called Stan. She put on some make up, grabbed her jacket, and set out early to work.

In two days' time, it would be the anniversary of her Dad's death, so she thought she'd give her Mam a bit of time. Evie walked through the streets to her childhood home, graffiti growling at her from walls and paving stones: `Loz woz 'ere,' `Vote UKIP', `Jobs for Brits'. Middlesbrough, narrow and boring, angry and ignorant, not long since voted worst place to live in the UK.

She quickened her pace the last two streets to her Mam's and let herself into the narrow hall. Desiderata hung on one side, exhorting the family to go quietly. Ironic, thought Evie, as her family were all blessed with foghorns where voice boxes should be, though she and her sister had tempered theirs over the years. A crucifix lurched at a slight angle on the other side. *Why'd you want a dead Jew on a stick for an ornament*, Evie had once heard someone say on TV, and she'd never been able to see it the same since. She heard her Mam call out.

`Evie, is that you, pet?'

`Yes, Mam, it's me. How are you doing?'

Evie's mother, Beulah Frances Coburn, shuffled into view, looking thin and far too weary for a woman who was only in her fifties. Evie hugged her, noting how the worn lines of her face flanked an incorrigible twinkle in her eye.

`Come through, pet, I've just boiled the kettle.'

They went into the little middle room.

11

`I've not had time to clean up yet, so you'll have to not mind the mess.'

Evie ignored the apology. Beulah was pure North East stock, brought up to measure her worth by the sparkle on an ornament or the amount of dust on a window sill. Her house was host to massive collections of ornaments, knobbly pieces of china and crock decorated in the gaudiest of colours and boasting copious lashings of curves and crevices, like faults in a rock. These were a challenge to the very art of dusting. So when Beulah apologised for the mess, Evie knew that it didn't mean that the house was untidy. All it really meant was that Beulah hadn't yet had time or inclination to visit the contours of her Mabel Lucie Attwells with a Johnson's cotton bud.

The tea was brewed before Evie had her coat off and her backside parked in one of the lovely old brown leather chairs with its unwittingly tasteful velvet cushions. Beulah sat down opposite.

`I'll be mother,' she quipped innocently, and poured the tea, hot and strong, into china cups which nested neatly on china saucers. Beulah took out a small gold tin, once host to Victory V lozenges, now her tobacco stash, and rolled herself a perfect cigarette in half the time it took most people to shake out a packet of Lambert and Butlers.

`Mam.' Evie couldn't help herself. `I thought you'd stopped after that last bout of flu.'

Beulah looked Evie directly in the eye.

`I have,' she asserted, not a flicker of guile in those discerning eyes. `I'm not smoking *as such*. I just have the occasional rolly.'

`Oh Mam, what are you like.'

And that was that. They caught up on things, not that there was much new to say. Beulah moaned about not seeing their Geraldine, and said she was sure there was something up. She asked after Stan, Evie said he was alright. Beulah recounted stories of Bingo, and old Mrs Cornet up the road going in for her bunions, and Evie told her about her friend Jeannie, and how tired she was.

Neither of them mentioned her dad.

12

Evie left after half an hour with a buzz in her head and that same old hollow in her heart. They say that by looking at her mother you can see how a woman is going to turn out. Evie hoped not. She knew that she couldn't, wouldn't, take on a life like Beulah's, depending on the ITV news and the Sunday People for truth about the world, and the local Mecca for any excitement.

She walked at a pace down the street, swallowing the urge to howl out loud. She wanted her dad. He'd have understood her, helped her to believe that the future could be different. His loss had left a gaping hole in her very being.

Evie got to work on time, and Roy, the chip shop manager, gave his usual friendly welcome. For four hours Evie chipped potatoes, deep fried fish, cleaned up fat, and smiled a lot at the scores of customers who came for their daily cholesterol fix (although according to her Mam, the chips weren't fatty *as such* because they were cooked in vegetable oil.) Then she washed her hands, shed the chippy smelling overall, checked her lipstick and sprayed herself with *Impact*.

Jeannie arrived dead on time, smiley as ever, and they went to the pub and chatted. How are the kids, your Mam, work, the usual. Jeannie fixed Evie with a look.

`Go on then. What was all that about this morning, then?'

Evie took a swig of her lager.

`Oh I don't know, I just get so fed up. I mean I know it sounds daft, Jeannie, but Stan's just so bloody obsessed. I know it sounds daft, but there are times when I really do wonder if only I was a pigeon, I wouldn't get more attention. Stan knows every feather, every shade of colour on those birds, what form they're on, how much food they need, everything. D'you know, he even has their droppings analysed sometimes, just to make sure they've got the right diet. But he hasn't got a clue about me most of the time.'

Jeannie laughed, spluttered.

`Surely you wouldn't want him to have your droppings analysed?'

Evie gave a wistful smile.

13

`Ha ha. No, but I wouldn't mind him cooing in my ear now and then, spending a bit of time caressing me, at least knowing when I'm aroused. D'you know what, Jeannie, I don't know when he last really saw me, Evie Amanda Cutler, properly, I mean.'

`Evie, he's a *man*, for goodness sake. Men don't do that Pet, it's all Hollywood dreams. And I tell you what, I'm not even sure I'd *want* my Eddie to look too closely at me these days. This old body wouldn't take too much analysing, I can tell you.'

Evie smiled obligingly. Yet, rightly or wrongly, she wanted the magic back with the bloke she fancied, not the impostor who had crept in somewhere over the hours and days and weeks and months and years of monotony that their life had become.

`I suppose you're right', she said to Jeannie. She finished her drink, took the empties to the bar and ordered another, and they started to have a bit of a laugh. If there was a pivotal moment for Evie, it was somewhere in that moan and laugh session that passed for conversation. It was becoming ever more apparent to Evie that if life was to change, then she had to change it.

Which was why, after three more halves of lager and lime, she found herself persuading Jeannie up the road to see Jack Donaldson, the local palmist and Tarot card reader. If Evie's future wasn't here in Middlesbrough, in the footsteps of her foremothers, then she wanted to know where the heck it was.

And Jack was about to give her a number of important clues.

Two
Down the Loft

Birmingham Roller Pigeons

A long time ago, Pensom set the standard of the roller as 'should turn over backwards with inconceivable rapidity for a considerable distance like a spinning ball'; that standard still holds true today. The pigeon must be somersaulting with sufficient speed to give the illusion of a compact, tight ball. If it doesn't do that then it is not spinning with the degree of quality that is required for a Birmingham Roller.

Graham Dexter, *Winners with Spinners* 1997

Once down the garden, Stan assumed the usual position, looking through the barred and netted windows of his pigeon loft, resting his arms on the wooden sill.

`No chance of a bloody shag today, then, might as well see you lot do something.'

Evie was right about one thing, at any rate. Stan did talk to his pigeons. On that decisive Thursday, he was being frank, very frank indeed.

`I'm pissed off with it.'

Stan fancied that a little red hen cooed at him sympathetically.

`It's okay for you, spread and tread, spread and tread.' The hen beat her wings, perhaps a little smugly.

`Me, I wake up every sodding morning with a stonking great hard on and she doesn't want to know.'

Stan straightened up, shook out a bunch of keys, searched through them. `You'd think a man could expect a bit of sex now and then with his own bloody wife.'

He found the correct key and prepared to unlock. `I mean, what's the matter with that.'

More birds were now hanging expectantly on the wire netting, hungry, alert, agog for the next revelation. Stan sighed, exhaling his frustration into the air.

His mood lifted, slightly. His loft was calming, a magical work of art which he made more and more comfortable the more time he spent in it.

`At least make a feature of it,' Evie had said when he first designed it, `if we have to have it taking up half the bloody garden.'

`What d'you mean, a feature?' Stan had asked. `It's a pigeon loft, that's all.'

`For God's sake, Stan, 'she'd said, `put a bit of tasteful colour in it, make it look nice.'

Stan had complied, and feature it was, the heavy wooden slats stained dark red and the window frames a deep bright green. An old brass knocker adorned its yellow door, heavy brass bolts added security. Up one side of the loft there grew a Russian vine,

16

immaculately pruned and shaped, its thick leaves turning colour with reassuring regularity. Vivid hanging baskets festooned every corner of the roof, pinks and purples clashing boldly with the paintwork. Metal placards screwed on here and there added a unique touch: a road sign nicked years ago when he was drunk, *Loft Lane*, and a Homer Simpson picture, courtesy of Damien. The door jamb was inlaid with painted card suits. All the loft needed now was a chimney and a washing line, and he could hire it out for canal holidays.

Stan undid the padlock, slid back the door and stepped into the loft. The cacophony of beating wings, scratching feet and hungry coos intensified, signifying his life's work, years of careful breeding, training and attention. There they were, three kits of twenty beautiful, well-bred pigeons, their heads rocking slightly on elegant necks. They thrust forward eagerly, subtle rainbows of colour glinting in their plumage, chests proud, throats warbling incessantly. Stan swelled a little himself, preened slightly. An onlooker could be forgiven for thinking he was going to coo back at them.

He opened the far kit box.

`I hope you lot are going to cheer me up now.' He began to chase them out.

`Come on, come on, away with you, you buggers.'

Stan shooed the pigeons out of the loft with the aid of a plastic carrier bag tied on to an old mop handle. Then he stepped outside, took a great mouthful of tea, folded his arms and prepared to watch and wait. The birds lifted effortlessly into the waiting sky. He knew that it would take a few minutes for them to gain height and to begin to perform.

Stan's thoughts returned to his domestic problems. Surely a man was entitled to a bit of desire, and surely a wife might be expected to respond now and then?

Surely.

He took another sip of tea, put on his shades as the morning sun brightened the sky. As far as Stan could tell, most women would be really pleased to be wanted. Yet when he tried to touch Evie, what did he get?

A reprimand.

Stan folded his arms, keeping an eye on the rhythmic circling of the birds, his face slightly flushed.

True, he might have got his timing wrong when he slid across the bed towards Evie. But then again, you had to wonder, if not then, when, for Christ's sake.

And when he'd got out of bed and caught sight of himself in the mirror, he thought he wasn't a bad looking bloke. Six foot tall, good musculature, mop of dark hair, green eyes. Nothing wrong in that department.

True, he was wearing shorts with **I Luv Rollers** written on them. When he first got those, Evie had said `very nice, Stan', so he thought she liked them. Today, he suddenly thought them ridiculous, and quickly pulled on his dressing gown.

True, he had then farted.

Stan hadn't used to feel bad farting in front of Evie, but now it seemed like just another unwelcome betrayal by his body. He swigged more tea: the birds were up now, almost ready to roll. He continued to revisit the morning.

Fleeing his embarrassment, he crossed the flowery bedroom carpet and pulled back the nylon velour curtains, praying that the wind would be light. The cloud looked to be hardly moving. Stan knew that first appearances could be deceptive, and studied the movement of the young trees in the garden. When he noticed only the gentlest of sways in their branches, the lightest of flutters in the early autumn leaves, he smiled despite himself.

Sod Evie: at least he could fly his pigeons, see if they had come on the roll. At least down the garden he wouldn't be rejected. You could trust a pigeon to never let you down.

Oh yes.

So Stan went downstairs, soft footsteps trained to know just which creaks to avoid, and proceeded through the living room to the kitchen. Not long since he'd decorated it, tiling it himself, plain beige with an occasional fruit or harvest scene. *I mean*, he thought to himself as his memory traversed the labours of his conjugal love, *harvest scenes – how much more can a woman ask for?*

He filled the kettle, blue to match the rubbish bin and bowl, a pound for the pair from a car boot sale. The kettle was from Argos, Evie insisting that electrical equipment be bought from a reputable store. Most other stuff came from the lads, you never asked where they got it.

Once the kettle was switched on, Stan walked through to the bathroom, an extension on the back of the house. Cold air enveloped him, and he shivered, turning on the shower and letting it run while he peed, and then while he brushed his teeth. He looked at himself in the mirror for the second time that day, in close up now. A few lines circled the sockets of his eyes, hints of grey peppered the stubble on his chin. He scrubbed hard to ward off decay, forcefully spat out the toothpaste, and pulled out his tongue to check for fur quotient. He grimaced, abandoned the unsatisfying image he had created, stripped off and walked into the shower. Hot water ran over him with the soothing caress of which he'd felt cheated just moments before.

Now, in the garden, Stan was irritated, remembering himself doing all the nice things that a husband should do. Once showered, he'd made the tea, china mug for Evie, small size, milk and no sugar, giant mug for him, on the side of which was written **I Luv Rollers**, just like on his underpants. He took the tea up to Evie, even tried a cautious kiss.

And that had been that.

Stan worried about Evie sometimes, the set of her mouth a little tight these days, so different from the upturn that it used to have: but then he worried about all sorts of things, not least of which was where the next mortgage payment was coming from. And whether the black bald hen would lay. Stan sighed once more, a deep and solitary event, his frustrated breath dissipating in the morning air. He switched off his domestic channel, gave his attention to the birds, which were starting to perform and demanding his full concentration.

`You're kitting well, at any rate,' he noted, as the birds flew together, luminescent feathers twinkling in the sun. One or two of those birds would be influencing the rest to stay up, but you'd never know it unless your eye was trained. Stan's eye had been trained for over twenty years. He watched with anticipation, as twelve birds did backwards somersaults in the air, rolling in unison at high speed before gracefully stretching out and rejoining the team. Twelve! Come on, you buggers! And you could bet your bottom dollar that if his mates Frank or Doc or Akbar were here, the birds wouldn't be doing a bloody thing.

Stan stood for twenty minutes, gulping intermittently at his tea, talking to his little beauties all the time, picking out each bird individually, and marvelling at the spectacle they made.

`Go on, go on, break on the turn, break on the turn.'

He focused on a blue, its blue grey feathers sleek and oily. `By, but you're a cracker. Definitely breed from you next year.'

Then a red.

`Wow, if you fly like that in the All England, I'm in with a chance.'

Stan's spirit soared, wondering which bird to pair with which next year, whether to mark that mealy hen's tail feathers with a bright dye to help him keep an eye on it, wondering how far the blue of the sky stretched for. His thoughts flew along until he became aware of Evie's voice wafting into earshot.

`Stan,' he heard her calling, `Stan. Your breakfast's ready.'

`Coming,' he shouted back.

As ever, Stan had timed the morning routine immaculately. The old birds were beginning to drop, and came down fully on cue to the rattle of the corn tin. Stan fed them, trod the path to the back door. He'd fly the youngsters later, and feed the stock birds. But first, he'd get fed himself. The smell of frying bacon beckoned, and he welcomed the security of his plate of bacon, eggs, sausages, tomatoes, four slices of white bread, more hot sugared tea.

'You're a star,' he told his Evie, as he settled into his chair. He cut his breakfast into chunks, sausage to go with the tomatoes, bacon with the eggs. Then he cut the bread into squares, and on each square placed one or other combination ready to fork them into his mouth, one by one, once he had opened the morning paper.

Half Human Hedgehog Found in Carrier Bag! the headline screamed, and Stan began to lose himself in a world full of fantasy, women, football, and adverts for products that could provide him with a lifestyle he would never be able to afford.

`Stan, have you heard a word I've said?'

`Sorry, pet, I was miles away. Time for work already?'

`I'm telling you, I'm going to me Mam's first for a bit, she's not been well, and then Roy wants me to get in early. The money'll come in handy. See you later.'

Stan looked up, noticed the close fit of Evie's short black skirt, and the stretch of black Lycra over her chest. She had on a turquoise polyester jacket over the top, setting off the light streaks in her hair. A shock of arousal churned his belly. Then he noticed the cheap tatty shoes, which Evie had bought from the catalogue last year, her `everyday shoes,' not doing justice to her slim ankles. He avoided meeting her eyes in case his own revealed his shame.

She deserved better.

`Yeah, see you later.' Stan retreated into his breakfast and his paper.

Once finished, he took his plate to the kitchen, washed up, dried up, and cleaned all the shiny new surfaces. Stan was particular about the state of the house, even more so since he lost his job four years before. He noticed a lot now that he hadn't used to.

The morning post fell through the letterbox. Three letters. An electric bill, red. A weight of anxiety hovered around Stan 's heart as he wondered how they'd pay it. A letter for Evie, stamped by the local college.

Evie. The weight intensified. He loved her as much now as the day they'd married, and couldn't understand why it seemed as if they were constantly between each other. He wished he could take her away, somewhere fabulous, just the two of them on their own like it used to be before the drudge set in. Daft thoughts: no good thinking about what you can't have.

The third letter surprised him. It was addressed to Stan Cutler, and postmarked Netherlands. Fancy that – Stan Cutler had a letter from the Netherlands.

Now, what could that mean?

Three
Fool's Journey

Card O – The Fool

The Fool represents the beginning of a new journey. He reminds us that life is full of surprises, that we have unlimited potential, and that every moment can be spontaneous. The Fool heralds a change of direction, one that will guide you onto a path of adventure, wonder, and personal growth (or in Evie's case, down to the local fortune teller).

His message is to trust your natural responses. If you are facing a decision or moment of doubt, the Fool tells you to believe in yourself and follow your heart no matter how crazy or foolish your impulses may seem.

As fate would have it, Jack Donaldson had two cancellations that afternoon, if Evie and Jeannie would care to wait for fifteen minutes. Evie raised her eyebrows at her friend: the universe was on their side. She chuckled.

`Hope I can remember what he says.'

`We could write it down for each other?'

Jeannie didn't have to make the suggestion twice. Evie grabbed her arm, and the two women nipped out to the newsagent's, bought a pen and a pad, then flew back into the shop, seating themselves on high back chairs. Evie looked hard at the receptionist, a woman with a heavily powdered face reminiscent of the Sahara desert; she hovered between the desk and the curtain behind which Jack sat telling the future.

`You'll have to pay up front.'

Evie nodded, and they paid up. She began to calculate how much the shop must take each day if every consultation was the same as hers and Jeannie's, twenty five pounds for a full reading and twenty for a quickie. She and Jeannie were both having quickies, just manageable if they made the weekly shop at Aldi's for the next couple of weeks or so instead of Morrison's.

Stan would have a dicky fit if he knew how much Evie was blowing but then sod it, he always had enough for his pigeon corn, and goodness knows what he'd spent on the loft these last twenty years. Evie wanted her palm read, and she was going to have it.

If the shop were open from nine till six every day, that would be two hundred pounds a day; six days a week, forty-eight thousand pounds a year and twelve weeks holiday. Take off eight thousand, say, for running costs, and you're still doing pretty well. Evie whistled softly to herself: why couldn't she do something like that? She had to get to life beyond the chip shop.

Sahara face smiled professionally, put the money in the till, and ushered the women behind the curtain where Jack sat, about to reveal the secrets of their destiny.

Jack Donaldson was in his sixties. He must have been bonnie at one time, but now displayed a gauntness common to large boned

24

men. There was something surprisingly shabby about him. His fingernails were long and yellowed, slightly curved at the end. His hair was more fawn than grey, his teeth uneven. He looked at the world through transparent watery eyes, and smiled.

`Who's first?'

Jeannie tilted her head towards the client chair, for Evie to go first. Evie lowered herself into a padded velvet covered seat, which moulded to her shape. The table between her and Jack was covered by a dark green chenille cloth, like the ones that Evie's relatives always used to have in front rooms saved for best, a small fringe reaching down towards the floor. Four packs of Tarot cards sat on top, and Jack Donaldson searched Evie's face with his eyes.

`Tarot or palm?' he said. She deliberated briefly. The Tarot cards were pretty, their pictures like doorways to another world. On the other hand, the palm reading might be good because the palm was a part of Evie's body, the lines of destiny physically hers, growing and changing with her life. Evie remembered someone telling her that the Greeks used to read palms, and let's face it, they'd done alright for themselves; they'd had all those philosophers, hadn't they, as well as inventing that lovely aniseed drink someone had brought her back from holiday one year.

`Palm please.' She'd taken off her wedding ring so that Jack wouldn't have unnecessary clues.

`Place your hands palm down on the table.' Jack spoke with authority, and Evie did as she was told. Jack contemplated them for a moment without touch. Evie's heart was quickening with anticipation.

`Your thumbs are distanced yet pointing towards each other. I would say that you are married' – he paused, looking slightly puzzled – `or at least in a very close relationship: but there's a gap between you and the man you love.' Evie tried not to blink. `You work with your hands, and they show strength and courage. Sometimes you feel frustrated with what you're doing with them, and would like them to be more flexible, more energetic.' He paused again, this time looking Evie in the eye. She was determined not to respond, not to give anything away. So far, he was being accurate, but general. So what. He lifted her fingertips, suffused them with surprisingly sensual warmth.

`The length of your fingers shows an artistic talent, probably in some kind of performance. I'm not quite sure what it is, except I'm certain that it's visual. Could be painting or photography, but no, I'm sure from the length of your fingers that it involves you performing in some way.'

Evie stilled her brow, her mouth, tried to make her face a mask. It wasn't easy. Excitement tingled through her veins. Performing. Evie loved to dance, had lessons all through childhood to her teens, had even dreamed once of being a professional, whirling around in sequined dresses like they did on *Strictly*. It had never happened, just another dream that she'd given up for Stan.

Stan with two left feet.

She concentrated on Jack's voice, as he turned over her hands to reveal her palms. The silence clung to the room: she was aware of her heartbeat, loud and insistent. Jack spoke gently.

`I see a strong life line here; your health is good and robust. You will live to be in your eighties, possibly nineties.' Evie shrugged inside. Longevity wasn't big in her family just now. Nearly a year since her dad had died from lung cancer, never even reaching sixty. He'd worked all the hours God sent, labouring for a better life, saving for a retirement he would never know.

She fought a tinge of bitterness. Jack was spinning a line. He could see nothing.

`And here, on your lines of affection, I see that you have a child, just one. I think it's a boy?' He ran his finger lightly over her palm, causing it to tingle. He raised an eyebrow. Evie felt her cheeks flushing slightly: it was getting harder to remain impassive. `Your fate line tells me that this is a time of great change for you. There has already been unrest, recently. Some time within the last year. It could be a death, or perhaps a separation. Something you couldn't stop happening. There's sadness, and regret.'

Now he was getting closer.

`But these feelings won't last. As your loss becomes more bearable, it is keeping you in touch with the value of your life, and will open up new opportunities, a new beginning for yourself in ways that you may not yet understand. Look,' he said excitedly, indicating a line on Evie's hand, `your line of fortune gets stronger as you go through life. It reaches all the way to the finger of Apollo. Great, unexpected things can happen to you, and you know, you will never be short of money, you will always have enough, though you may not know that yet.' He paused for breath. `Yes, my dear, it's looking like the best is yet to come. You must be optimistic. You must take control of the changes you want.'

He prattled on then, and for some reason Evie was distracted by a sense of wanting to cry. Jack was right: he had to be, otherwise she might as well give up. The best had to be yet to come. She could see her Dad's face so big, smiling, the gap in his bottom teeth giving him a distinctiveness that she had loved. She saw his eyes, so alive right up until the cancer had dulled them with its pain. Death had freed him from the suffering. Sometimes she felt like the pain of her grief just got worse.

Jack's voice was strong.

`You will travel, young woman, there will be opportunities overseas. You will look deep inside yourself and find parts that you didn't even know you had, and you will succeed. What I can't see is if the partner who loves you will be with you. There is a question mark in your hand, a slight gap within your girdle of Venus. There will be a short break, but then I don't know if there's someone new or someone old.'

He looked Evie in the eyes and must have seen the emotion. As if on impulse, he reached out to his pack of Tarot cards, pressed them into her left hand, and told her to shuffle them. She was spellbound, compliant. He told her to pick out a card and to give it to him.

Card number eighteen.

`Ah,' he said, `Major Arcana.'

Evie had no idea what he was on about.

`The Major Arcana shows the journey of life,' he explained. `And in each lifetime we have many journeys. We are all born the Fool, Evie, much to learn and little to carry. As we complete each loop of our journey, so we become the Fool again, ready to leave our baggage behind, to move forwards, to meet people and experiences from which we can learn. When the Major Arcana shows, it means change is coming.' He laid the card on the table, and smiled.

`The moon,' he said, `very apt. The moon is a card of three levels. A full moon, a crescent moon, and here, look, a waning moon.'

Evie looked more closely at the card. Moons, dogs, two pillars, dew drops falling from a full moon onto the ground. Evie thought of tears watering plants, making new growth.

`This represents the emotional you, the mental you, and the spiritual you. It is a strongly female card. It represents lunacy.'

She laughed, spoke for the first time. `That's about right, I suppose.'

He stopped Evie with his hand, before she could belittle herself `Lunacy,' pronounced Jack, `is a truly wonderful characteristic. The influence of the moon, its tides, its cycles, is ever present. This card represents for you the urge to be in touch with your inner self. It is very creative, and at its best, it is the quality that blends you with nature, risk, achievement, and light. There is just one caution. Lunacy can turn to madness if you become too bound up in an excess of emotion. You must remember two things to steer the right course.'

Evie was all ears.

`One, remember to connect to the outside world, and secondly, remember that the light of the moon must shine on everyone.' He fixed her with his eyes. `In other words, beware rushing into something without thought for others.' He paused. `Trust yourself, trust yourself deep down, remember your values, and then go with your moon into a starlit sky.'

He dropped the card. The consultation had finished. Evie was dumbstruck. A screech from Jeannie broke her trance.

`Evie Cutler, you'll be on the stage yet, you dark horse.' Evie blinked, made a watery kind of smile, swapped places with Jeannie, and took over the pen and pad. She knew that her reading had been a mix of lucky strikes and generalisations that Jack must make to everyone, and was surprised that it had so much power. Yet as she listened to the reading he gave to Jeannie, and wrote it down, Evie realised that their fortunes couldn't possibly have been just interchangeable spiels. Jack had Jeannie down as having four children, and although she only had three, she'd lost a little girl at birth, stillborn: every mother's nightmare, labouring to deliver the lifeless body of a child strangled by its own life line. Evie saw Jeannie glimpse the memory as Jack spoke. Good with words, Jack said, and that was true too. Jeannie worked in the town bookshop, she'd just found the job after years of backbreaking shifts at the local newsagents. Reading was her passion, her safety valve; it kept her sane. So she and Evie couldn't have swapped readings, not really – apart from the best being yet to come, that is, which he said to Jeannie as well, and which was a relief for them both.

Jack didn't do the card thing with Jeannie, and outside, linking arms, Jeannie reckoned that he'd fancied Evie, but Evie knew better. It was something much spookier: he'd seen something in her eyes that had made him want to encourage her, to reassure her. It was magical.

When Evie got home, she could see that Stan was pleased to see her, and accepted his offer of a cup of tea. She went for a bath, soaked the day out of her bones, went down to cosy up in front of the fire.

Stan was going out, that's why she could remember the day so well. Thursday – you could set your weekly calendar by it, same routine for Stan for the last twenty years. Thursday night was lads' night out, rain or shine. If your wife was giving birth, you'd to get drunk to celebrate; if someone had died, you'd to drown your sorrows; if you'd been made redundant, you'd to show the bastards that they'd never have you beaten.

That night, Evie didn't much care why Stan was going out: she was just glad to see him go, leaving her space to digest the different elements of her day.

Four
In the Shed

Rollers are both unique and strange creatures, not dissimilar to the people that own them...

Graham Dexter, *Winners with Spinners* 1997

Stan was curious – a letter from the Netherlands. Who on earth would be wanting to contact him from all those miles away? He took the neatly penned envelope to his chair by the fire, opened it carefully along the flap. He spread out the single sheet of typed paper, and read.

Dear Stan Cutler,

My name is Jan van Deuzen. You may know my name, I am a Dutch pigeon fancier and visited England five years ago. I am writing to you from Utrecht, in Holland, for myself and a friend. For us the hobby is comparatively new, but our club is beginning to thrive and some of our fanciers are now starting to breed some good birds. We know of you of course as one of the great pigeon fanciers of England, and we would very much like to come and meet you, to enjoy your pigeons, and to learn from you.

So, Stan, we want to know if the two of us can come and visit you and your friends next month or the month after - maybe early October? We would like to see your birds, and to meet also the great Doc Weaver, and if possible to go to your Midlands region to see Gordon Stoneman. We would like to come in three weeks' time, flying to Leeds/Bradford airport, which I believe is near to your good selves. It would be me, and Allan Kychen. Please could you telephone me as soon as possible or contact me on my e-mail, jan.666@agw.com Phone numbers are 030 289 4353, or my mobile is 030 95 128542. We look forward very much to meeting you all, my friends.

With best wishes to our fellow pigeon fanciers, Jan van Deuzen.

Stan let out a breath, re-read the letter. *One of the great pigeon fanciers of England.* Men from Holland wanted to come all this way, especially to see his birds.

Where would they stay? How would he feed them? What if his pigeons wouldn't perform? He went straight to the phone, and dialled Doc`s number. He got the answer phone.

Hello, you're through to Jim and Maggie Weaver, sorry we can't get to the phone, we're either out or in the bath or somewhere, but if you leave a message, we will get back to you as soon as we can. Thank you.

Bloody answer phones. Stan was brief.

`Doc, it's Stan. Give us a ring as soon as you can.'

Stan 's impatience was stifling, knowing that neither Frank nor Akbar would be around until later. He picked up the *Daily Rag*: he put it down. Nothing for it but to go to the loft and survey his livestock. Gorgeous. Look at that little mealy, the white down on its neck emerging from a chocolate-coloured ring, the beautiful ash red of its feathers, its eyes like that of a toy teddy bear, deep and dark ringed by a soft pink. Worth a fortune. Not that he would sell, although he'd considered it from time to time when they'd been really broke.

Stan had read recently about an increased trade in racing pigeons, that it wasn't unusual to get twenty thousand pounds for a top racing pigeon. And he knew one bloke, an Arab he was, who'd paid twice that for a prize Birmingham Roller. But that wasn't what it should be about. Stan bred his own, swapped with other respected fanciers for a breeding season, or lent them out to keen newcomers to the hobby. He didn't agree with selling them, just like he didn't agree with Middlesbrough FC buying in foreign players, however bloody good they were, and then charging the earth to get into a match at the Riverside stadium. It was the spirit of the hobby, the breeding on home territory, the sense of belonging that was important. Any bugger with money could buy good stock, it meant nothing. Stan's mind was racing as he turned out the young birds.

`Holland,' he told them, proudly, his little confidantes. `They're coming from Holland to see us.' He watched them into the sky.

33

Same sky as Holland, but how different were the gardens onto which the sun shone over there? All the pictures showed windmills and rivers, flat fields. Holland wasn't really far, but Stan had never been.

Stan dreamed away a full thirty minutes, watching and imagining, until the pigeons began to drop, circling lower all the time. He fetched the old corn tin, filled it up, and shook it at them, rattling it and calling to them to get in.

`Howay, howay.' They were coming closer, pecking greedily. `Come on,' he clucked, `come on, away with you now.'

Fed, watered, admired, and locked up, Stan left the pigeons to their own devices, and went back into the house. A card was sitting on the mat in the hall.

We called to read your gas meter. We will call again tomorrow, a.m.

Shit. More bloody bills. No time to lose: what a stroke of luck that he'd been out in the garden, that they hadn't been able to get in. Stan went directly to the back shed, unlocked it, and clambered over to the far corner, behind the rusty old bike that he was going to do up one day. He fought his way through cobwebs and hints of damp and lifted an old rug. There it was! The spare gas meter. Stan heaved it up from its corner and manoeuvred it into the wheelbarrow, gathered up the smelly old rug and threw it over the lot. He wobbled his way out of the shed with the wheelbarrow, pushing it to the back door. He heaved the meter into the kitchen, and placed it outside the cupboard under the stairs. Then he went back to the shed, collected his tools, and brought them back to the house, stopping to switch off the gas main, under the sink.

Stan opened the gas cupboard, looked at the reading on the gas meter. Far, far too high for a man of his means. Meticulously, methodically, he wrenched every bolt, undid every nut, until the meter came easily away from the wall. Then he placed it in the wheelbarrow, covered it with the rug, and pushed the new load down to the garden shed, where he hoisted it into the corner, covered it over, and shut the door. He ran to the house and connected the replacement meter, the one the gasman read last time, the one the gasman always reads. He tightened bolts, turned on the mains, and turned on the fire up full, switched on the gas cooker, and put on the central heating. The meter had run only a week since the last reading, just as well to top it up again. Sweating, he replaced the tools, and locked the shed door. He smiled to himself: he might not bring much money in, but by heck he knew how to keep the bills down. He settled down to the oblivion of daytime telly, wishing away the rest of the day until he'd be seeing the lads.

Evie arrived home at about five o'clock. She had, he fancied, a queer look on her face. He could see that she'd been drinking, probably with Jeannie, and was slightly flushed.

`How'd your day go, Evie love?' Stan was up on his feet to make her a cup of tea. `There's a letter for you.'

`Thanks. So so. How about yourself?'

`Aye, not so bad.' Stan went through to the kitchen, thoughts racing, made a fresh brew, and brought it to Evie, who was sprawled on the sofa, cheap shoes off, feet lapping up the warmth of the fire.

`This is on high – we'll have a huge bill.' `No. It'll be alright. What's in your letter?' Evie looked into his eyes.

`Just a college thing. I think I'm going to go and do an English class. I'm not sure now though. In fact, I might just do the performing arts.' She paused, and Stan discerned a faraway look in her eyes as she watched the blazing fire, its fake flames licking the air, crackling with pent up energy. Stan followed her gaze. When he was a lad, he used to throw salt on the fire to turn the flames blue. So many colours in that fire, so many shapes. Faces, mountain ranges, animals, wild dragons. Dreams. What did Evie see? He didn't know what to say.

`I've had a letter as well, look, it's from Holland.' Evie blinked, looked at him.

`What's that for, then?'

Stan passed the letter to her. `Pigeon men.'

`Oh aye.'

Her attitude changed, then, almost dismissing the contents before even seeing them, soon passing the letter back.

`So where will they stay? You'll have to clear that room out, mind. Maybe Damien'll go and stay at Susannah's for a while. So how else has your day been?'

Long, he wanted to say, long and lonely, and to be honest with you, I've missed you.

`Not so bad, you know, the usual. The birds are great, and I think I've decided to pair that mealy cock with the red badge hen. That cock`s a hell of a roller, and he kits well. The hen's a good roller too, a bit deep mind, but very steady, very consistent, so I think they'll make a good family.'

Evie gave a half-hearted smile and stifled a yawn. She stretched.

`I'm knackered, Stan, I'm going for a bath.'

Stan watched her put down the empty teacup, a slight ring forming on the cheap wood table. He was tempted to follow her. He loved her skin after a bath, but the shadow of the mornings events stopped him. He went instead to the kitchen, where he peeled potatoes, pricked sausages, and when Evie came down, bangers and mash was ready on the table. She was wearing her pink dressing gown; she looked young, her face fresh and clean, and her hair still damp. Still a faraway look in her eyes. She kissed Stan on the cheek, the air around them ever warmer, and then slipped deftly away just as he thought he might circle her waist with his big hands.

After dinner, Stan and Evie sat at opposite ends of the sofa.

`It's hot,' Evie said, `shall I turn the fire down?'

`Just right, meself,' lied Stan, wiping a bead of sweat from his forehead. `Give it a little while.'

They looked towards the TV in the corner of the room, neither of them interested, neither knowing what else to say. At seven, the phone rang. It was Doc.

`Stan? What's up, mate?'

Stan told him briefly about the letter. Details could wait until they were in the pub. He needed to see the lads, to feel the excitement again. Doc arranged to pick him up as usual in half an

36

hour. Stan hung up, went to the bathroom, and washed his hands, his face, and the back of his ears like his old Da had shown him, and his armpits. He sprayed himself with *Lynx*, half price, from the car boot sale, and lots of it. You never knew: the adverts might come true. He went upstairs, found a clean shirt, and put it on. He snuck into Damien's room and took a bit of gel for his hair. Damien was never in on a Thursday, he'd never know.

At the sound of a car horn, Stan ran downstairs, blew Evie a kiss, and left the house. There they were, Maggie in the driving seat, Doc stuffed comfortably into the passenger seat, ready to pick up Frank and Akbar en route, just like every other Thursday night. Asylum beckoned. At least in the pub Stan wouldn't be saying the wrong thing or making the wrong moves. He opened the back door and relaxed into the comfort of the familiar seat with a great sigh of relief.

Five
Retreat from Play

Card IX – The Hermit

The Hermit suggests a period of withdrawal, a desire to turn away from the bustle of society to focus on the inner world, seeking answers within through quiet and solitude. There comes a point in life when you might begin to question the obvious (or in Evie's case, the value of a Thursday night out supping ale in the local halls of debauchery).

The hermit suggests a sense that there is a deeper reality, the search for which can feel a solitary quest. At some point, however, diversions having been stripped away, the fool on their journey will slowly re-enter society and meet up with a friend or mentor, to receive help and, in turn, help others as you progress.

Once Stan went out, Evie turned off the TV and poured herself a glass of white wine. Butterflies inhabited her stomach. The letter from the college had been an offer of acceptance, even though she'd applied slightly late. All she had to do was to go and enrol. Evie was chuffed, and terrified at the same time. It had been difficult to focus on Stan's excitement over his letter, her own initial interest dampened when she'd seen it was from pigeon fanciers.

Evie could have gone out as well, of course: people never tired of telling her what a lot there was to do in Middlesbrough, what with pubs, Bingo, and some of the local new clubs. The girls used to go out regular at one time, you could have set your watch by them at eight o'clock on a Thursday night, and some of them still did.

Evie remembered those nights with mixed feelings. On the one hand, when Damien was little, that Thursday date had been a lifeline. She'd have to get ready, have to put her make up on, and then more often than not get drunk as a lord. Over the years, though, it had stopped being enough. Everything was just a variation on the same theme. Escape from domesticity, that was the first objective, with rediscovery of youth becoming an increasingly common agenda.

Evie sipped her wine, wondering when she'd begun to get uncomfortable, bored even, at some of the girls' behaviour, especially now they were well and truly women. She'd used to be amused at Mam calling her contemporaries girls, even when they were in their thirties and forties. Now it was so easy to do the same. Some of them would flirt with anything in trousers, go out like mutton dressed as lamb, some of the girls had one-night stands, and one, Sue Gibson, had been having an affair for twelve years, and still hadn't been found out. Was it only her and Jeannie who were completely faithful to their husbands, for better or worse: she sometimes wondered which it was. The furthest she'd ever get, they used to tease her, would be to go and ogle a group of male strippers.

Evie tried watching male strippers at the local Mecca on the night that Marty Massive and the Muscle Mavericks were on, a night she could never forget. She'd never played Bingo in her life, but after her dad died, she tried to give Mam a bit of support to get back into the swing of things. She went with her and her friend Aggie.

From the second that they went into the big shiny-mirrored hall of the Mecca, Evie felt as if she'd been sucked into a secret alternative galaxy, filled with women dressed to kill. An aura of strictness, order and earnestness contrasted with a tinsel sea of peroxide blonde or shiny copper hair: layers of shimmering Lycra clothes were sprayed onto women of all shapes and sizes. They all massed together into various queues, so that from an aerial view they formed an undulating carpet of fluorescent mosaic.

The queues were for ticket books.

`Pink, blue, gold, jackpot, green, white, or yellow,' the woman behind the Perspex shield shouted. Mam and her friend Aggie rescued Evie, getting her the right combination, pink and blue for the smaller games, one gold for the special, and one which would give her a chance of the big game. Someone on the North East Mecca Map would win over one hundred thousand pounds that night. Evie paid up, prepared to move on. The cashier looked at her kindly.

`Don't forget yer dabber, mind.'

`What's a dabber?'

Mam grabbed her by the arm, smiled apologetically on her behalf, and yanked her toward another kiosk.

`Yer dabber, to mark your card.'

Evie smiled at the memory of her Mam pushing into the next queue, remembered the selection of large, brightly coloured felt pens designed to obliterate the numbers on your card as they came up. Dab, dab, dab. You didn't even have to draw a neat line through like when she used to play the children's box version when she was little. Just a great splodge on the end of a hard felt knob, placed without precision.

Another unwelcome reminder of sex with Stan.

`What's your favourite colour, pet?' The vendor smiled encouragingly.

`Purple.' Evie smiled gratefully, gave her a pound. Dabber in hand, she went with Beulah and Aggie to a table near the front, and waited.

`Won't be long, pet. Always best to get to the front, see more of the action.'

Evie could swear that Beulah and Aggie were virtually rubbing their hands together in glee. She'd looked around the room. It was packed, just packed with the women in Lycra, some of it clinging like a second skin over young, in your face, curves, some of it barely winning the struggle to keep spreading sagging flesh at bay. The women were like an amoeba, in perpetual motion and perhaps even multiplying in their seats. The noise was incredible, and no one seemed to be self-conscious about who could hear their conversations.

You got how much? Two thirty an hour? I wouldn't get out of bed for that, you might as well stay on the social.

Anyway, I've got to go and have it out next month. The doctor said you don't even have to be cut open these days, so they're taking it down me flue, save any scars. Our Jimmy'll have to miss out on his Saturday nights for a bit though!

I said to him, right, you can bugger off, mate, no daughter of mine's being taken up the back of an alley for her first date out, right, you go out with our Michelle and you treat her like a lady, right, or else you don't get a second chance. I called her as well, mind, fancy letting him do it and then only getting upset because he wouldn't take her for a meal after. You've got to laff.

It was all depressingly familiar, and Evie found herself trying to mentally shut them all up. It was only the caller who could manage that, though. He was a smarmy looking glitter coated man they called Larry, and when he got up on a chair with the lights momentarily dimmed save for a revolving reflector ball right above his head, Evie couldn't believe the abrupt shift in atmosphere: you could almost hear the concentration in the

41

silence. Larry gave out the rules of the game, and suddenly he was away, shouting out numbers that displayed in red on electronic signs which were dotted about the room. Once he was into his swing, the speed was phenomenal, and dabbers dabbed constantly, creating the sound of relentless rainfall. Every time a woman's raucous voice shouted `House!' a great sigh was audible around the hall as nineteen hundred other hungry women scored another near miss. After thirty minutes of frenzied activity, Larry announced a fifteen minute break, and Evie's party queued for pints of lager and trays of chips which were covered in red sauce and little brown hard bits like old scabs about to peel off a knee. They were barely sat down before the Bingo started again, the women responding to `clickety click, sixty six,' and `number seven, I'm in heaven,' the smarmy caller holding them rapt with the power of fortune on his side.

Suddenly, a commotion erupted at the next table, as a red-haired woman of about forty seemed to be choking, desperate coughing becoming a sick wheezy silent scream as foam erupted from her mouth, her face turning puce. In a flash, Evie was up and across to help, her knowledge of first aid leaping from the recesses of her unconscious mind where it had lain since she was a Girl Guide.

`Let me through, I know what to do,' she yelled, muttering under her breath, *keep the airways clear, loosen her clothes, make sure she's not near any heavy furniture or breakable objects, maybe do that chest manoeuvre if she really was choking.*

She heard Larry screaming louder through the mêlée, relieved that someone else had seen the seriousness of the situation: she could use the help. Then she heard what he was shouting.

`For Christ's sake, what are you lot waiting for down there? Grab her dabber, table number fifty three, someone GRAB HER DABBER!'

A woman whom Evie took to be the redhead's friend weighed up the situation rapidly, and just as Evie was moving glasses out of the way, she caught a sniff of sweet perfume mixed with sweaty crotch, as the other woman also climbed over to get to her friend.

42

She yanked the green felt implement from the redhead's hand and snatched her pile of cards, moved swiftly back to her own seat, and shrugged apologetically in Evie's direction.

`Shite, hen, it's the big game, it's the big game. We canna stop now.'

Larry's voice boomed out.

`Two sexy ladies waiting for a date, eighty eight!'

The redhead's friend dabbed manically, marking two cards at once. Evie went to the redhead, thumped her on the back and then did the honours to help dislodge what turned out to be a large wad of chewing gum, accompanied by a quantity of foaming lager. Evie felt stunned. What if the redhead had choked to death, right here on the floor of the Mecca? Why was her friend concerned only with marking the cards? What use would money be then? Evie imagined Stan 's paper heralding the news. *Bumper Bingo Bonanza Won by Fated Foaming Female.* The redhead sat up.

`Can I get you anything?' She shook her head.

`No, I just inhaled me lager, I'll be alright now. Thanks.' Evie was kind of glad to get away, and go back to her own seat, if only to get a calm breath of air.

Later, when the Bingo had finished, the redhead had recovered enough to give her full attention to Marty Massive and his crew, and Beulah had poured a Southern Comfort from her bag into Evie's glass. Marty and the Mavericks came on stage to a great roar from the audience. They did a few acts, wearing leathers, dressing up as firemen. It was hard to take them seriously, even though they were fit, when they were in G-strings, a large helmet and a pair of heavy-duty boots and yellow woolly socks. One fancied himself as James Bond: another carried a large plastic machine gun and posed as Arnie, approaching all the front tables and menacing them with his weapon. Evie didn't see much hint of real sexual prowess, and thought that the gun was probably the only tool he could rely on. Great big thighs, tight backside, and stomach like an oiled concrete slab, yet the bump in his G-string no larger than a Morrisons economy sausage. He turned

43

and wiggled seductively, displaying a dagger tattooed on his arse. Evie was fascinated by the spectacle, watching it all from the outside, just like she did when Stan approached her in bed. Only with Stan it was white cotton shorts with **I Luv Rollers** on them and a big red heart. Very attractive.

Suddenly, the stripper grabbed the erstwhile foaming redhead and hauled her up on to the stage, inviting her to cover him in baby oil. Then he had her pull off his G-string with her teeth while he swiftly hung a silk towel over his crotch. He practically forced her to put her head under the towel which was now all that hung between the screaming women and his manhood, presumably in hopes that she would lick it, suck it or at least blow it a bit of hot air. The audience were going wild. If only he knew, Evie thought, how precarious his manhood was. What if she choked again on his parts, froth obscuring any blood drawn, the audience deceived into thinking that he was having an uncontrollable orgasm right there on the stage, the grimace of agony on his face tragically mistaken for an expression of ecstatic release.

Evie got a grip on herself, just in time to catch Beulah and Aggie screaming wildly, `Get 'em off, get `em off, we want a stiffy, we want a stiffy.' Beulah saw Evie looking: she leaned over and pressed her mouth against Evie's ear.

`It's alright,' she yelled, `I don't fancy them *as such*, it's just a bit of fun.'

Evie smiled weakly, but suddenly felt hot, the taste of bile rising in her throat. She made her excuses despite Beulah's protests and called a taxi home.

She never went back to a Mecca after that.

On that Thursday night after the palm reading, Evie's reveries were jolted by the phone ringing. It was Geri, her older sister. Geri, she who had married into money and got away from it all. Geri the social worker, keen to help the less fortunate, and now a senior manager. She didn't call often these days, not since she'd moved to the new development over Sedgefield way. Sedgefield, jewel of the North East, once the constituency of Mr `call me

Tony' Blair. Mining cottages replaced with exclusive designer estates housing a smattering of `B' list sporting celebrities, handy for Newcastle but far enough away not to have to mix too closely with the salt of the earth locals. There was a new golf course, and good value murder mystery dinner weekends at Hardwick Hall. Evie knew that there was no shortage of young and old men to see to the buildings and maintenance, better than manning a booth at a heritage park.

Geri's deep, designer voice trickled down the phone. `Evie. Dah-ling. How are you?'

Evie responded cautiously. She'd never got used to being Dah-ling. Maybe Geri was after something.

`I'm alright, Geri, I'm well. How about you?'

`I'm fine, Evie, fine. Listen, I'm over your way tomorrow night, wondered if you fancied a meal? There's something I want to talk to you about. Bit of a surprise, really.'

Wow, an honour indeed. Geri and eating didn't really go together. Evie was intrigued.

`Tell me now, Geri.'

`No.'

An echo of authority travelled down the phone lines. Evie could imagine Geri taking children into care, telling their parents `**No, you cannot have the bairn back!'** She could imagine her at a case conference, making her assessments, arguing the toss, getting things to go her way.

`You'll have to wait. It's a surprise.'

Geri had her there. Evie felt compelled to go. And anyway, she fancied seeing her sister.

`Alright. We'll meet at the new Italian on 'Boro Rd. I've got something to tell you, too.'

`Fabulous, Dah-ling. I'll see you at eight. Bye.'

Geri hung up, business like, no messing, no great phone bills. Evie went over to the bureau that she'd picked up at the second-hand shop, took out the college prospectus and snuggled in her dressing gown on the sofa, to read it again, cover to cover. She would go in the morning and register, and she'd start the next week. English, with a drama module in it. Evie wanted to be dramatic, to be European, exotic. She sipped her wine, and smiled.

Six
The Cabbage Club

In the advent of the NBRA, fanciers had a new challenge. New clubs sprouted up all over the country in the knowledge that they could all compete for the National honours. Clubs now have to be vetted to ensure that each has an adequate quality, entry level and quantity of competitions. It is also required of clubs to have annual general meetings, a record of members, published results.

Graham Dexter, *Winners with Spinners* 1997

Stan's night out was a bit special that Thursday, as it was the Annual General Meeting of the Old Cocks Invitation Roller club. He, Doc, Frank and Akbar were the main club members, the other two, Sam Shipston and John Hooper, came on the flies but not to the meetings. They could usually be found in the Cabbage Club for the Thursday night bevy, so Stan would probably see them later on. Frank, Doc and Stan discussed their agenda while Maggie Weaver's car sped them towards the Middlesbrough suburbs. She pulled up outside Akbar's house, and Stan nipped out to ring the bell and summon his friend.

The Akbars' front door was painted deep blue and had a brass knocker in the shape of an eagle on the front. Akbar's house was right on the outskirts of town, a three bedroomed semi plus loft conversion. It had a large bay window with leaded panes, through which a warm glow always seemed to radiate. A tidily kept garden fronted the house, liberally planted with hardy fuchsias, in vivid pinks and purples.

Jasmine Akbar – Jazz, as Akbar called her – came to the door, a strikingly fine-looking woman, blue black hair, deep brown eyes and full smiling lips. She always dressed in a bewitching mix of Western and Eastern clothes, silk trousers, sometimes a sari, sometimes skimpier top, always beautiful colours. Tonight she was wearing turquoise. Jazz spoke with a seductive hint of Punjabi accent, and Stan felt slightly frightened by her, in the nicest possible way. He would hate to offend her, and so although he'd known her for thirteen years, he always called her Mrs Akbar, or Mrs A. Tonight, Jasmine was beaming at him as usual, brown eyes twinkling in welcome.

`Hey, Stan, Akbar's just in the bathroom. Step in a minute.'

Stan walked into a light green hallway, with pictures of family members strewn liberally around its walls. He passed through a stripped pine doorway into the front room, a mêlée of noise and light. Akbar's two sons were playing with friends on a PlayStation; the baby, Bel, was hurtling around in a baby walker, dinner rusk in her chubby little fingers and round her deep red mouth. She squealed in delight when she saw Stan, and headed straight towards him. Stan was torn between a desire to pick her up, and running quickly away before those mucky fingers went all over his best trousers. Jasmine sensed his discomfort, and came to his salvation, positioning herself between the baby and Stan. For a second, he wondered how Mrs A stayed so clean – never a splodge of rusk on her silk – and decided it must be part of the magic that she seemed to carry round with her.

`How's things then, Stan?' Mrs A`s voice was deep. Stan felt a slight tingle, aware of how, if he allowed himself, he could easily fancy her to bits.

`Not so bad, you know how it is.' He gestured toward Bel. `Little un's coming on though, eh? She'll be a heartbreaker that one, when she grows up.'

Jasmine smiled at Stan, turned her head as she heard her husband's footstep behind her. A pair of brown hands encircled her full yet shapely waist. Stan registered the slightest pang of envy, the pang turning to the pleasure that always accompanied seeing Akbar.

`Stan my man, how you doing, old friend.' Akbar shook Stan 's hand with the usual firm grip, pulling him out of the living room and away from domestic bliss, amid a flurry of goodbyes and kisses. He and Stan went down the path and into the Weavers' car. They headed off to Great Broughton, winding their way from urbanity to the semi-rural village. They all thanked Maggie Weaver profusely for her unfailing good will and for the lift.

The old pub at Great Broughton boasted original beams. The beautiful circular rosewood bar was always polished to perfection, mirroring the well-kept wooden panels which encased the three rooms designed around it. Stan was always amused at how Frank's head all but skimmed the beams, Frank's long skinny frame a sharp contrast to Doc's, whose portly belly was supported by a frame of five feet seven, even when he wore his Cuban heels.

Doc bought the first round from the young barmaid. Stan, like the others, couldn't help but be attracted by her slim hips escaping from low slung jeans. He and Akbar both agreed that they could give her one, lucky lass. Frank was quieter; Stan always thought this was because he was raised by a mother and five sisters. Maybe they taught him the value of respect, or maybe he just learned the art of keeping lecherous thoughts to himself. At any rate, Stan thought it neat.

The men settled down round the long table near the log fire and studied the menu.

`Think I'll have a steak.' Stan felt like big food, celebratory food.

`Nice bit of fish for me. By, it's been heck of a day.' Frank yawned widely and took a gulp of his Guinness.

`Yeah, I'll go fish. Got to keep the old waistline trim for the ladies.' Akbar nodded toward the barmaid again, winked conspiratorially at Stan.

Doc went for steak and ale pie in suet pastry. `Can't see as that'll affect the jocking dieting.'

`You? You don't need to diet, Doc.' Akbar jested, looking at Doc's spreading gut, but Stan gave him a quick warning glance. Stan had known Doc for nearly thirty years, knew that under that gruff exterior lurked a sensitive ageing man, whose dreams were stifled beneath the veneer of a successful career and a conservative marriage. Stan had a lot of time for Doc. After all, it was Doc who had helped him into the hobby all those years ago when Stan was just nine years old. Doc`s fifteen year advantage had seemed glamorous at the time; now it carried the mark of earned esteem.

The guys ordered their food, and Frank got the second round. His long legs loped gracefully, and when he ducked again beneath the beam, he grinned at the others, his crooked upper teeth adding charm to his shy demeanour, the crinkles round his piercing blue eyes spreading to meet the first signs of silver at his temples. Stan tried to recall how long he'd known Frank, must be sixteen years. Another good guy, and Stan thanked him when he placed the drinks on the table, folding himself down into an armed chair, crossing his legs to reveal odd socks.

`Cheers.' The four men raised their glasses.

`Been fishing lately, Frank?' Doc was a keen fishing man as well as pigeon fancier, and had met Frank at a charity fishing weekend, in honour of the memory of a mutual friend.

`Not bloody likely. Hey, did you know that there's a fine line between fishing and standing on the riverside looking like an idiot?'

Doc responded, `Suppose you've been spending too much time in that garage of yours. You know what work is, don't you Frank?'

The guys waited for a second.

`It's for those who can't fish.' They groaned, then Akbar spoke.

`Anyway, Frank, how's that loft of yours coming on? I've heard it's so big you can fit a family in it.'

`It's coming on good. Come round at the weekend to have a look, I'll be felting the roof, you could give me a hand. There's four kit boxes, two for the youngsters, one for the yearlings, and one for the old birds. Then there's two breeder sections. Nice big corridor space at the front of every box, and I'm having me phone line extended down the garden. And I've got some great waterers for if I'm away.'

Stan focused intently: not that he was ever away, he reminded himself, but loft design was a big hobby with him. `How d'you mean, waterers?'

`Well, I've got the water piped down to the loft, and I got these little automatic feed waterers from John Mettle's, that shop that a lot of the racer men use. They're small olicups, fed from me mains header tank, just keep them on all the time and it's piped through to each cup. Constant fresh water – I'm really pleased with them.'

`Don't they get mucky?' Doc asked.

`No, they keep really clean, I've got a V perch over the top of them.'

`Brilliant.' Stan was impressed. `I'll come and have a look at the weekend. And I'll give you a hand with the roof, Frank.'

`Think you'll make a better job of it than when you went to Sheffield and put that felt on wrong way up for old George?'

51

Akbar innocently reminded them off the young Stan 's enthusiastic mistake.

`Yeah, and he never knew till it peed it down and found the nest boxes full of water next morning.' Doc chuckled.

`Alright, alright, I've done a few since then. How is George, anyway, anybody seen him?'

`Not since the All England last year, mate, he didn't fly this year and I haven't been across to see him. Ooh look, I think that's ours.' Doc's eyes lit up at the sight of steaming plates being carefully carried over by the waitress. She placed them on the table; the guys passed round condiments and tucked in, on a mission to leave plates so clean they barely need to be washed up.

`Mmm, real jockey's whips – that's what I like when I go out.' Frank covered his chips with salt and vinegar.

`Ow. That's hot.' Doc had forked a huge mouthful of steak and ale pie into his mouth, and was shifting it from cheek to cheek to prevent burning.

`Serves you right for being a pig.' Akbar was forthright as ever. Stan picked up the conversation.

`So what are you gonna pair up next year then, Frank? I'm thinking of doing a bit of out crossing myself, what d'you think?'

Fifteen minutes later, meal finished, Stan had decided to borrow a pair of Frank's best breeders to investigate the quality of the ensuing hybrids.

`My round.' He took the orders, went to the bar while the waitress cleared the table. Once done, Doc took out a notepad and pen.

`Right, I now declare the AGM of the Old Cocks Invitation Club officially open.'

The Old Cocks Invitation Club had an unusual status. Most of the clubs up and down the country were organised on a geographical basis; but this rogue version was set up by the four friends to ensure maximum enjoyment without hindrance from some of the more confining rules that seemed to take over the national organisations. This club was based on friendship and

52

flexibility. Members could fly anything between twelve and twenty birds in a kit, and the judging criteria were more concerned with quality rather than quantity of breaks. Each year, the club invited other individuals to take part in the spring fly. Every Roller man admired the club as all of its members were top men in the hobby.

The guys always approached the AGM with serious intent, reviewing the progress of the club, its rules and regulations, its ethos, and deciding which honorary invitations would be made this year. They kept records so that the winning flyers from the club could go forward into national competitions. By custom Doc wrote the minutes. They were not always totally accurate, but they always did the trick.

`Right then, are last year's minutes agreed?'

`Certainly are, Doc,' the lads agreed. `Right then. What about fundraising?'

`What fundraising? We never got any last year. I don't know how we've managed to break even.' Frank was straight to the point.

Doc flushed slightly. `Well, we had some reserves.'

`What about a car boot sale?' Stan fantasised the pleasures of rummaging around, mooching.

Akbar agreed. `Bloody good idea, mate. My turn for the drinks. What are you having?'

Doc narrowed his eyes slightly. `We need to put some thought into this, especially if we want a judge from America this year.'

`Well, why do we want a jocking judge from America?' Frank had a bit of a thing about Americans.

`Cos it's really good to think internationally.' Stan still hadn't spilled the beans about his letter, enjoying the build-up, thinking wide.

`Anyway, we agreed it last year, and you've just unanimously agreed the minutes, so shush,' said Doc.

`What d'you mean, unanimously?' Frank never did complete his formal education.

`We'd like to help you there, Frank, but all three of us agreed not to.' Stan's retort was too quick for Frank, though it raised a smile from Akbar, who was just returning from the bar with shorts all round.

`Okay, so what else apart from a car boot sale?'

`Auction? We could all put some pigeons in.' Akbar always bought well at auctions.

`Aye, that's not a bad idea, we'd have to do it at the Blackpool show mind, we wouldn't get enough people just for us.'

`What about some guest fliers this year? I'd like to see Gordon Stoneman come round with us. He flies some right good pigeons.' Stan felt enthusiastic.

`He's fun too. Likes to have a bit of a giraffe.' Frank agreed.

`What about Phil Madeley?' Doc intervened.

`No, his birds are too long in the roll, he wouldn't know quality if it smacked him in the mouth. He's a big Bill Pensom fan, bit out of date really. Anyway, he's a bit of an arsehole, doesn't pay his dues on time and such like.' Stan, clearly, wasn't keen.

Doc laughed.

`Talking of Bill Pensom, did you see that article in the American Roller Journal? There's this guy, he interviewed Pensom years ago, and keeps on making this quote about Bill saying that a good bird rolls like a bull. Course, he didn't realise that this was Bill's Brummy accent – he meant roll like a ball. So this Yank's spent the last twenty years trying to breed pigeons to roll like a bull.'

Frank grinned.

`Typical. Hey, what about getting Graham Dexter? He's just come out with those new books, *50 Questions Answered for the Less Experienced Roller Flier* and *50 Questions Answered for the More Experienced Roller Flier*, fucking brilliant. He might even judge for us.'

Stan's eyes lit up.

`Good idea, I'd like to see him compete though rather than judge. His old birds last year were a treat.'

54

An hour later, the meeting was over, minutes folded up neatly in Doc's pocket, ready to give to his surgery administrator for typing. Doc paid the bill and ordered a taxi. Stan looked shrewdly at his friend as Doc announced that this last necessary extravagance was catered for from the membership fund. Stan knew that this fund covered much more than it should, and suspected that Doc put in a few extra pounds while keeping figures on paper always accurate should they be scrutinised. He knew that Doc subbed his friends without it being glaringly apparent, so that no one lost pride, particularly for those who equated their lack of income and status with aspects of their self-esteem. It was a fine line matter, and Doc walked it well. Stan always imagined that he'd see Doc alright one day, if ever his boat came in.

The next port of call was the Cabbage Club. To get to the club, the taxi headed out of the village onto increasingly busy roads edged with houses and street lights, punctuated by pubs and late night shops. Then the town suburbs thinned out again as the driver turned off towards more subdued surroundings. Suddenly, he took a sharp right up a dimly lit lane, and pulled into a muddied turning circle lit by the last orange street lamp, its glow barely illuminating the heavy earth beneath. The lads were laughing as they poured out from the taxi, and the driver grinned conspiratorially as he pocketed his tip.

Akbar led the way, unlocking a large barred gate and holding it open while the other three trampled, slightly giddy, onto the darkness of a roughly gravelled path. The moon was just winning over the cloud to shine enough light for them to pick out the shapes of intermittent sheds and fencing on their route. Doc fastened the gate after them as they made their way along, the faint smell of rich earth and manure wafting on the light wind.

`So what's this letter from Holland then, Stan ?' Doc was wondering why Stan hadn't said anything yet.

Stan 's eyes brightened in the dark, ready to forget the restraint that he'd exercised all evening as he'd focused on the light formality of the AGM.

`It came today. It's from one of the Dutch lads, Jan van Deuzen, I think he came over about five years ago for the All England fly, but I didn't meet him.'

`You mean Cloggie?' Akbar clarified.

`Probably. Anyway, him and another bloke, Allan someone, they want to come and stay in October, `specially to see our birds, Doc, and we'll bring them to see yours twos, as well.' Stan waved towards Frank and Akbar.

`They want to stay a few days – give us a chance to show them some real rollers, hey?'

Frank grunted assent, trying to keep his strides slightly smaller.

`Probably don't know a roller from a tumbler. Least they won't be as bad as the Yankees.'

The men laughed.

`All bloody height and no quality, that lot.' Doc vocalised for them all. The Americans were notorious.

`Yeah well, typical of the Yankees, the bigger the better but no real understanding.'

The men rounded a corner, and a hut with lights on, larger than the rest, came into view. The faint hum of music and voices carried across the air.

`Might even invite me to go and judge one of their competitions.' Stan mused, the possibility of a little excitement in his life feeling disproportionately attractive to him. None of his friends realised quite how much – how could they, it was only today that Stan had realised the utter desperation of his current lot. Usually, he kept a bright face on things, especially round the lads.

`Can I come – a few nights in Amsterdam wouldn't go amiss, hey, lads?' Akbar gave a smutty laugh.

`Don't think he lives in Amsterdam,' said Stan, `though I suppose it's probably not that far away.'

`If you were determined, like.' Frank stated this matter of factly, and they all laughed. They were now watching their step carefully in the dark, on terrain covered with allotments. The path was narrowing, and the noise getting louder. They were approaching the Cabbage Club.

The club, unique, was established in 1963. It had started as an allotment shed, just like all the others around. Old Ted Frampton was known for his prize marrows and cabbages, and his ways of telling a story. On Saturday afternoons, he was in the habit of selling off his excess vegetables for a very reasonable price and with the added bonus of a nice cup of tea. Being a man of cooperative nature, he encouraged the other lads to do the same and bring along any extras from the allotments. Over time, it became routine that the nice cup of tea be mixed with a can or two of beer. This was a hut where the men could catch up with each other, unwind, and take home a nice little parcel of vegetables for the wife.

It took ten years for Ted to extend the hut and another ten to get the drinks licence. The club was still membership only, comprising of the allotment holders, local pigeon fanciers, fishermen, and their friends. Its atmosphere never strayed far from that initial ethos of cooperation and relaxation, and although Ted was long since dead and gone, his ashes turned to fertilizer for his precious allotment, he was oft remembered and quoted in the small and cosy bar.

On arrival that night, the lads were greeted by shouts of `ey up,' and `you're late tonight, thought you weren't coming,' and the sound of lively banter. The room was smoky and warm, and it took only minutes to find a table and furnish it with drinks for the four friends, where they were joined by Sam and John.

`Anything exciting 'appen at the AGM?'

`Same old shit, my friends, same old shit,' reassured Akbar, and updated them on who had been chosen as guest flyers, a decision which was supported with enthusiasm. Alfie Elliot, an elder racing pigeon man, wandered over to their table.

`Evening gents. Still playing with those daft old rollers?' The question was posed with a twinkle, and was responded to in good heart.

`Still breeding them bloody great racers, man?'

Alfie was respected by all in the club, as there wasn't much he didn't know about pigeons. He passed the time of evening with them for a while, then donned his cap and took his leave.

Stan, Doc, Frank and Akbar sat and planned into the night the details of the Dutchmen's visit. By closing time, they'd established that Jan would stay at Stan's, and Allan at Doc's. They'd discussed whose pigeons must be seen and agreed some places of interest that they could take their guests. Doc's mouth was already watering at the agreement that they would be going to a favourite Indian restaurant. By the time they left the Club, all four were in excellent spirits and looking forward to an exciting visit.

When Stan got home, replete with food and drink, he collapsed into bed beside his lovely wife. The day had, after all, gone well. Much better than he dared expect this morning, and it took only seconds until his jaw dropped and he began to snore into the night.

Seven
Reach for the Stars

Card XVII – The Star

People look to the stars for inspiration. You know that they are always there; you just can't always see them. People navigate by the stars; use them as a guiding light. Stars offer a glimmer of hope in dark times, a barrage of brightness in time of celebration.

In the Tarot cards, the Star is there to remind you of hope when grief or despair has been present. In Evie's case, the Star gives her a glimpse of a different future. She may not yet know what it is, whether it's more stimulation or more spuds to peel.

But it shows that there is light at the end of the tunnel, and the tunnel is provided from an unexpected source.

Evie hadn't heard Stan come in, and next morning he was fast asleep when she woke up. It was a great day, bright blue sky, sunlight's energy permeating the air. She got out of bed and headed straight into the shower. If she got to college early, she could register and still be at work in loads of time. Friday, the chippy's busiest lunchtime. Lots of local people still ate fish on Fridays, a hangover from a culture of Christianity, most of whose rituals were as dead and buried as Christ himself.

Evie would have to have a word with Roy about her hours, but she wasn't sure yet what she'd need. She squished her free sample Oil of Olay foaming cream on to its accompanying white net puff. `One dab,' the advert promised, `will clean and moisturise your whole body.' Sure enough, white foam erupted like Mount Vesuvius from the puff, and Evie let the creamy suds flow all over her skin, fancying that she could feel its texture becoming smoother.

Obviously, she'd have to think about these things more, if she were to get into performance. What if she became an actress, was invited to do a nude scene, how would her body hold up? She washed her shoulders.

Lady Godiva perhaps.

No, too crude. Anyone could wear a great long wig, and anyway, Evie was allergic to horses. Lady Macbeth? She could remember Polanski's film, had managed to persuade Stan to go with her because he'd heard that there was a naked woman in it. Was it Helen Mirren? Evie couldn't remember now.

She could remember the hand coming out of the sand at the beginning, though, the soft chants of the witches, `hubble, bubble, toil and trouble'. And she remembered bits of Lady Macbeth's speech, a tortured mind rambling ineffectually at the indelible blood on her hands.

`Out, damned spot! Out, I say!' Evie said it out loud in her shower, molten bubbles coursing prolifically now into the shower tray, her confidence growing by the second. `What, will these hands never be clean?' She spoke boldly, staring as she envisioned a madwoman might do, then letting her lids fall closed, feeling her body moving majestically along a stage, the audience hushed in anticipation, silence draping heavily around. She searched for the next words, something about a nightgown, she thought. She moved swiftly on, howling now, with the parts she could recall.

`Now, wash your hands.' Evie raised her arms, pushed her soapy hair back: she *was* Lady M., could feel the pain, the guilt, and her sheer desperation.

Her lunacy.

Suddenly, a cold hand grasped her shoulder, and Evie screamed, nearly losing her footing on the wet tiles. A man's face was close to hers; she could smell his morning breath and hear his heavy breathing.

`Feeling frisky, pet?'

Evie looked into Stan 's grinning eyes, felt her nakedness exposed in his eyes. She bellowed.

`You daft bugger, you could have had me over.' He carried on grinning, the presence of the ever ready erection imposing hopefully on her thigh.

`Well I heard you talking and singing, I thought you were in a good mood.'

A shadow passed across the lens of Evie's eyes. Stan saw that he had got it badly wrong, and looked perplexed. She sighed, not sure if she was more exasperated by Stan 's lack of culture or her own pretensions.

`I was being,' she announced, deliberate and purposeful umbrage in her voice, `Lady Macbeth. Now go away and leave me to rinse off.'

Stan whimpered out like a dejected dog. The burden of guilt that only a minute ago she had been acting now weighed like a stone in Evie's heart. By the time she was dried and dressed, Stan had a cup of tea ready. He looked at her kindly, as if to let her know that her lunacy in the bathroom had been forgiven.

`You look gorgeous,' he informed her, `going somewhere special?' She gave him a smile. He deserved that, he really did.

`I'm going to the college,' she told him, `to enrol for that class. The one I said about, before.'

She saw his apprehensive look, felt suddenly tender towards him, and put her arms around his neck.

`To be honest with you, Stan, I'm a bit nervous myself, but I'm that excited. I just want to do something different. You know, our Damien doesn't really need me like he did. I mean, we hardly ever even see him. And I don't always want to be out with the girls. You always said I had a good brain, I just want to go and see if it still works. Bit of a hobby, I suppose, you know, like your pigeons. Something I can get lost in for a while.'

As she hoped, Stan seemed to identify with that, and visibly relaxed. He kissed her, softly, on the cheek, and she felt the real warmth in the way that he held her. She felt safe, comfortable, and in that moment, she could just have snuggled up with him in the armchair and settled for the familiar. She could have stopped everything that was going to happen, just by reconciling herself to a life of security and safety, maybe even to routine sex, predictable maybe, stale yet comforting.

But she didn't. She squeezed him hard, and told him not to worry, to have a good day, and that she'd see him later. She left the house feeling buoyant.

Joining college was a lot easier than Evie had thought. She was surprised how confidently she braved the big stone steps, and asked where to go, who to see, and what she had to do. There were a lot of people around, mostly students and staff she supposed, but she didn't feel intimidated, more like she was supposed to be here. She felt neither conspicuous nor invisible. She knew that her clothes, black jacket, jeans, a tight top, and wedge shoes, were okay. Nobody stared, nobody ignored her. Within half an hour, she was registered for English. She had a reading list, a timetable and a library card. It felt fabulous: *Evie* felt fabulous. Two evenings and two afternoons a week. Not much to negotiate with Roy, it should be fine.

Evie whizzed down to the chippie and broke the good news. Roy was mixed about it. He'd always said she was bright and should get herself back to school, but then what on earth would he do without her. She put his mind at rest. Three hours a week, that was all she needed. Tuesdays and Wednesdays, not the busiest times. She could work until one thirty. If he wanted, she'd go in half an hour earlier. It was the best she could offer, and Roy agreed. He would get his niece to cover her hours in term time, she could leave her baby in the back and would be glad of the few quid extra.

Evie couldn't wait to tell Jeannie. She rang her when she got in, but kept it short, she couldn't let Stan hear her sounding so enthusiastic, although to be honest, he was a bit preoccupied and seemed surprisingly mellower than she thought he might be. His news about the Dutch pigeon fanciers seemed to have done him good. Evie smiled inwardly.

She felt pleased that Stan was quite happy to have a quiet night in with a few lagers, his pigeon yearbook, and a couple of videos while she went out with Geri. Evie thought carefully about what to wear to meet her designer sister. It was like a new Evie was about to emerge, although she wasn't yet sure what form she was going to take. She did know that whatever it was wouldn't involve much polyester. She perused her wardrobe, settled on a long black skirt, tight black ribbed top and a deep purple skinny cardigan. There had to be some black so that she didn't feel like a beached whale besides her tall and emaciated sister whose body was crowned by a great mop of wild auburn wiry hair. Their Dad used to joke that Geri could make her fortune hiring herself out on Halloween as a broomstick, but she never laughed: her weight was far too serious a subject.

Evie shod herself in suede wedges and pinned her hair up, and, having elongated by six inches, sheathed herself in a long grey fitted coat that originally came from Wallis, which she'd bought for fifteen quid in the nearly new. She felt good, creating a cocoon, silky and elegant, in which the butterfly that she was to become might gestate.

Evie welcomed Stan's offer of a lift to Giorgio's, and enjoyed the gentle kiss he proffered her before she got out of the car. She felt a strange flutter inside as she left him, a sense of foreboding. She shrugged it off, and launched through the stainless steel rimmed glass doors into the art deco black and white tiles of the hottest new restaurant in town.

It was as yet quite empty. Middlesbrough folk were in the habit of assailing restaurants after a good few pints, so for now there were only three or four groups of people eating. Music was slightly gauche, *Pink Martini*, low volume, engaging yet unobtrusive.

Unlike Geri, whose presence obtruded all over the place. She was perched on a high leather seated chrome legged bar stool, and dazzled in tight designer hip hugging silk combats, as far removed from army surplus as you could get, pockets everywhere neatly zipped so as not to cause unsightly bumps or folds. She had on a light green chamois top and a loose deep green jacket. Her hair was as unruly as ever, dark and streaked with red, purple and damson, and she wore green contact lenses. Her nails were long and alternated turquoise and bottle green. She wore a ring, an emerald, real of course. The sisters kissed carefully, twice, once on each cheek, Evie being careful not to smudge her Yardley's best, knowing that Geri would be taking care of a Dior red.

Evie had for aeons approached Geri with caution, and her appraisal of her sister was automatic and swift, having felt no malice towards her for years, just a certain boredom with her relentless pretensions. Not boredom *as such*, of course, being her mother's daughter, more a little ennui with Geri's faddish behaviour which Evie had only recently realised was associated with a degree of unhappiness. On that Friday night, Evie had to admit that Geri looked genuinely pleased to see her, and felt a twinge of emotion that she barely recognised as sisterly love.

`Dahling.'

Geri took hold of Evie's hands and broke out into an uncharacteristic smile.

`Evie, you do look good.'

She meant it, and Evie smiled back.

64

`So do you, Geri, you look fabulous. What are you drinking?'
She giggled conspiratorially. `Pimms, Evie, Pimms. But this is my
treat. I've so much to tell you. Now, what's it to be?'
Evie settled for the same, and in the space of two Pimms No.5's, a
drink that she had never requested before, Evie learned why Geri
had had to see her. Evie was nearly breathless with her sister's
excitement, and by the time Geri was on her Secret Life Story
Chapter Three and continuing, Evie's chin was getting closer to
her chest, and it was all she could do to stop her tongue hanging
out.

Evie realised that Geri's was a common tale, and kicked herself
mentally for not having realised things sooner. Eight years ago,
Geri had found out that Henry, her awful, snobbish, tight
buttocked, professionally coiffed architect husband, was having
an affair. She'd told no one, despite at that time going through
the trauma of counselling and treatment for infertility problems.
(*Thank goodness, Dahling, that I hadn't conceived. Now we'd have
some poor child under our feet, probably cursed with his father's
pompous nose, and I would have had to stay at home to look after it for
another eight years until Henry designed it a suitable apartment in
some redbrick university town.*) Apparently, Henry had made it
very clear that he would continue to have his affair, but would
not press for a divorce unless Geri let him off with a good
financial deal. Geri had no intention of giving him a good
financial deal, and in turn, had made it very clear that if he
wanted a divorce, she would take him to the cleaners for
infidelity and psychological trauma. (*My counsellor was simply
fabulous. So gullible, so amateurish, so warm and accepting, quite
frankly I could have feigned any old garbage and got her to testify in
court. And Henry knew it. Cheers!*) For the last eight years, then,
they'd lived an arrangement, he being free to be unfaithful as
long as he was discrete, and she throwing herself into her career,
her gym and her hobbies. Geri's mouth curled into a cynical
smile as she described how she'd hung on his arm at social
engagements whilst indulging her bulimic habits in all the best
toilets. But at least the bank account was in joint names.

Just recently, though, things had changed. Geri had a fling on a two week cleansing spa holiday in the Seychelles. It wasn't her first, but it was the first time in her life that she'd met someone who really satisfied her sexually. (*To be frank, I'd given up trying or wanting good sex, just resigned myself to a good fake moaning session if I wanted something particular from Henry, or else resorted to D.I.Y., or even a bag of Thornton's continentals for half an hour or so. Managed to keep two down all night last month, you know.*) What really shocked her was that the Seychelles lover was on her wavelength. He liked her. He challenged her when she faked anything, understood her genuine passion for social justice, and loved the spiritual side of her, to which she let him be privy. She liked him.

Evie saw the light in her eyes at this revelation, and could see that Geri meant it when she said that on returning home, she just couldn't carry on living a lie, feeling too old to be any longer interested in pretence; pretending to be in a successful marriage, pretending to eat loads and then throwing up in cold hard lavatories all over the globe, pretending she didn't feel lonely at times. (*Let's face it, a toilet bowl's a toilet bowl, whether it's down a garden and made out of cracked crock, with a long chain hanging down towards it, or whether it's part of a sunken marble suite - which, incidentally, are a nightmare, you have to virtually lie on your belly to vomit tidily.*) Geri faced Evie square on.

`I think Dad dying was the final straw. When we put him in that hole, threw that dark tacky mud on that silly wooden box, I thought, well, Dad, you're on your own now. And whatever else I do, when I go in that box, I'll be on my own. I could hear his voice as he stood on that darts mat – *it's not your last throw that counts in this game, it's the next one*. It haunted me for weeks, Evie. I hear him saying it every morning when I wake up.'

Evie saw into her sister for the first time in ages. She knew only too well, of course, exactly what Geri meant. In a disarming gesture of affection, Geri squeezed her arm.

`So, Evie dear sister, I'm getting a divorce. Henry's agreed to give me a good deal.'

Evie glimpsed a passing sadness in her eyes.

`In fact, he's moved out already, apparently he'd been thinking of moving to his penthouse in London for a while. I'll miss him, of course, in a funny sort of way, but I think it's best. Come on, let's move to our table.'

The corner table was perfect, near the blacked out windows, the women able to see out while passers-by couldn't see in.

They ordered, Evie going for salad, sea food penne, garlic bread, Geri making her order very specific so that she could acknowledge her obsession with being skinny rather than have to ingest and then regurgitate large plates full. (*When I say small portions, I do mean very small portions, do you understand me? Just one plain green salad, a very small plateful of whitebait, maybe ten at most, and then a mere taste of carbonara sauce with only about twenty pieces of pasta. Have you got that young man? Good.*) She poured glasses of red wine. Funny, Evie wondered if Geri was getting drunker now that she wasn't throwing up so much.

`So, let's drink to freedom. And then I'll tell you the rest.' And so Geri went on for another two hours, with not even a single visit to the lavatory. She was thinking of changing career, although not one hundred per cent sure, and had just completed a six-month weekends course on Feng Shui. She pronounced it by grunting down her nose, so that it sounded like Fung Shoy. (*Balance in the home, Dahling, perfect harmony between the elements, wind and water, good relationships thrive in the right environments*), and arranged to come and `do' Evie's house the following month. She listened to Evie's news with real enthusiasm, her new found self carrying a sort of freedom and generosity which Evie had never associated with Geri, even sounding dead chuffed about the college.

If she was honest, Evie enjoyed her sister's company for the first time that she could remember. There had been a sense of primal bonding at their Dad's funeral, but this was different. Evie even felt understood when she was whingeing about how bored she was with Stan.

67

Geri was waiting for her divorce settlement, a vast amount of money. She was going to redecorate the house, using her newfound spirituality to guide her. And then she wanted to go away, to have a long weekend on a city break. She flung out the idea as they got their coats and made moves towards the waiting taxis.

`Amsterdam, Evie, Paris, Florence, somewhere exotic, somewhere really European, decadent and magnificent. I'm asking Fee, she's been a good friend to me over the years. So how about you and Jeannie coming too? My treat, Dahling. Think about it. I'll call you soon about the Feng Shui. Ciao, Evie, ciao.'

Evie felt stirred. She could hear Jack Donaldson's voice, *you will travel, young lady,* and just caught a glimpse of the stars before a grime streaked cloud hid them from view. When she got home, she dreamed of canals, of gondoliers, of museums, of bright clothes, and dancing. She smiled in her sleep, into her pillow, the very air whispering around her – *the best, Evie, is yet to come.*

Eight
Clearing the Cobwebs

Card XII – The Hanged Man

The Hanged Man tells us to literally hang around, to be patient and to realize that the best approach to a problem is not always the most obvious. Sometimes, we just need to stay put while looking anew at what's around us – in Evie's case, in her cupboards, around her house, under her bed.

When we most want to force things to happen, that's when we need patience. Seeing a problem from a new perspective is always a good idea. Ironically, when we stop trying to solve problems in the way we think, we are more likely to find what we are looking for.

September came and went, and Evie acclimatised to doing classes and course work. She noticed that Stan seemed on a bit of a buzz, and in a way, they didn't really see that much of each other. He seemed dead excited at the visit that was coming up from the Dutch pigeon fanciers, occupied himself with making arrangements, visiting other fanciers, clearing out the spare room.

The sex was still lousy. Well, not so much lousy as non-existent. Evie felt as if Stan and she had fallen somewhere and got stuck in a fissure, hanging in there like a piece of stale bread jammed between the breadbin and the kitchen unit. Once fresh, delicious to taste, raring to be spread with real butter and savoured, now fit only for the bin or the toaster. If they weren't careful, they'd be doomed to end their days as a stodgy bread and butter pudding, like so many of the other fatty stale couples that Evie saw all the time in the streets and in the chip shop queue. People in the North East had the lowest life expectancy in England, and Evie wasn't surprised.

Once she'd decided it was just a case of being stale, Evie felt optimistic and was inspired to freshen up her whole environment. She was keen now to Feng Shui the house, brush out those dusty old corners, and maximise the energy. She knew that Geri would be delighted to have an excuse to try out her new hobby, not to mention getting her nose into Evie's business. So on the last Thursday of the month when Evie knew that Stan was going to be out doing pigeon things, she arranged a day off and Geri came over to do her magic, as planned. She arrived in typical style, dressed in a black boiler suit with red belt, red Doc Martens, and red bandana decorated with a black Chinese character. She carried a red sackcloth bag with hidden goodies in, and sniffed depreciatingly as she crossed Evie's threshold.

`Stagnant,' she declared, more as a matter of information than judgement. Evie stood back as Geri passed through the front hall, wrinkling her nose disdainfully, narrowing her gaze. Her eyes flickered to the comfy living room to the left, taking in the whole environment, her head slightly cocked to one side as if she was even listening for the sound of the house. Evie waited with baited breath as Geri nodded to herself, excitement in her eyes.

`Oh yes, Evie, I'd quite forgotten. What tremendous clutter you have, such mess, such stale energy everywhere.'

Evie could almost hear the saliva forming in Geri's mouth. She felt slightly offended but knew her sister to be right. The place had about as much energy as a tortoise in a marathon. Evie swallowed her pride. Geri put her hand on Evie's shoulder and smiled, really warmly.

`Chill out, Evie, we'll have great fun.' Evie tried to believe her.

They sat first at the table in the little middle room, and Geri produced from her goody bag a compass and a map of the house. Evie laughed.

`Blimey, I know you haven't been for a while, but you won't need those.'

Geri raised an authoritative eyebrow.

`Evie, you must take this seriously. For all you know, there might be a dragon under the house, you've certainly got poison arrows aimed at you from the front, and you need all the help you can get.'

Evie sobered instantly – wow, if this was true, it was no wonder things were bad. Over the next few hours, she began to see her house through fresh eyes, starting in the kitchen.

`Evie, the kitchen should be a source of nurture and care, the very heart of strength giving. It's important to keep it clear of obstructions, and the surfaces clear of clutter. Just look at this, all the corners are full of rubbish.' Evie looked at the room with dismay: Geri was right. Every surface had gadgets and devices on, mainly provided by Stan through somewhat dodgy means.

`I know. It's just so difficult getting everything in the cupboards, never been a very big kitchen.' She could hear her self-pitying tone, instantly picked up by Geri.

`Okay, it's small, but how many of these things do you really need and use?'

Geri made her account for each item. Within five minutes, they'd identified as useless a toasted sandwich maker (popular with

71

Damien until three years ago, but never used since); a water filter jug that hadn't had the cartridge renewed for as long as Evie could remember; a bowl which seemed to just collect rubbish, holding five coins, a piece of string, and two cigarette lighters; two dog eared cookery books covered in stains; a hideous vase which Mam had given her and which she felt guilty about putting out; and a fat reducing grill which Doc had given to her and Stan, which they'd tried once and never used since. And the three washed out bean tins on the windowsill, which Stan collected to rattle his corn in, had to go too.

Geri went out to her car and came back with a large cardboard box.

`I had a feeling I'd be needing this,' she said sternly, and the lot went in. Then they threw out unwanted crockery from the cupboard, ice cream sundae glasses (not a huge need for these in Evie's house), three of the most scarred out of a collection of far too many saucepans, two of the huge Pyrex bowls Stan kept on getting (still leaving two which was more than adequate), and one of the two cafetières which they had had as anniversary presents, one being quite enough for a houseful of dedicated tea drinkers. Evie began to feel surprisingly light. Geri clapped her hands with satisfaction.

`Now then,' she said, `luckily the sink isn't in the south, so the energy in here should be fundamentally sound. You've got a lot of metal in here, Evie, a lot of yang energy.'

Evie was uncomprehending. `And?'

`Well, you want quite a lot of yang because it brings activity and life. But too much can be bad for relationships.'

Aha. So that was the problem. Too much yang. `So what do I do?'

`Just bring in a little more wood and earthenware. Maybe change the breadbin from that hideous stainless steel to wood or unglazed crock. Hang a wood chime. Just a couple of little things, but not lots to put on the surfaces – see how much better it is already.'

Evie noted these possibilities, and felt really good moving through the kitchen to the bathroom. This turned out not to be in the best position, which would be the east, but she could redress the balance by a simple addition of some evergreen plants, perhaps one on the sill and one in a hanging basket. Geri cautioned Evie to keep the toilet seat down and the plugs in the plugholes, to prevent the Qi energy from being needlessly sucked away. It seemed that she needed all the energy she could get.

Next, the middle room. Geri chose to call this the dining room, which Evie supposed it was, strictly speaking. After all, they had their breakfast and sometimes their tea in here, so yes, *Dahling*, dining room it was. Geri set to work.

`Evie, these lights have got to go. I mean look at them.' Evie looked up at her six lamped central piece, complete with wavy fluted pink flowered glass lampshades that matched the two wall lights in the alcoves, which Stan and Damien had done. Surely they contrasted well with the floral wallpaper?

`But Geri, I can't afford to do too much here. What's wrong with the lights?'

`Too dim, darling, too dim. A dining room needs to be bright and bold, and have a feeling of spaciousness with it. You could change these for up lighters, or even just change the shades to something open, something clearer and plainer: these little flutes just keep the light in their own space. We can soon spruce up though without spending any money.'

Ten minutes later they'd moved the table to the southwest aspect of the room – which was, obviously, much more auspicious when meals were eaten mainly by family members – and thrown out the pile of papers stacked up in the corner.

`And you need a mirror.' Geri paused. `I've got just the thing for you at home, it's a lovely round one with a simple frame, it'll soften the energy of the square table. I'll bring it over.'

The front room turned out to be reasonably positively aspected, and was certainly the room in which Evie felt most relaxed. The colours were soft and plain, and it was kept tidy. The front room was still equated with visitors and Sunday best. Evie was more than happy to reposition a chair and to get rid of the big crock

73

dog that Stan had found at a car boot sale and kennelled on the hearth. It turned out that his small aquarium brought good energy into the room, particularly as Stan kept it so clean and fresh. There was also some original wooden panelling on the walls, stripped and stained, which grounded the energy well. Geri suggested buying a money plant to put in this room, to enhance the general wellbeing of the family, and increase the chances of prosperity. Evie noted this one in capital letters, although she couldn't quite imagine how a plant would bring more money, but hey, anything was worth a try.

Geri spared nothing, and thoroughly enjoyed herself, her own pleasure emanating an energy which it was impossible not to catch. She discovered changes to make everywhere, and Evie was well ready to go for them, making a long list of what needed to be swapped, what to be thrown out, and what to be bought. Her favourite was the bedroom, which Geri disparaged instantly. It began when she opened the door.

`Evie, Evie, so much trapped Qi. I can sense it before I begin.'

Her nostril quivered.

`You'll have to move the bed, for a start. You're facing the door with your feet, just like a Chinese corpse. Bad luck or what.'

She strolled over and knelt on the floor, peering underneath the bed.

`My God, this room is being used as a cupboard, not a boudoir at all. Look at it.'

She dragged out the good suitcase, old, brown, and covered in dust. Beulah would have had a fit. There were another two canvas bags of Stan's, full of pigeon rings and pigeon record books, and other paraphernalia.

This must have been his idea of clearing out the spare room.

Geri yanked out a cardboard box, full of old shoes, wellies, and even an old hair crimper, long since forgotten. Piles of magazines under Evie's side, and books. A red rag rug, that Beulah had made years ago and which Evie didn't have the heart to throw out.

Geri pronounced on the lot.

`This needs to go, the Qi is so stifled that your sex life will suffer, and your sleep will be of a poor quality. There's some hope for the rug, mind, you could do with a bit of fire in here. That's a gorgeous red, Evie, you should put it out – add a splash of passion to the place.'

She held the rug up, and it was suddenly obvious that it was indeed quite beautiful. Originally, Evie had not fully appreciated it, having been too aware of Beulah's martyrish curses as she'd created it, each woven piece an act of self-inflicted torture.

`This,' she would say, gritting her teeth, `used to be your father's favourite waistcoat. Until he got so fat.'

She would force it through the matting, to just the right length. Then she would tear up another garment.

`And this,' she declared, tearing up a skirt, `was your sister's, when she used to be a decent girl. Before she went off the rails.'

Beulah would set her face hard, and her bitter memories seemed to have woven themselves into the rug with the material. But now, with Geri holding it up to the light, you could see the magnificent hues of fire in the fabrics, and even remember Beulah's pride when she'd completed it. It was a gift of the heart, capturing a family history like an American quilt, and it was really quite beautiful. Geri laid it on the bed, her attention distracted.

`Now this, Evie,' she declared as she wandered over to the huge mirror facing the bed, `this will drain your soul at night. Evie, how long have you had this?'

Evie hesitated, blushed. Stan had brought it home from a car boot sale about three years before. He wanted them to see themselves having sex, but it hadn't quite worked out. The only time they'd really tried to, Evie didn't much like what she saw, whereas Stan had liked it so much that he'd come far too quickly. Fortunately, Geri didn't wait for an answer.

`Mirrors in bedrooms need to be to the side of the bed, not opposite. If it has to stay in the room at all, it needs to be covered at night.'

Another thirty minutes, and they'd moved the bed to the optimum position. The box of rubbish was in the yard, ready for the tip. The mirror went into the hall, to reflect energy into the living room, and the red rug was shaken and laid down on the floor. It was beginning to look something like. Evie wanted the curtains to go – suddenly, cheap velour didn't quite do it. She fancied heavy cotton, possibly cream to tone with the red. There was all kinds of potential now. She poured out two glasses of white wine from the fridge, to celebrate. Geri gave it cautious perusal.

`Hmm, Moselle. Yes, why not.'

The wine was well chilled, and Evie used her best glasses, a present from Jeannie for her crystal wedding anniversary. Stan had forgotten it until he'd seen the gift. So what, Evie had told herself; but she'd been hurt.

She opened a packet of biscuits and some pâté, specially bought, with a big hunk of cheddar cheese. Just a light nibble. She noticed but didn't comment on Geri's willingness to have some.

`Thanks, Geri.' Evie raised her glass. `That was really good. So how's things with you?'

Geri concentrated, her thirty-seven well-preserved years momentarily apparent in the lines around her eyes and jaw.

`Well, it's all happening. Papers are in with the solicitors, Henry's been back once to pack up some more stuff. He's being terribly nice but it's really weird, talking about who'll have what. He's been generous, I'm keeping the house in return for waiving any claim on his pension. I don't want him to maintain me, but he's giving me a lump sum, which is about half our savings and the share values. I'll be alright for money, so I'm luckier than most.'

She took a sip of wine, and absentmindedly crunched a biscuit. She looked wistful. `The house is quiet, but I'm used to that.'

She sighed, shook her head, as if getting rid of cobwebs.

'So anyway, Evie, overall I just know it's a good thing. And,' she leaned forward conspiratorially, eyes twinkling, `I want us to do that holiday I was on about. I've decided where to go.'

Evie's heart beat a tad faster, her breath hung.

'Guess where?'

She closed her eyes; anywhere would do.

'Amsterdam, *Dahling*, Amsterdam. Five days, four nights, good hotel, flying from Teesside, all on me.'

Evie squealed.

`Brilliant. Geri, I can't wait. How much spending money d'you think?'

She was immediately working out how much she could put on one side from the chip shop money, and obviously Jeannie would be tight.

`Well, up to you, but Evie.' Geri gave her a big sister look. `Evie, I know money's tough. Well, the fact is, that's one thing I've got loads of. I'm going to give you an early birthday present.'

Evie was thrown, because she didn't know if she could in all honesty take money from Geri, even though she had it.

`It's no good looking like that. Evie, I've missed so much these last few years, and part of what I've missed is you. I want to give you £500.00. And' – she held a hand up like a stop sign as she anticipated any discomfort or inclinations to refuse – `you could do me a very big favour by being generous enough to accept it. Since Dad died,' she went on, her eyes meeting Evie's with the mutual understanding that seemed to be around these days, `things have changed a lot. The money is just a gift, I'm not being superior. On the contrary. I think I've missed out a lot on you, let alone your Damien, and it's my loss. So it's just a pressie, I won't be doing it all over the place. I want to give you this, the holiday, the cash. A one off celebration. Please.'

There was a tear in Geri's eye. What could Evie do but take her hand?

`Cheers, Geri,' she said, emotion replaced by the raising of glasses.

At which point dear old Stan crashed in, full of enthusiasm and insensitivity.

`Geri,' he said, and shook her hand in his clumsy way. `Well, this is an honour. You girls had a good time then? What's that mirror doing in the hall, Evie? Thought I'd met meself going out as I was coming in.'

He chuckled at his wit, his amusement a solitary event. He shrugged, and defended himself in his usual way.

'Oh well,' he grinned, 'the old ones are the best.'

Evie had that old familiar feeling of mild embarrassment. *No, Stan*, she thought, *the old ones are the old ones.*

After Geri left, Evie thought about the holiday. She hadn't been abroad in years, not since they'd done a coach tour to France for a cheap weekend. Damien had been about four, hated the whole event, and cried all the way there and back. They'd been the youngest people on the coach, everyone else seemed to have booked through SAGA holidays. Nice enough, but a bit overwhelming for a twenty two year old with a lot of life in her.

So, what would she need? Not sure yet, but clearly, she would have to go shopping, and the 'Boro Road wouldn't do. A trip to the Metro centre would be good. Evie phoned Jeannie to see if she'd come: she would, of course, and it was sorted for the next Thursday. She went to see Beulah, just to go through the motions of asking her too. She wouldn't come, but Evie knew she'd have got brayed if she hadn't asked. Anyway, she was excited, knew that her Mam would like to know what was going on. Evie stopped off at the post office on the way and filled in an application for a new passport, had photos done. She'd get Doc to sign the necessary.

Beulah brewed up, and mother and daughter sat facing each other. Evie didn't comment when Beulah rolled up: they were her lungs. She told her about the trip with Geri. Beulah looked unsurprised, but pleased. She'd never liked Henry, and had probably been more hurt than either daughter had known when Geri had estranged herself to live up to his lifestyle. Evie detected a note of caution regarding her daughters' newfound friendship, curtailing the discussion, in favour of more general talk, but Evie had insisted on telling all about the Feng Shui. Then Beulah moved to tittle-tattle, not really very interesting.

Until she got to Stan.

`How's your Stan, then? You never both come round any more, has something happened?'

Evie answered her casually. `Same as ever, Mam, same as ever.'

Beulah had that shrewd expression of hers on. Silence hung for a while. Eventually, she spoke in a different tone.

`Reading between the lines, Evie,' she began, in a tone that meant something heavy was coming – `I would say that something isn't right between you two. Would that be right?'

Evie narrowed her eyes, curtained access to her soul. The trouble with Beulah was that she was so alarmingly accurate. Her senses were like those of an old witch, hearing the slightest incongruity in the tone of a voice, and spotting an angsted aura at a million paces. Exasperating. Evie focused on her, hard.

`Well don't read between the lines, not when you haven't been invited to. It's rude.'

Beulah didn't flinch, took an extra deep drag of Golden Virginia, and blew it right into Evie's face, spitefully.

`I'm right, then.' she asserted. `Well, don't act in haste, Evie, that's all I can say. There were times, you know, when I could have left your father. But I hung on, and I must say, at the end of the day, it paid off.'

It took a minute to register the words. Evie had no idea what her Mam was on about. Dad had been perfect. *Perfect.* He never argued, never shouted. He always, always let Mam have her own way. Evie could hear his gorgeous voice so easily, liquid sex, Auntie Bridie from next door had used to call it. Whenever Mam had asked him anything, big or small, that voice would answer smoothly, so understanding, so respectful – `it's up to you, pet, whatever you want.' Not like the tyrants that some of the women had to put up with, oh no. Funnily enough, in the corner of her memories, Evie could just glimpse Mam tightening her lips sometimes when he'd said that, although she'd never known why.

Admittedly, dad had one or two eccentric little quirks. The missing bottom teeth which he had removed so that he could just fit the stem of his pipe inside it, so that he could smoke while he was riding his old Lambretta scooter. His insistence on going to Bridie's once a week for a tealeaf reading, even though he maintained that he wasn't a superstitious man.

Funny, Bridie hadn't come round since Dad died, now Evie came to think of it, and she hadn't heard Mam mention her much.

Then there was the endearing way Dad used to soak his horny old feet in a bowl of soapy water on a Saturday night, Geri and she competing to rub them down with soap, him giving them a thin bar of Cadbury's Dairy Milk by way of reward. Mam fetched and took the water away, but never joined in. Too busy. Evie's Dad had been a little gem. How in heaven's name could Beulah have even thought of leaving a man like that? Evie glared at her.

`Don't be daft, Mam, you might have got fed up, but you can't have really thought of leaving him. It's much different from being a bit chewed.'

She coloured slightly, realising that she'd given herself away. She saw Beulah's look, scornful like a draconian headmistress.

`So I was right.' She sighed, and for a second, she looked uncertain which avenue to pursue. The scorn presided.

`Evie, you're a bright enough lass, but your love for your Da leaves you blind, always did. Do you think you've got the monopoly on an unhappy marriage, do you really? I loved your Da, but by, he was a difficult old sod as well.' Her eyes looked far into the distance, searching for remote memories. Once located, she brought them to life as if they were yesterday.

`I remember once, the first time we'd ever saved enough money to go on holiday, I was so excited. He borrowed the old Ford Popular off your uncle, and we'd got twenty pounds in spending money saved up. We went to a caravan at Mabelthorpe, d'you remember, Evie? You were just two.'

No, Mam, I was two. Why was Evie feeling so tight, so defensive? Beulah, clearly, wasn't really waiting for a reply. She went on.

`We got there and unpacked, you kids thought it was great, right by the beach. We went straight down, and you both had a donkey ride. Well, at any rate Geraldine did, you screamed and screamed till we took you off its back.' This thought seemed to amuse Beulah, and her eyes crinkled as she remembered. `It was lovely, everything was lovely, until it started to rain. The first day, we played as much as we could in the caravan, silly games, and cards and things. We went to the club in the evening, nice people, the couple who ran it. They had a daughter.' Her face hardened. Something bad was coming, something a daughter probably didn't want to hear. Evie's chest tightened further, and Beulah continued.

`Well, your Da charmed her like he always did with the lasses, and they gave us free pop and crisps for you every night. We got to be regulars, of course.' She paused. `On the fifth night, Evie, he went there before us and by the time we arrived, he'd gone. Him and the daughter.'

Silence dominated the room as Evie tried to block out her words, even as she felt for Beulah, could see her with her kids, bewildered and alone, but still thinking no, that couldn't have happened, having no ability or inclination to picture the scene that her Mam was recounting.

`I didn't see him again that night. He came in at dawn.' Beulah looked Evie in the eye. `He'd blown all the money, so we left, and d'you know, Evie, although I still loved him, I never ever trusted him again.'

Evie's heart thumped.

`She was just the first, Evie, just the first, and I won't bore you with the details of the rest. We'll just say he played close to home, and that was the hardest thing.'

Beulah inhaled deeply, blew out a huge smoke ring.

`But I never left him, and in his way, he was a good husband and a good Dad to you girls. And I've no regrets, I had a good life. So think on, Evie, think on what you've got, not what you haven't got.'

With her unique ability to throw in a hand grenade and leave it exploding anywhere other than her own front yard, Beulah shook herself down and went on to talk about the everyday trivia of life, so that when Evie left, her mind was like a roller coaster of confusion. She supposed that her Mam's idea of a good life was

81

different from her own. And she couldn't feel badly about her Dad, couldn't really believe the enormity of her Mam's revelation. Dad was perfect, and that was that. And she knew that Stan was a good man, salt of the earth and all that, but then Evie wasn't her Mam, ready to settle for second best. She'd been so bored these last few years, and now things were starting to look up.

It wasn't fair. Mam hadn't helped at all with her prying and wise woman advice; she had just muddied the waters. Evie wished she hadn't gone round.

But she soon began to smile as she imagined the little changes in the house, and of course the trip away with Geri. Nothing was going to spoil the excitement. She returned to her dreams, planning her outfits, planning her colours, shading in the pattern of her butterfly wings.

Nine
Shake your tail feathers

Listen to as many people's views as possible...... Listen carefully and remember. Ask as many questions as you can..... ....encourage comment, criticism and evaluation from all interested parties...... Continue to be critical, be humble, continue to learn ...

Graham Dexter, *Winners with Spinners* 1997

Stan was pacing, went for the umpteenth time to check the loft before setting off on the drive to the airport. The lawn was tidy, twice mown in the last week. The fuchsias in the hanging baskets were looking well, bar the odd chewed leaf that he hadn't been able to protect from the pigeons. The loft was pristine, smelling sweet. All was well in the garden, the sound of cooing, as ever, calming.

Stan had borrowed Maggie and Doc's Renault Espace, which carried some little responsibility. Much better than his old Honda Accord with string holding on the passenger door, and a gear stick that won't do third. Loft checked, he took Maggie's key ring gadget out of his pocket, aimed it at the car, and ping! He was rewarded by a flash of indicators and the clunk of doors unlocking. Stan grinned, vocalised an automatic `yes,' fist moving skywards in a gesture of triumph.

The car was a breeze to handle, radio controls on a stem on the steering wheel, air conditioning, electric windows, and cruise control. It took till he was way over the flyover and on the road to Leeds/Bradford to try out every control. He programmed the CD stacker before he left, and sang along to Shania Twain, *That Don't Impress Me Much*, imagining Shania in the very seat beside him, slender thigh within squeezing distance and silky hair twinkling in the sunlight. And Stan would find something to impress her, for sure.

Clear roads and an easy pace ensured that Stan arrived at the airport with time to spare. He parked up in the short stay car park and moseyed over to WH Smiths. He'd not had time to read the paper before leaving home, and was beggared if he was going to pay for another one, so just picked up his favourite on the pretence of looking through to sample. The headline today was, spookily, about planes - *Headless Pilot Manages to Land Passenger Plane before Dying* - and conjured gruesome pictures. Stan found the images disturbing – it was one thing to know about Michael the headless chicken who survived for eighteen months in California (allegedly), as his brain stem was intact, but another to consider a human being doing something similar.

84

How on earth would he see the controls? Stan discarded the paper, went to check the arrivals board. The Amsterdam Jet2 flight was on time, just another fifteen minutes to go.

Stan bought coffee at Starbucks, beguiled by the treat of vanilla, banoffie and toffee flavour. By the time he was half way through the large and very expensive (one twentieth of his dole cheque) mug, he was feeling nauseous. Still, at least he'd found out what he'd been missing, and was reassured that a Yorkshire Tea Bag was much nicer, more than adequate to offer his guests, and at a much more reasonable price. He looked around, watching people intently. Two men in suits, mobiles on, businessmen, good tans and plenty of gold mined by the poorer people of the earth, no doubt. A young man and woman, her tiny with a shapely arse and trousers so low they might fall off any minute, light blonde hair, him brown eyed and hair well cut, body well-muscled and worked out. Young love, probably just going on holiday. An elderly man pushing a woman in a wheelchair. Life could be worse after all, although there was something very special about the way the couple were talking and expressing affection, despite the ambulatory limitations. Three women, off for a good time perhaps, or off on business, hard to tell. Neatly suited, well groomed. A man and a small child, maybe eight years old, hair slightly tangled, both with brown hair, anoraks, worn jeans, walked hand in hand, engaged with each other in a way that Stan could never remember doing with Damien. A lump threatened in his throat.

Pre-empting any indulgence in unexpected emotion, Stan went to the Gents. Once he'd relieved himself, he washed his hands, regarded his eager green eyes in the mirror, eyes full of longing and anticipation. He scrubbed up well, and could see where Damien got some of his good looks. Stan winked at his reflection, left the Gents, and made his way to Arrivals. The Arrivals board informed him that the plane from Amsterdam had landed.

He took out a sheet of paper from his pocket, and unfolded it to make a sign – **Stan welcomes the Dutch**. He held it up, scanning the faces of the increasingly frequent groups of passengers. Many people smiled at him, said hello to the Englishman with the friendly welcome.

After a few minutes, two likely looking men walked through the gate. One of them, a man about Stan 's age, came forward: he was wearing a sporty jacket and a cap with a badge on. As he approached, Stan saw that the badge sported a picture of a pigeon, and bore the letters ANPR; he knew this stood for *Association for Netherlands Performing Rollers*. His heart almost missed a beat as the fit looking man announced himself as Jan. Stan shook his hand with delight.

`Stan, I want you to meet my friend Allan.' Jan gestured to the man beside him who was tall and blond, around 30 years of age. As Stan greeted him, he just glimpsed something in Allan's blue eyes that he was unsettled by, something sly. He instantly reconfigured the assessment as shy: after all, you have to give a man the benefit of the doubt. Stan welcomed both men warmly.

`Can we get coffee round here?' asked Jan, `they only had instant on the plane and I could do with a fix.'

Stan registered a slight dismay, imagining the Aldi instant coffee powder at home: if only they could wait.

'Yes, there's a Starbucks over there,' he said, leading the party onwards. The lads sat down, and Stan ordered three regular filter coffees. Another six pounds out of his spending money. Jan pronounced his cold, and summoned a waitress.

He looked her in the eye. `This coffee is cold,' he asserted.

`I'm sorry sir.' She put her forefinger into the coffee. `Nah, that's okay – don't feel too bad to me.'

The Dutch men looked incredulous, which, to her credit, at least she noticed. `I'll change it anyway,' she quickly said. They laughed, and by the time the coffees were drunk, Jan had negotiated a full refund and given the money back to Stan.

Stan led them to the car, and they loaded in their luggage, soft bags full to bursting, plenty of room in the lovely Espace. Jan sat in the front with Stan, and they chatted while Allan admired the scenery from the back.

`So how are you, Jan? Sorry we didn't meet when you were over here last. I think Gordon brought you over and flew my kit for you for the All England. I was on a double shift – sod's law.'

`Yep, I remember of course. Your birds were second. Good quality, just a bit slower at kitting than they could be. Excellent show, though. Have you still got that little mealy hen?'

`Oh aye, she's one of my favourites. Frequent and deep in the roll. She's earned me the Quality Shield in the National this year.'

Stan spoke proudly: wasn't it fantastic that Jan had remembered such detail? By the time they got to the Middlesbrough flyover, Jan had carefully elicited the finer details of Stan 's best old bird kit. They were interrupted by a voice from the back.

`What's that smell, my friend?' Allan was speaking in the tone of a wrinkled nose, and Stan confessed that it was the River Tees, dumping ground of ICI and then some. It wasn't half as bad as it used to be, though an odour persisted despite the edict for the company to clean up their act.

`Not far to go. I'm putting you up at ours, Jan, and then you at Doc Weaver's house, Allan. Is that okay?'

The men agreed: they were looking forward to seeing some good pigeons. Stan drove first to Doc's house, an impressive three-storey dwelling on the Linthorpe Rd, the bit that had been bought up by the professional class when it was dogged and tired looking. Now it was a wealthy area. Stan pulled onto a wide drive with a forecourt, plenty of parking space, as this was also Doc's surgery. The large bay window to the left of the door was the waiting room, while that to the right housed the comfortable office and reception which was overseen by Maggie, and staffed by two assistants. This was a doctor's surgery of the old-fashioned kind, small and personal.

The men piled out of the vehicle, and Stan led them through the leaded glass door to the beautifully tiled hallway, original floor renovated to the best standard. The chandelier which graced the high ceiling suited well, exuding both the twinkle and the tinkle of welcome. Maggie arrived to greet them, explaining that her husband would be busy for another half an hour or so, and

87

ushered them through the well laid out kitchen to a large conservatory which looked out onto a generous well-kept garden. She paused for handshaking and a full introduction of names, and bade the men sit down on large padded sofas and chairs. It had begun to rain, albeit lightly, and the patter of the raindrops on the conservatory roof was strangely hypnotic.

While Maggie fetched tea, coffee and snacks from the kitchen, the men commented favourably on their surroundings.

`How long has Doc lived here, then?' asked Allan.

`Ooh, got to be twenty years by now.' Stan nodded in affirmation of his own recollections. `He used to practise in Acklam, just up the road, then they bought this and did it all up themselves. Maggie's got a great eye for decorating.'

`And is he a general doctor?' Allan was curious.

`Oh aye, sound as a pound and gives all his patients the best care.' Stan described his old friend with pride. `Good man, Doc. Been a pigeon man longer than any of us, never looks down his nose, bred some of the best pigeons you'll ever see.'

Maggie appeared with the tray, and sat herself down. `Now then,' she said in a calm and assertive tone, `what will you have? There's coffee, tea, cheese straws, tuna sandwiches, bacon sandwiches, egg mayonnaise. Help yourself now, don't be shy.' The men took plates and napkins, and filled their plates.

`So tell me, what do you do over there in Holland? Are you from Amsterdam?'

Both men began to speak at once, but Allan's voice dominated. `No, Jan lives in Utrecht and I am in a village on its outskirts. We are about an hour's drive from Amsterdam. Amsterdam is of course the place that other Europeans know the best.'

`My husband would very much like to go to Amsterdam, but I'm afraid I'm not a very good traveller, so we tend to do our holidays in Britain mostly. I flew to the States once, but my ankles were like balloons at the end of the journey and my blood pressure was through the roof.' Maggie smiled gracefully, missing the slightly uncertain response to her liberal self-disclosure and its subsequent images, and Stan was thinking that perhaps Maggie had given too much information.

`Aye, I'd like to go too,' he said, `perhaps we'll be coming over to visit your pigeons before long.' He looked hopefully at Jan, who nodded earnestly.

`I hope so, my friend, you would be more than welcome.'

Maggie persisted. `So what kind of work are you all in?'

Allan led the way again. `Myself and Jan, we work in one of the biggest diamond factories in the city. We were both at one time polishers, but now we are in management.'

`So do you know a lot about them? I absolutely love diamonds. My engagement ring is a diamond you know, a real one, cost fifty pounds all those years ago. That was a lot of money in those days.'

She showed her engagement ring, and Allan and Jan dutifully admired it.

`This is a very nice diamond,' Allan said, `who knows, it might have been polished in our factory.'

`What a lovely thought.' Maggie smiled. `Would you like another sandwich?'

The Dutchmen took more food and chewed. Stan felt slightly uncomfortable; the silence was companionable yet just slightly exclusive. He was relieved when it was fractured by Doc walking sturdily into the conservatory.

`Ah, here you are.' Jan stood up. `Pleased to see you again, Doc.'

`Jan, how you doing? Welcome to the 'Boro.' Doc and Jan shook hands, and then Doc turned to Allan. `You must be Allan?' Allan nodded, shook hands. `Maggie been looking after you, has she? Anybody want more tea?'

`No, we're fine,' Jan answered for himself and Allan.

Grabbing a sandwich and a handful of cheese straws, Doc headed for the door to the garden.

`Come on lads, it's a bit wet, but it's stopped raining so let's go and have a look at the birds, hey?'

The men needed no encouragement, leaving Maggie with a tray full of plates and crumbs. Stan smiled at her gratefully; he knew that she'd been feeding Doc excessively for years. They say that the way to a man's heart is through his stomach, but Stan wondered what troubles this compulsive feeding masked. He knew that his friend would like to travel more and that Maggie wouldn't. He wondered about the conjugal side of things, which Doc had intimated more than once was not satisfactory. So his friend got the best bread, enjoyed the finest steaks, and kept the best-stocked fridge in town. The fruits of such compensation spilled over Doc's trouser belt, and Stan prayed that he and Evie would never reach this state of compensatory stalemate.

Doc had two lofts, one small one for the breeders, and a larger one for the flying stock. The breeders' loft was a carefully converted garden shed, painstakingly treated in copper stain with smart brass locks on. The main loft was stained to match, constructed from wooden slats, with a nice bit of boarding at the front. Stan watched Doc mount the boarding, take out his key and unlock the main door to the first kit box. Picking up a broom handle kept especially for purpose, he chased out his old bird team. The birds instantly had the attention of all the men. They lifted quickly into the air and formed a kit, beginning to widen their flying circle.

On the ground, the men had all assumed the position, legs hip width apart, arms folded, shades taken from pockets to protect against the hidden rays of the sun. Within minutes, the birds turned on the wing and seven rolled together. The men turned too, and at the roll, all of them moved their hands into their pockets.

`They look lively, Doc.' Allan was favourably impressed. `Nice little blue checker there. What family is she?' Jan was ever curious.

`Originally, she's from Bill Barrett's stock.' The late Bill Barrett was revered as one of the earliest known fanciers, his name carrying great weight. `I had one of his best cock birds and paired him with one of my own hens. Great on the roll, his strain used to be a bit deep for my fancy, that's why I out-crossed him. Lovely bird, that, one of my best.'

`Tell me,' asked Allan, `what feed do you use for the birds?'

`Bit of a mix. Mostly wheat and maize, sometimes a bit of milo, a few peas. And just before a competition, if they seem to be going off the roll, I'll give them just Depurative.'

Stan smiled, knowing that Doc kept to himself the extra magic ingredients of vitamins and tonics that he crushed and mixed from time to time, or the occasional clean out with Epsom salts. It had taken him years to get these potions just right, and he wasn't about to give away all his secrets.

Arms were folded again as the men followed the birds around the sky. Up, round, on the wing, then nine rolled together, wings tightly in, the faintest gleam of sunlight catching their feathers. Doc stepped backward, experienced a sensation of sliminess under his feet. He looked down and cursed loudly, his face turning a bright shade of puce.

`That bloody cat. Excuse me gentlemen.'

Doc marched to the smaller shed, entered, and returned seconds later with a small shovel, a shovel especially assigned to this particular task. He shovelled up a mound of cat shit, walked over to the fence which demarcated his garden from that next door, and projected the slimy mess over the top of the fence with a practised twist and flurry. He used a plastic stool to enable him to reach high enough to avoid the carpet tacking which was meticulously set all round his fencing but which the cats, to his chagrin and Stan 's amusement, are extremely adept at traversing.

`This is yours, you mucky sods,' he yelled, marching back to the main loft. There he turned on the tap that was piped onto the loft side from the mains, and washed off the shovel.

`Vermin,' he stated, to no one in particular, `bloody vermin.'

Stan, who was used to this ritual, was watching the Dutchmen watching his slightly eccentric friend, and grinned.

`Do you have much problem with cats in Holland?'

Jan chuckled. `I used to have quite a problem, but now I have a very effective water device. I have a sensor that detects cats and instantly sprays them with water. Cats hate water, they leave your garden very quickly, I can tell you. Problem is, now and then it goes off to the wrong stimulus. My wife was not pleased when it caught her hanging out the washing and soaked her and the clothes. I had to adjust it slightly then, as you might imagine.'

`Worth the risk, though, hey?' Stan asked. `I used to have a sonic device that just gives them an ear blasting, but the batteries run out real fast, and the cats quickly get accustomed to it, so that never really worked for long.' He was keeping an eye on the birds as he spoke, and let out a satisfied `yes' as eight rolled together, perfect timing on the wing again.

The men kept their attention to the sky. Jan and Allan were constantly asking after specific birds. Stan had to admit that they had a keen eye, their five years in the hobby paying off. They were less impressed by depth than quality, endearing them to the English roller men. From Stan's point of view, they'd make good companions and good competitors.

When the birds were dropping, Maggie appeared with perfect timing and invited Allan to come in and take his bags to his room. There were two large guest bedrooms with en suites in the splendid house. Once there were three, but one of these gradually emerged as Doc's own little bolthole, its bed being more and more frequently used. Jan was happy to go to Stan's. He seemed to want to get to know Stan and his birds well, and Stan was ready for a bit of flattery. He suggested that he take Jan across to his house now to settle in, and that Doc should bring Allan over a little later.

Stan diverted Jan away from the Espace now to the battered old Honda, specially cleaned for purpose. Stan grinned sheepishly as Jan noted the piece of string on the back door – 'waiting for a part'. He reversed out of the driveway and began the short journey to his house. Jan seemed interested in the changing landscape.

`I'm always fascinated by your houses here. In Holland we make much more use of the roof space. In England this is quite unusual, hey?'

Stan mused. `Well yes, some people do loft conversions, but they're not usually built with them. Is that what you do in Holland, then?'

`Yes, we use all the space that we can, so that there is no wastage. And usually our houses are set a little further apart.' Stan was driving through council estate terrain now, having left Linthorpe Rd way behind.

`It varies a lot here, some houses are dead near to each other' – Stan was thinking of Beulah's old terrace – `and some people have a bit more garden space. Depends what you want and what you can afford.'

`Yes, of course.'

Through Jan's eyes, Stan became aware of the graffiti on the walls and the pavement, contrasts between really well kept gardens and some real dumps, full of long grass and rusty old parts from bikes, scooters, all things mechanical. He turned into his well-kept cul-de-sac, pulled onto the pavement outside his house, where path and front were immaculately kept, the grass short, small flowerbeds well-tended, winter pansies adding a splash of colour. He saw Jan cast his eyes over the frontage before turning to grab his bag.

Stan welcomed Jan into the small porch – 1960s, very trendy at the time – which in summer housed tomato plants, whose fragrance seemed to permeate no matter what time of year. Red quarry tiles on the floor were highly polished, adorned by a mat stating *wilkommen, bien venu, bem vindo*, which Stan had bought the previous week from the car boot sale in a spirit of cosmopolitan bonhomie.

Stan took Jan into the small hallway, showed him the front room, gave him the one minute tour of back room, kitchen, and then bathroom. Jan looked around politely, taking in a remnant of chintz here, a modern kitchen set there, a modern round mirror in the living room, the `Home Sweet Home' sampler in the hall, and the wind chime hanging over the sink in the kitchen. Stan suddenly glimpsed how difficult it was to look at each object in this house and try to jigsaw it together into a coherent picture.

93

He saw a house full of conflicting tastes, a split second of insight that passed before he could make head nor tail of it. He took Jan upstairs.

Stan felt proud of his preparation in the spare room, now dominated by a special bargain from Home Base, a large sofa bed created from heavy tubular metal, with a ladder up to its first floor, and whose sofa part opened out to double. Never mind that it was so big – it gave maximum occupancy in minimum space, a good buy. It was bright yellow, a sunshine colour. By, it looked well against the pale mauve wallpaper.

One of Evie's New Age posters adorned the wall, saying *It's not what you think you are – it's what you think, you are*. His dear Evie, she did have some strange ways. Anyway, Stan liked the picture, a kind of deep sunrise, simple and bright. Now he'd spent a day taking out the clutter of canvas bags, bird rings, pigeon books, old waders and so on which seemed to have accumulated in this room, it looked large and spacious to him. He wasn't so certain that it looked spacious to Jan, who seemed to be searching for something that he imagined might have been there, like an en suite bathroom. Stan compensated by pointing to the comparatively new B&Q silver chest of drawers, which just fitted nicely between the bottom of the bed and the wall.

`Make yourself at home, now, don't be shy, and help yourself to whatever you want.'

Stan left Jan to unpack his bag and went downstairs to make a brew. Soon Jan joined him, and they went straight to the garden. The sun had crept out from the hinterlands of grey clouds, and Stan took out cushions for the garden chairs. Jan was clearly wowed out by the loft, and of course fascinated by looking at the birds.

`So look at these beautiful barless mealies.' Jan picked out two young hens, silver grey and healthy looking, `whose line are they?'

`Mine,' replied Stan, pointing out his favourite hen to Jan. `They're both off Foxy Lady, she's a brilliant roller, and I've kept her as a stock bird this last eight years. Paired her to the red

94

checker cock, Lord Flaunty.' Stan was showing off his best birds, pleased that Jan seemed fascinated, taking mental notes. He wasn't so sure about the slightly curled lip on Jan, not quite a full smile, but, hopefully, friendly.

`You give all your birds names,' he commented. `I've never come across this before.'

`Only the stock birds,' corrected Stan, 'only when you know they'll be around a while. This one here' – he pointed to a blue badge hen – `this one's called Jamie Lee Bond. Her ring number is 7007 – get it?' Jan smiled. `And this one here, beautiful little mealy hen, she's Seven-of-Nine, same reason, 'cos of her ring number. And this cock,' he stated, pointing to a black strong looking mottled bird, `this is BFB – Big Fat Bastard. Brilliant bird, came off of one of my best pairs in the nineties, Hawk Lady and Bertie Bassett.'

Jan had to be impressed, how could he not: these were beautiful birds, in the best condition, and bred through years of experience and experiment. The men became entrenched in conversation on lineage and how to pair up until they were distracted by the sound of the gate at the back garden. It was Doc and Allan, and they'd managed to pick up Akbar on the way.

Then it was show time in the garden, as Stan flew first the young birds, then the yearlings, and then the old birds. Cries of `good roll,' `there's a beauty,' `which bird is that?', `that's deep,' resounded in the garden. Before they knew it, the skies were darkening in the late autumn afternoon and the birds were all fed and put away. Stan noted Jan and Allan exchanging a satisfied nod. He pulled himself up to his full height, and grinned.

Ten
Illusions and Delusions

If we are really honest about Birmingham Rollers, they are an optical illusion...The illusion is created and we look at the illusion and we perceive it either as something good or something substandard. Lots of things will influence that, the mood that we are in, perhaps the time of day, how far away the pigeon is and the actual style and quality of the pigeon itself. The angle of vision...is very important.

Graham Dexter, *Winners with Spinners* 1997

By the last day of the Dutchmen's visit, they'd seen all the best pigeon fanciers in the North East, and one or two in the Midlands as well. For Stan, this was the time of his life, showing off pigeons, showing off his guests. He'd bet his mates' birds could outclass Rollers anywhere else in the world. On this last day, all six men were to go round the 'Boro and end the day with a meal at a favourite Indian restaurant – great food, take your own beer. The women were coming too. Stan was looking forward to it.

And brill, the Dutchmen were so enamoured of Stan's pigeons that he'd decided to gift them ten of his very best stock birds to breed from. They'd asked him to sell some of his birds, but he wouldn't, not even for fifty pounds each bird. Instead, he planned to give them on permanent loan. That way he'd be helping his friends from overseas, without losing his carefully bred family strain, the fruits of twenty years of his skilled management and dedication. Just imagining the moment when he'd break this news to Jan caused a tingle of excitement in his body – he could just see the glee on his friend's face.

Stan rose early, wandered into the bathroom, and cursed as he nearly hit his head on the hanging basket of ivy that had appeared just next to the shower cubicle. Where the fuck had this come from? He'd have to ask Evie about it. He peed, washed his hands, and went into the kitchen to do his duties. Jan came downstairs, wearing a thick towelling robe of good quality, and greeted Stan enthusiastically.

`Good morning, Stan. It looks like the sun will come out for us today. What do you think, my friend?'

Stan agreed, he'd already noted the clear dawn, and there seemed to be little wind. Cold but fresh, just the way that he, and the pigeons, liked it.

`Aye, it's looking good. Jan, what about breakfast – full Monty?'

Jan patted his flat stomach and grinned.

`Not today, Stan, your English breakfasts will be my death. Perhaps a small omelette and some toast?'

`Okay then, but you'll have to wait a bit for that.'

Stan had tried to make them before, but they came out flat and rubbery, like a strange kind of Frisbee. Maybe something to do with the microwave, he wasn't sure. He'd have to wait for Evie to get up and rely on her better nature. This last month, she'd seemed a bit happier around the place, and had been friendly and hospitable these last few days. She was even coming out tonight, Stan was glad to say.

While Jan showered, Stan picked up the paper, read the headline – *Whole Platoon Eaten Alive by Werewolves* – and immersed himself in the gruesome details before turning to the usual parade of near naked women. He brewed tea to be fresh for Jan when he emerged from the shower, his hair gelled and spiked in a way that Stan could never get his own to do in a month of Sundays. He took a cup up to Evie, and asked her if she'd do omelettes for breakfast.

`But Stan, you don't like omelettes,' she murmured from her early morning sleepiness.

`I know, love, but that's what Jan wants, so I'd better have the same.'

`Mmm. Okay then, down in a bit.'

`Good lass.' Stan kissed Evie on the cheek, left her to have her tea in peace.

He sat with Jan in the living room while they drank their brew.

`What's on for today, then Stan? Did you say we were going to Frank's?'

`Yes, he's had a day off work so we'll start at his, then go to Akbar's, then a guy called John Martin, old chap, he came third in the World Cup this year, puts up some good pigeons. Then we'll go and see Doc's old bird team, and then back here to fly mine. It'll be dark come five, so then we'll take a rest and go into town tonight. Sound alright?'

`Sounds great. Will we pick the others up on the way?'

`Aye, and we'll borrow Maggie's car. Ey up, here's our lass.'

The sound of the creaking steps on the staircase heralded Evie's arrival into the living room. Like Jan, she was wearing her towelling robe: Stan was aware that unlike Jan, hers was a bit

98

thin here and there, that it was a good bargain from TK Maxx, and that it was nevertheless quite fetching.

`Morning, Jan, how did you sleep?'

Jan caught her eye.

`On my back.' They both smiled.

`Okay, very good. So, what d'you fancy in your omelette – bacon, mushrooms, tomatoes?'

Jan thought for a second, went for mushrooms and tomatoes. Evie was just about to move through to the kitchen when Stan gave a little cough and placed his order.

`And I'll have the same, love, only with some bacon with it. And a couple of them sausages from the butcher. And a bit of black pudding if there's any left.'

Evie cast him a glance, as if she was about to say something, but smiled instead. All the men had been out and about the last few days since they arrived, so she hadn't had much to do with them really, but she knew how much this visit meant to Stan.

`Okay, love, will do.'

By the time Evie had cooked, Jan had dressed into good corduroys and a neat sweatshirt, nice boots, maybe Timberland or something similar. Evie joined him and Stan for breakfast.

`So, Jan, which part of Holland did you say you were from?'

`I haven't yet.' He smiled again right into her eyes. `I'm from Utrecht. It's about 50 kilometres from Amsterdam.' He took a mouthful of food and ate with relish. `Mmm, the omelette is very good.'

`Good, glad it's okay.' A very slight pause ensued. `Funnily enough, I'm going to Amsterdam quite soon with my sister – in about ten days in fact. Where would you recommend that we go? What's it like for women on their own there?'

`Well, it's really quite safe there, because it's so liberal, people can always buy what pleasures they want, so they don't have to try and steal them from anyone. This is better, I think.' Jan shrugged.

Stan wasn't sure he'd heard right.

`I didn't know you were going to Amsterdam. When? Why?'

99

`I didn't have chance to say. You've been busy and we've just arranged it. Geri's taking me as a treat, to celebrate her divorce. So what are the things to see, Jan,' she continued. Stan had to hand it to her, very smooth. Would she ever fail to surprise him? `Well, what do you like? We have wonderful museums, as you probably know, and if you like theatre, we have the Leidse Plein Theatre, which has interesting shows. Then there is the architecture, of course, and then there is the sex side which you English seem to be so keen on.' Jan smiled with this bold assertion, and went on. `Dutch food is not brilliant, but we have lots of restaurants which do cuisine from all over the world. I would recommend the Thai ones and the Vietnamese, but of course it depends on your taste.'

Evie took a forkful of breakfast, digesting all this information alongside her food.

`What about bars and clubs – which are the ones to go to?' They chatted on, Jan recommending the Piano Bar, suggesting that if they stayed near the Leidse Plein they would be able to find anything they want. Stan was noting the animation on Evie's cheeks and in her eyes, fighting to let his pleasure outweigh the knot of jealousy in his heart.

`And then, of course, there are the diamond factories,' Jan was explaining.

`What, you can look round them?' Evie sounded intrigued.

`Oh yes, we have guided tours for tourists, you can look at the history of the diamond trade in Amsterdam and see the stones before they are polished – it's quite fascinating. Go to Gassan – that's where I work.'

Stan could see Evie imagining diamonds that they would never own in a million years. He rose abruptly and began clearing sauces from the table.

`Ah well, time to go, it all sounds very nice, I'm sure.'

He saw Evie look up sharply, she was probably thinking how fabulous it would be if he worked in a diamond factory, instead of being on the sodding dole. Couldn't blame her for that. She finished eating, rose from the table, said goodbye and made her way upstairs to get dressed. Stan encouraged Jan to the car, and they set off on their final fly day.

Frank's house was first port of call, and Akbar was already there with Allan. The house was neat and simple, an ex-council house which he bought and customised to accommodate his height. The front door had the top light window taken out and the door replaced with a specially built longer one. The kitchen units were mounted on a six inch plinth, the lights high and embedded into the ceiling. Stan admired his mate's skills; Frank was a joiner by trade, meaning he could make all necessary changes himself. Stan envied Frank's pride and joy, his specially made king size bed, which he'd built inside the main bedroom and which could probably never be moved out. The house was furnished plainly in deep russets and creams, the same carpet all the way through from the stairs up, and polished wooden floors downstairs. Frank maintained that he couldn't be bothered choosing lots of things to match and so just got the simplest things he could. Stan couldn't help contrast how good it looked compared with the messy jigsaw he'd noted his own home to be.

And as for freedom – well, as the only bachelor in the group, Frank had a whole alcove shelved out for his trophies –pigeon trophies, fishing trophies, snooker trophies from his younger days, an Aladdin's cave of cups, plaques, and cut glass vases that Evie would never allow Stan. Although Frank said very little about his sex life, Stan knew that he was seeing a married woman and suspected that Frank was the father of one of her children, but Frank played things very close to his chest, and her identity, although Stan had mentally narrowed it down to one of two possible candidates, was a well kept secret. Akbar had commented that the lad next door was getting very tall, but Frank had never been drawn.

He was flying an old bird kit and a young bird kit, and started with the old birds. Impressive, of course, and Allan in particular thought it the best they'd seen, while Jan still expressed preference for Stan 's.

`No, these are tighter in the kit,' insisted Allan, `they may have slightly less quality but they have great formation.'

Stan nodded, an astute enough observation.

`I 've bred this kit from a kit I had five years ago, taking the best kitters out and pairing them up as stock birds', Frank explained. `So they're all brothers and sisters, or at most cousins, and I just keep on throwing out the ones that won't kit properly. It was a bit of a risk with the quality and the length of the roll, but it's been a good experiment.'

The lads all nodded, respecting Frank for breeding in this unusual way, having the guts to try it out.

`Aye, I've had a few good teams let me down in the competitions because of kitting,' Stan admitted.

The young birds were less tight in the kit but good on the roll, and Jan was particularly keen on a little grizzle that took his fancy, a pretty bird and a frequent roller. Frank would never part with it though, and Stan thought ahead again as to how pleased the Dutchmen would be when he made them his present later on. His chest swelled ever so slightly.

Akbar's was next on the agenda, and Mrs A welcomed them as ever with her charming ways. The lads went to the garden, she brought out fresh tea, and a whole spread of delicacies. Akbar's kit flew, but they weren't in good form.

`Some good birds, just that they think they're on their holidays.' Stan's remark summed it up and raised a laugh, saving Akbar from revealing how disappointed he was.

`Ah well, I'll just have to fly my real team when I get back tonight, instead of this lot that I just keep for show.'

Then it was off to John Martin's, who lived in a ramshackle house and had some of the most consistently lively rollers in the 'Boro, having kept pigeons of one kind or another all his life. He had lost most of his seventy-odd year old teeth and some of his hearing, but kept a thatch of white hair. He was delighted to see the lads, and immediately made them a brew of very strong tea. Allan had trouble swallowing the treacly mix, soft lad, but

102

swallow it he did as John regaled them with the story of how he was a founding member of the Birmingham Roller Club.

`Course in them days, we didn't bother with all these fancy meetings and journals, just flew our pigeons. Hobby's changed a lot. There's men now'll just buy ready made stock, like Manchester United bloody football club.' John snorted with derision, a snort which became a wheeze. He toked on a foul smelling pipe.

'Where's the skill in that, man? It's all in the breeding, the way you pair 'em up, the way you fly 'em and train 'em, you don't need much brass for that.'

Allan leaned forward.

`Tell me, John, what's the most important thing to consider when you're pairing up, then?'

John didn't hesitate.

`Remember, only outcross when you really have to. You've to keep on inbreeding, and you can go as close as mother to son or father to daughter, definitely cousins. Half-brother half-sister is a good cross. But don't be in a hurry. When you narrow down your line too much, though, sooner or later you'll start to lose quality. Test it out over a number of years, keep on experimenting, and always record what you've done.'

What that man didn't know about pigeons was nobody's business, and everyone nodded at the sage old man, who continued to send up smoke signals, and to wheeze. He sat a few moments, and then took the men outside to his loft, where once again they were treated to the spectacle of the lovely Birmingham Rollers, men on a mission.

At the end of the day, they finished their flying at Doc's house. This time they discussed how to allocate kitting points, whether the birds had to stay tightly together or whether they could have some leeway, so by the time it was dark, Stan was confident that the Dutch men had learned loads and were well satisfied with their day.

By seven thirty, Stan, Evie, Akbar, Mrs A, Doc, Maggie, Frank and the Dutch lads were sitting in the Star of India, carrier bags full of beer and wine stashed behind the counter to be opened by Mr Bashir, the owner of the restaurant, and his son Mohammed. Everyone ordered his or her favourite dishes. Doc couldn't choose as usual, so ordered two starters, onion bhaji and mutton tikka. Maggie frowned at him. Evie interjected.

`Doc, I thought you were going to Weight Watchers?' She raised an eyebrow. Doc coughed.

`I am, I've been going for thirteen months. I tell you what, it's marvellous. I haven't put on a single pound in all that time.'

Stan sorted out drinks, made sure everyone got what they wanted. Was there anything in the fact that as conversation flowed, Evie turned her attention to Jan, he wondered, then told himself not to be so silly.

`So Jan, tell me about your diamond factory.' Jan laughed.

`My diamond factory. I wish it was. No, I used to work as a polisher but now I'm in management. I oversee the whole process from when we take the diamonds in uncut to when we ship them out again, cut to precision and polished up. It's very satisfying.'

`Blimey.' Akbar was impressed. `So you're handling rocks worth a fortune every day of the week?'

`Oh yes, some are more expensive than others of course, but we have had some beauties over the years.'

`So don't you ever get tempted to nick one?' Frank was curious. Allan looked quickly at Jan, with almost a split second warning glance. Jan laughed.

`Of course, but it's risky.'

`Risky. Surely it's impossible?' Akbar was fascinated. Glances were being exchanged left right and centre now. Stan almost held his breath.

`Well, it should be, but you know, there is always a loophole.'

`What do you mean,' said Stan, `a loophole?'

`You just have to be clever, Stan, look for the loopholes. There's always a loophole, someone too daft to see what's in front of them.' Jan sounded smug, his cheeks were pink. `Between you and me, we've got away with one so far. And we wouldn't say no to another.'

`Jan, you forget yourself.' Allan intercepted Jan with a harsh look tempered by a terse smile. He addressed the table. `You don't want to take any notice of him, he's a wind up merchant. If only it was true – but let's change the subject. More naan bread?'

Evie poured Jan another beer. Stan was certain, as he knew Frank and Akbar were, that Jan was probably telling the truth, but accepted that now was not a good time or place to ask more. Doc missed everything due to the attention needed to eat his two starters in precisely the correct sequence. He was flushed, the red wine easing him towards a splendid state of bonhomie.

`This tikka is marvellous,' he announced.

`Probably cat,' said Allan, the clichéd remark attracting a slightly embarrassed look from Stan. This was their favourite Indian restaurant, and he wanted no offence to be caused. Doc was smiling affably.

`So did we tell you my favourite cat story, gents?' Stan knew what was coming and sat back. Doc had the floor.

`It was the summer before last. I was out in the garden, turned my back to go fetch some corn from the shed, and blow me, when I got back down there was a bloody great Tom in with the birds. Big grey moggy it was, claws out and eyes wild, thought it was his birthday.'

An outraged gasp echoed round the table: every fancier's nightmare.

`Well, I was between a rock and a hard place. If I'd shooed everything out, I'd never have got the birds back, because they'd have fled in panic.' Everyone nodded agreement. `But then again, I knew if I went in the cat would go wild.'

Maggie interjected enthusiastically.

`I was there – I'd seen it from the kitchen window – you could see already how vicious the cat could get. After all, they are wild animals in a way.' She paused, Doc nodding at her to continue the story as he cut up bhaji and dipped it in yoghurt sauce.

`So, I ran out straight away with Doc's padded winter coat, and a pair of padded gloves, because I knew he would want to go in and get the cat, I thought it would protect him. It was awful – as soon as he was in, the cat just went berserk, springing around faster than you could ever imagine, claws out and screeching so loud. Doc was turning every which way to try and get the damn thing, but it was so vicious – it even bit through the gloves into Doc's hand, blood spurting out. I thought it was going to go for his face.'

Doc took up the tale.

`It tried to, it was a right little sod. Don't mind telling you I was pretty scared, but I was determined to get it – bloody vermin. Anyway, this went on for about five minutes, when suddenly, in the middle of all the leaping around, it went to ground for a second too long, and I just managed to get my foot on its neck.'

Maggie's face looked serious at the memory.

`He had no choice. It was him or the cat. So I watched this cat as Doc just stood on it and stood on it until it died. Took it about five minutes. I can see its eyes now, wild and agonised, hear its yowling, loud at first and then becoming quieter. I swear it was looking right at me.' Her eyes were flashing now. `But I knew there was nothing else he could do.'

Everyone had stopped eating, transfixed by the imagery of the dying cat under Doc's feet.

`So,' Maggie went on, `after it was dead, I let Doc out – he was trembling all over, poor love – and got him some hot sweet tea and we saw to his hand. Then we had to decide what to do with the cat. I noticed it had a collar on, so I had a look, and there it was, a nametag, `Oscar,' and a phone number. So I put it in a box, tried to lay it out so it looked peaceful, and rang the owner. It was a woman.'

Doc and Maggie exchanged glances. Doc forked more food into his mouth.

`So, I rang up and told this woman that I was dreadfully sorry, but I had found her cat in the road, dead, and it had probably been knocked over. She was terribly upset, came round straight away. Doc couldn't bear to see her, so I had to deal with it all. I always remember, she said to me how peaceful he looked in his box, and did I think he had suffered? All I could see was this howling agonised face, but I said no, I expect he died a very peaceful death. I gave her a nice cup of tea, and off she went, crying. Came round the next day and put a note through the door, saying how kind we were.'

Maggie gave a wry chuckle.

`Anyway, about five weeks later, we had another pesky cat in the garden, a young tabby, and we didn't want to risk the same thing again. So Doc trapped it, and we put it in the boot of the car and drove right out into the country side, way past Guisborough, and let it out.'

Jan and Allan were leaning forward, the English lads sitting back, knowing what was coming next

`And do you know what? About three days later, we were in the car with the local radio on, and an appeal comes on the air regarding a lost cat, exactly the same description – young male tabby. And,' she said, in hushed tones, `the cat's name was Madison. *Madison*. You know, the Odd Couple, Oscar and Madison. Had to be the same woman, didn't it?'

The Dutch visitors were silenced for once, looking slightly disarmed by Maggie's pleasure in telling the story, so Doc once again denounced all cats as vermin, and finished off his starter. Plates were cleared away, Stan made sure that everyone had more drinks, and Akbar returned to the diamonds.

`So d'you actually handle the diamonds then, Jan?'

Jan sat up straighter. `Not really anymore, not in terms of cutting and polishing. But I used to be a polisher, and so now I manage the other polishers as well as checking some of the orders and overseeing the whole process.'

`What do they look like before they're polished?' Maggie wanted to know. Jan was only too happy to oblige, and began to tell them about the different grades of diamonds, how many are usable, and how they were transformed from a rough stone to a priceless gem.

`So they're not all really valuable then?' Evie asked.

`No,' said Jan. `But when they are, you can get some real beauties. You can get different cuts as well – a square cut will give you thirty facets, then we do different ones like an emerald cut, or a marquise – very intricate, very pretty.'

Evie seemed impressed. Stan wished he worked in a diamond factory.

`You'll have to let us know when you have a sale,' she said. `I'd love a real diamond. But not yet a while, not unless we win the lottery.'

Stan looked at her, longingly. He'd love Evie to have a diamond, to buy her the biggest rock around. No chance of that though. Akbar's interjection was timely.

`So where's this loophole, then, you know, in the system?'

'Well it's really since they brought in computers,' Jan began, `and of course, that's one of my fortes. So if you can beat the computer, you're in. As long as you're careful, of course.' He gave a boastful smile.

`And part of being careful, of course, is not to talk too much.' Allan glared at his boastful friend's beer flushed face. `Enough of this – where's the main course?'

The English lads raised their eyebrows.

Doc coughed. `So who do you think has got the best kit you've seen, then?' Allan took up this invitation gratefully, and by the time the table was filled with the excellent Indian food, the men were talking pigeons while the women were talking jewellery and clothes.

Stan couldn't believe his luck at being surrounded by such great company, and Jan and Allan made his night by pronouncing his birds the best they'd ever seen, congratulating him on the perfection of his breeding plans and the quality of the roll. Akbar, Doc and Frank supported the Dutchmen's praise and evaluation. Before he knew it, Stan found himself proposing a toast.

`I'd just like to say,' he said, faltering slightly. Evie nodded encouragement – she'd never known Stan make a speech or a

108

toast. `I'd just like to say that this has been a right honour to have your company.' He cleared his throat. `To come all the way from Holland just to see our birds. We're chuffed to bits.' He raised his glass. `So I've decided, Jan,' he continued, `to give you some of my best breeders to take back to Holland. Permanent loan. Yours to keep but in the spirit of loaning back to me at some point or anyone else who needs a bit of help. My present to you, in friendship and to remind you of the 'Boro. Cheers.' He sat down, blushing, and a gasp escaped around the table – to give away breeders, so many top breeders, was typical of his character and one reason why Stan would never have any money.

`I couldn't,' said Jan, although Mrs A and Maggie exchanged a glance at this, noting that the protest was both rapid and unconvincing.

`Jan, man, you know you can,' said Akbar, and then began to giggle at the rhyme, and then they all began to laugh, relieving the tension.

`Least I can do,' said Stan, `it would be great to think that you're flying the Cutler family pigeons right over there in Holland. I'd be honoured.'

`It's you should be honoured,' said Doc, pulling apart the last stuffed paratha, and looking at Jan. `Stan 's never sold a bird in his life, and he only gives them to those he trusts. None have ever gone abroad before.'

`I'll guard them with my life,' said Jan, putting his hand on his heart. `Thank you my friend, I just don't know what to say.'

Everyone picked up little bits of conversation, and by the time the beers and wine were finished, and coffees drunk, all agreeing that the meal was gorgeous, almost as good as Mrs Akbar's cooking though no one could ever match her samosas. Only Frank was sober enough to notice Allan and Jan laughing conspiratorially in the Gents toilet, and the way they stopped when they saw him. He let the moment pass, but he didn't forget it.

Eleven
The Wheel of Fortune

Card X - The Wheel of Fortune
In Greek mythology, there are three women known as the Fates who spin the destiny of us all at the moment of our birth. The wheel of Fortune represents levels higher than the everyday realm. In Evie's family, there are also three women, one of whom, Geri, has just helped give the wheel of fortune a little push around.
The Wheel of Fortune represents unexpected encounters and twists of fate. You can't predict surprises, naturally. But it is said that when the energy of the Wheel arrives, you will feel life speed up, you may feel whirled around, and not quite be sure where you're going to end up.

The day before Evie and the girls were due to go to Amsterdam, she was faffing about what to wear. She never had got to the shopping trip at Metro, with one thing and another, and anyway, she'd told herself, she could always buy things over there. So there she was, thirty-five, trim, hair fresh from the salon in a bold shorter cut, and suddenly her whole wardrobe looked wrong. What would they wear in Amsterdam? Not, she suspected, polyester from the Hartlepool cheap warehouse that masqueraded as a retail designer outlet. She rang Geri.

`It's me, Evie. What are you wearing, Geri? I don't know what to take.'

Geri laughed that confident `don't worry' laugh of hers. `Don't worry, Evie, just a few things. Combats, they're always good for carrying things and travelling, a good dress, my Armani trousers, a few tops, that nice Donna Karan jacket – just a few casuals.'

It didn't help. Geri always looked like she'd stepped off a Milan catwalk, whereas the closest Evie ever got to that was feeling good enough to have stepped off the pages of the Grattan spring/summer catalogue. Beulah used to have Kays years ago, and the girls would sit looking at the pictures of the men in their white Y-fronts, tracing the bumps of their penises with their fingers. Occasionally, there would be pale blue Jockeys. Evie could suddenly see those well shaven hunks as if they were there in front of her, hair dark and Brylcreemed down. But this wasn't helping her decide what to wear. The biggest name she'd owned in clothes apart from her grey coat was a Dorothy Perkins smart black suit that she'd bought for her Dad's funeral, and that had had its label ripped out when she bought it from Boyes. It seemed too formal for a girl's weekend. She rang Jeannie. Her uncertainty was greater than Evie's, but she seemed to care less about it. Her raucous tone was calming.

`Wear anything, Evie, by the time you've had a couple of bevies you won't even care. Anyway, you always look good, legs right up to your arse. We'll have a great time, you'll see.'

She was right. Why did women always seem to be looking at themselves from the outside in, whereas men looked at life from

111

the inside out? Evie compromised and decided to go on a quick shopping trip in town. She had the money from Geri, after all. She bought a pair of nice combats from Next, and was surprised how good they looked. She liked the feel of them low on her hips. She bought an ankle length skirt that was similar style, lots of pockets and zips, and a zipped hooded top. When she got home, she laid them out on her bed with a favourite dress she'd had for ages, courtesy the Good as New shop where she'd got her coat, and added three tops and a jacket. What about shoes? She decided on low wedge boots, she'd had them for years but they were comfy and would suit any weather. After all, it was November so she needed to be warm. She threw in a pair of heels, just in case. She packed the things she wouldn't be travelling in into a light holdall bag, and then laid out her shoulder bag stuff – passport, tickets, money, make up. Anything she'd forgotten she could do without, and anything she could buy there would be a bonus. She started to feel footloose.

Stan came home just as Evie was waiting for her taxi. He'd been meeting up with Frank, some business deal in the offing. She didn't ask too closely, and didn't have to wait too long to find out what it was. Stan kissed her on the forehead, and slyly took out of his pocket two hundred quid.

`Don't tell me this is my pocket money?' Evie held his gaze. He tried to look casual.

`Wish it was, pet. No, Frank and Akbar and me have all put in, we want you to buy as much tobacco as you can – Golden Virginia if you can find it, easiest to sell.'

His lines seemed studiedly casual.

`So how much tobacco does that mean me carrying?'

Stan shifted now on his feet.

`It won't take up much room, just get as much as you can and pack it round your luggage. Should be about twenty cartons I think. Jeannie could take some, stuff it in with your knickers – you know you girls, you carry that much rubbish it won't make any difference to you.'

112

Evie felt cold, felt as if she didn't know him. She could see that from his point of view, this was a simple and obvious request. The wife's going abroad; she can bring us some baccy back. Harmless, logical. It was, however, the last thing she wanted. She was going abroad, with friends, for the first time ever. She was leaving her mundane life behind, just for four days, no son, no husband, no chips. No responsibility to have to do anything. And more, she wanted to forget Middlesbrough, the foraging round, the waiting for the crumbs from someone else's table, the dodgy dealings, always looking for a chance to make a quick buck. She wanted nothing to do with it.

Evie looked Stan in the eye.

`Stan, I'm sorry but I'm not taking baccy in my knickers.' She handed him the money. `You take that right back, and the lot of you can stick it up your own orifices.'

Stan looked shocked, as if he didn't understand. Perhaps it was the word orifices that took a second to sink in, but he soon got the gist.

`But while you're there,' he began, more in hope than judgment. All these years, she thought, and still he couldn't get an accurate read out from her face.

`No, Stan. I'm sorry, but I'm not doing it. End of story.'

He looked at her then with disappointment. Evie could see he felt the distance just as she did. A horn blared outside. She couldn't wait. She gave Stan an awkward hug, picked up her bags, and went.

`Acklam Road, please,' she told the cabbie, and smiled as she waved to poor old Stan. Maybe he would think that the smile was for him. But actually it was for the feeling of escape as Evie went first to Jeannie's house, and then to Teesside Airport. Amsterdam, here we come, she was thinking, let's hope this is a trip that will change my life.

They met up with dear Geri and Fee at the front of the airport. Geri had parked her flash Audi cabriolet (part of the divorce settlement) and secured it for the four nights they were going to be away. She looked stunning, as ever, big hair freshened with some light pink streaks, effortlessly flowing long casual dress, elegant square-toed shoes. Evie used to hate her looks when she was married, she seemed so toffee nosed with it, but lately it was something from inside that made Geri look so good. Evie just hadn't realised how unhappy and tightly wrapped she must have been when she was married to Henry, and there was a new fun side to her which suited her well.

They checked their baggage through, and headed straight for the bar, even though it was early afternoon. Fee was straight in her leather handbag. If Geri had risen from humble beginnings to greater and mightier heights, Fee had gone out of her way to do the opposite. She came from good stock, what used to be called landed gentry as far as Evie knew, and had gone to boarding school and then finishing school. She did management studies, became fluent in French and German, and went into the magazine world. It wasn't long before she'd moved sideways to fundraising for charities, and she'd met Geri years before at a training week for women in management. She couldn't help her residual plummy tones, and Evie had learned not to despise her for them. Reading between the lines, she suspected that Fee's moneyed childhood had been somewhat sullied by some kind of male violence, although Evie had never known the details. She had a great compassionate side and had clearly been a constant support to Geri.

`What are you having, girls?'

Geri and Fee had gin and tonics, Evie and Jeannie went for dry cider. It went down a treat, long and cold. They wandered in various combinations around the duty free, and Evie and Jeannie found themselves at a table topping up their glasses while the other two shopped.

`Eeh, Jeannie.' Evie wore a relaxed grin. She felt ridiculously happy.

Fee and Geri came back laden with champagne and chocolates – `a little something for our rooms, girls.' They had one more drink, and toasted Henry and the great divorce settlement. By now, Evie felt confident enough to get on the plane. She'd been terrified but trying hard to block the terror out. After the three drinks, however, she'd reached a kindly plateau, rational enough to know that statistically flying was safer than being on the A1, and that the pilot probably wanted to get home safely too, and mellow enough to think that if she died, at least she'd go out happy. Once boarded, she relaxed easily, and of course the flight was short and they were all in good humour. The fifty minutes passed quickly. They landed safely at Schipfol airport and from there went by train into town. It was brilliant; the coaches had two storeys, like double decker buses, and were full of interesting looking people.

When they got into town, Geri sported a taxi to the hotel. The hotel was dead posh but really friendly. It had an Italian restaurant with a lovely view of a great looking square, lots of cafés and shops and open air seating, which turned out to be Leidse Plein, which that guy Jan had gone on about. Evie's room was fabulous – big double bed, sofa, table with lamp, TV, and luxurious bathroom, all done in cream and gold. Mint. And, hanging in the bathroom, were big thick fluffy towels and a gorgeous towelling robe, three times the weight of Evie's old one at home. It had the hotel initials on the pocket – NH – and was really smart. She ran a bath straight away, and phoned Jeannie, who was in the room across the corridor. They squealed at each other, and just as the bath was ready, there was a knock at the door and it was Geri and Fee, Geri holding the champagne she'd bought at the airport. Evie told Jeannie to come over as well, and they all drank a toast to freedom and friendship. One glass led to another, and before she knew it Evie had had a bath with all the girls crowding in the bathroom and chocolates fed into her mouth, and then slept for an hour on the bed before getting up to go out into town.

Geri had the evening planned; they were going mooching round the shops, (all open till ten o'clock, very different from the 'Boro), then for dinner, then to the Red Light area, and finally clubbing. She walked ahead with Fee, and Evie walked with Jeannie, taking in all the sights and sounds they could. Suddenly, a sickening crunch occurred on the right, the sound of bone hitting concrete – a young woman had got her cycle wheel stuck in a tramline, came straight off. A man quickly went to her, his mobile out, calling an ambulance. Someone else put a coat over her. A crowd was forming. Evie and Jeannie didn't stop, just looked long enough to notice the clear liquid that had formed a small puddle by the woman's head, bits of blood around it. Cerebral fluid. She was about Damien's age: somebody's daughter, somebody's sister, somebody's friend, somebody's lover.

Wow.

They moved on, crossing back to Geri and Fee, who seemed hardly to have noticed the whole affair, while Evie's head was full of how fragile life can be. Geri and Fee were giggling at something in one of the windows. Two minutes later, they passed a crowd of men on a stag night, their laughs and shouts vying for airtime with the siren of the swiftly responding ambulance. Fire-eaters thrilled the crowd. It all seemed surreal.

From then on, the girls walked down to the canal side, and chose a window table in a ribs restaurant. They ordered large plates of ribs and two bottles of wine, one red, one white. It was a clear evening, just perfect. Evie stretched her legs out, felt comfortable in her baggy combats and little tight top and hoody. She knew she looked good, and once she decided to stop worrying, had begun to approach the whole evening from the inside looking out. There were so many things to see.

Once Evie and the girls had eaten, any thoughts of serious shopping had long since gone, and so they made their way to the Red Light area, ending up outside a sex show theatre. And once they'd decided to go in, there was no holding back. Geri paved the way.

`Wet or dry?' demanded the man outside the booth. `Whatever are you on about, young man?' Geri put on her mock stern face, teetering slightly on Miss Whiplash heels and thrusting her Wonderbra clad cleavage towards him from the neckline of her cashmere coat. Any closer, and he'd probably have offered her a job.

`Drinks, ladies, drinks. Forty euros gets you four drinks each, twenty euros if no drinks.' He paused. `Why, whatever did you think I meant?'

Geri looked him in the eye.

`Then it's four wet ones, for us, Dahling.'

`Never doubted it for a second. Enjoy the show.'

Geri picked up the tickets and led the way. Evie had no idea what to expect, she thought perhaps it would be a bar with a small stage, but in fact it was like going into the cinema – an aisle lit up by coloured bulbs, rows of theatre seats. She felt a flutter of foreboding, and not without due cause. As Geri boldly went towards the front, so an Asian woman, wearing nothing but a skimpy bra, the shortest black leather miniskirt in the world and a pair of black ankle boots, grabbed hold of her and took her straight to the edge of the stage. Evie looked on amazed as the woman proceeded to lie back, put a banana in her vagina – displayed with no decorum whatsoever, as dear old dad would have said – and invited Geri to take a bite. Which she did!

Evie had to admire her sister; she didn't flinch, just bent over and took the bloody bite. Howls and shrieks filled the theatre, Geri turned around, took a bow and ushered the girls into the second row. The audience was going wild, clapping, laughing and whistling.

The acts were pretty graphic. There was a young Asiatic dancer, who was beautiful and sexy. Evie felt stirred, but aware of her vulnerability, too. There was a double act, tall hunky blond guy with a blonde woman; they both undressed, she sucked him to erection point, and they shagged on a revolving stage so that you could see every angle. There was an inevitable air of eroticism about it right to the point of penetration, then it became clinical, as she lay motionless while he dutifully went in and out, making sure that his manhood could be well seen. After about thirty thrusts, she changed position and then he did it again. Pretty boring, Evie thought: by now the blonde might as well have been

117

a blow up doll, or, even better, a sheep, for at least that would have made for greater entertainment value.

Then there was a nun and a priest who did the same, the nun stripping to a basque and stockings. The priest, when he took off his cloak, turned out to be a flabby-bellied has-been in his forties with a face like a cat's backside, revolting. However, credit where credit's due, the woman straddled him as he lay flat on his back, squatting over him and then pumping herself up and down on his manhood, her feet flat on the floor in a series of squat thrusts. That took some muscle action, if Evie's attempts at the Legs, Bums and Tums class were any indication. The blonde earned her money alright, and on such an ugly specimen. Suddenly Roy`s chip shop was acquiring a reasonably attractive hue in Evie's mind's eye, and she knew that she'd rather scrape potatoes any day than that particular member which had just been displayed.

Next Miss Dominatrix, dressed in skimpy black and wanting a man on stage. No one would go, of course. Geri shouted out raucously to the hordes of men around them.

`You're all talk and no trousers, come on you lads, get your bits out for the girls.'

`I will if you will, love.' A drunken Englishman bellowed from the row behind.

`In your dreams.' Geri dismissed him in her casework manager's voice, and focussed on the stage. Some poor lad was pushed onto it by his mates, forced to the floor and into a dog collar where he received some well-choreographed lashes from Miss Dominatrix. He was laughing to begin with but then clearly began to get too confident and tried clumsily to lash her back, and was instantly removed from the stage. Miss was not amused, and she made her feelings clear by shouting at him as she reached her final stage of undress, ready to do sex with the whip handle.

`You could have had me if you'd waited,' she taunted at him, but she was by now looking ugly and the audience hissed.

The final act was heralded by Batman music. A tall black figure ran down the aisle, cloak flying out behind him. Strobes were flashing, the music pounding, hot ice was pouring on from the wings. The black figure leaped onto the stage with a great bound, where a blonde woman was wrapped around a pillar, wearing nothing but a black thong and half-cup bra beneath a sheer black negligée. The white blonde of her spiky short hair contrasted boldly with the black of the mask on her eyes and her other attire. She hooked one arm around the pillar and flew round, to be caught by Batman and have her breasts and crotch unceremoniously fondled. She was pretty wooden, and it looked like nothing unpredictable was going to happen.

Suddenly, to the delight and horror of the audience, while the blonde woman disrobed from her negligee and lay down upon the rising dais, so Batman leaped off the stage, and he was heading for the front two rows. Evie looked at Jeannie anxiously – please, please not us. It was like being on the bus when mad Mary gets on and everyone desperately tries to avoid her eyes in case she targets them. But mad Mary is always brilliant at picking out the most vulnerable and easily embarrassed passenger – and so was Batman. Straight over to row two, tugging on Jeannie as she wailed pitifully and hung on to Evie's arm. Before she knew it, somehow Batman had hauled Evie over Jeannie's lap and carried her onto the stage. There was a second when Evie couldn't move, but then, a sort of euphoria came over her as she realised that she was enjoying the attention – not *quite* Lady Macbeth, but a stage – and an audience. Close up, Batman was gorgeous, short moustache and beard, and a soft voice.

`Don't worry,' he whispered, `you don't have to do anything you don't want to.' He mesmerised Evie on to the dais, got her to lie down next to Blondie. Close up, the face was ferrety and manic, but she smiled affably enough. Batman bent over again, whispered in Evie's ear.

`Just do everything she does, go with the music.'

This meant performing a series of stretches and hip movements, which came extraordinarily easily. The audience were cheering away, and when Blondie took off her bra, they urged Evie to do so too. She was almost tempted but not quite confident enough.

119

And when Blondie took off her thong, Evie didn't quite know where to look. She sat up and turned to the audience, opened her arms.

`Help!' She could see Geri, Fee and Jeannie standing up and egging her on. `Go, Evie, go,' they were yelling.

Muted exhibitionism was one thing, but when Evie realised that not only was Blondie on all fours, but that Batman had now taken his dick out of his leather knickers and that she was sucking it, she thought maybe time to move. Batman moved his face towards Evie.

`Would you like to do this?' he asked, as if it was a favour he was giving rather than asking. Evie covered her face with her hands, peeping despite herself through her fingers: she'd never seen someone else do this up close, and it seemed light years since she'd given Stan a blow job. What would he think now? She shook her head, stood up, desperate to be covered with a blanket. She clambered off the stage to tumultuous applause which Batman initiated by waving his arm toward her even as he shagged the hapless Blondie, now flat on her back, and good old Jeannie ran up and took Evie's hand, guiding her back to her seat.

`Oh my God, oh my God,' they all gasped, and Evie was breathless with excitement, but at least she thought she was safe.

But no. She was just recovering when Batman carried Blondie down from the stage, literally threw her across the audience's laps, and then started pumping again. Everyone was laughing, and then he was shagging her doggy fashion in the aisle. Gross, impersonal, graphic sex, literally in their faces. Evie needed a drink. The girls wanted to know everything.

`What was it like?' `You were brilliant.' `You should have taken your top off.' `Did you fancy him?'

One large gin and tonic later, and they could see Batman for themselves, close up. There he was, in the bar, wearing a pair of old jeans and a Batman t-shirt, looking gorgeous. He smiled benignly.

`Have any of you got a cigarette, girls?' he asked. Geri and Jeannie nearly fell over themselves to oblige.

`Cheers,' he said. `How did you enjoy the show?'

They murmured encouraging answers, and turned around to watch the next act from the balcony. It was as intriguing to watch the audience as the show. An elderly couple who must have been in their eighties arrived and assertively made their way to the very front row. Some of the men were really into it, some of them looked like they were bored but thought they shouldn't be. Once again, Evie wondered how Stan would respond, but decided that she didn't want to think about him. He'd just see her watching this show as an excuse to justify all the porn he'd ever used, a platform for experiment.

The blond guy came down to the bar, and started talking to Batman. They both smoked, drank a beer. They were bored stiff – or not, rather, but waiting to be stiffened again, right on cue. How must it affect their other sex life, if they had girlfriends, if they ever failed to get it up on stage? What would they do? The ultimate humiliation, in a theatre full of people.

Evie and friends left soon afterwards, and got a taxi back to Leidse Plein. The others wanted to look in a porn shop, but Evie had had all she could take for one night. She wanted to drink and to dance, to perform some more. She suddenly thought of old Jack Donaldson. Was this her fate, live sex performance? She hoped not, yet had definitely enjoyed a bit of exhibitionism, and the power of making an audience laugh. They went to Maxims, a laid-back club, and as they danced the night away, getting chatted to and chatted up, Evie felt a million miles away from all domestic chores, young, attractive, and alive.

It was fabulous.

When she woke the next morning, Evie felt like someone had poured sawdust down her throat. She hadn't smoked cigarettes for a while now, but that was how it felt, like she'd had a quick twenty washed down with whisky. In fact, she hadn't even tried any wacky baccy yet. She felt exhausted. Jeannie rang, full of life, full of the energy that she'd had to perfect to get her through the

121

days with her demanding family, and her exciting new job. She was about to shower, and Evie could hear *Summertime* coming over on her radio. As soon as she'd hung up, the phone went again.

`Morning, Dahling.' It was Geri, sounding brushed and flossed. `Meet you for breakfast in ten minutes – we're going shopping, so eat.'

Evie grunted, a sound that Geri was evidently used to taking as assent, as she hung up immediately. Evie knew, suddenly, that she wanted some time alone, to browse, to take in this wondrous city without obligation or socialization. She went next door and broke the bad news to damp towel wrapped Jeannie.

`Jeannie, I'm not coming shopping. I'll meet you all back at the hotel a bit later. I need a couple of hours to myself.'

Jeannie looked hard at her friend.

`Don't be so bloody daft, course you are. You can't leave me with Geri and the fabulous Fee.'

`You'll be fine.' Evie's mind was made up. `You know they're both alright – look at how they were last night. Go on, trust me.'

Jeannie knew when to give up. Fifteen minutes later, she was dressed and gone, ready to have a great time in the shops. Evie knew that both Geri and Fee would be generous to her, they didn't need Evie for this morning.

She took a leisurely shower, dressed in her new skirt and a tight sweater. It was mild for November, and she put her jacket over the top. She didn't really know where she wanted to go, just wherever her feet would take her. She drank an orange juice down at the breakfast bar, freshly squeezed, it was gorgeous. Then she set off, straight past the shops, which looked interesting enough, she just didn't want to be inside them right then. She passed stands of flowers, and although she knew it would be pointless to buy any for the room, she couldn't resist just one flower and pinned it onto her jacket. She wore her shades and carried a light rucksack. Why did she feel so different here from at home?

An hour later she found herself up by the University, with no idea how she'd got there. She browsed in bookshops, saw one fabulous antique shop full of clocks. You had to press the bell to go in, so she had, as if she was a serious punter. The cheapest item was three thousand euros, so Evie asked if she could photograph it to `consult with my husband'. It was Victorian baroque, green and pink, mint condition and kept under a perfect glass dome, the sort of thing her dad would have liked. He'd had a bit of a thing for clocks, and she wondered what he'd have made of Amsterdam.

Evie browsed in a poster gallery, and decided that she would head towards the Rijksmuseum. She looked up and down canals and imagined the boats that must have passed this way. The water was soothing, the bicycles, hundreds of them, fascinating. She had to remember they were coming and try not to step out into their path, although the noise of them gave fair warning, the creaks and groans of functional wheels and adequate chains. She remembered the young woman from last night. Had she lived or died? There was Evie, frightened of a plane, and it had turned out to be safer than a bicycle.

She was tiring, and she was warm. A small café, hanging baskets outside, plants in the window, beckoned. *Sneeps*, it was called. Evie glanced through the window; it was busy but not overcrowded. She walked in, the sweet smell of cannabis greeting her. She knew it was legal over here and understood it to be harmless enough. People were sitting around, two guys were playing pool, and there was a food menu. Evie got herself a beer and ordered goats cheese and honey toasted on rye bread. It sounded different at any rate.

It was only when Evie looked around more carefully that she noticed there wasn't a whole spare table, they were all partly occupied. She saw one by the window where there was just one woman sitting, a bit younger than Evie, hair her colour. The woman looked tired, and had a book open in front of her, a notepad and pen at her side. Evie asked if she could take the spare chair, and she nodded toward it.

123

`Help yourself.'

Evie smiled, sat down, and stretched. She felt really mellow just being here, didn't need any drugs. She glanced the book on the table, was surprised to see an Open University symbol on it. She read the title, *Introducing Social Science, D104*.

`Don't ask.'

`Sorry, didn't mean to be nosey. I was just curious.'

`It's okay.' The younger woman took out a cigarette, Camel Light, and inhaled hungrily. `I'm just trying to get my brain started again. Harder than it looks.'

Evie smiled, thought she knew that feeling.

`Yeah, I've just gone back to college myself, it takes a while to crank up the gears again.' The woman nodded, and Evie left her to read in silence. When the toasted bread and cheese came, Evie groaned out loud with the pleasure of the taste. The woman looked up.

`Good food here.' It was a statement, not a question.

Evie nodded agreement. `It's gorgeous.'

Evie ate slowly, savouring each mouthful, swilling it down with beer, cold and refreshing. She must have been salivating out loud or something, because she suddenly realised that the woman was watching her, smiling. Evie gulped.

`Sorry,' she said.

`No. It's good to see someone enjoying themselves.' Evie dabbed her mouth with a napkin.

`Are you just here for the week?' she asked, turning over her book. Evie recognised the manoeuvre; it meant `anything to stop me having to study even though I need to.'

`Another two days after today,' she replied. `How about you?'

`I live here.' The woman looked Evie straight in the eye. `For now, at any rate.'

`Where are you from?' Evie knew as soon as the words left her lips that it wasn't a good question.

`Here and there.' She lit another Camel Light.

`Sorry, I didn't mean to pry.'

The woman smiled. `That's twice you've apologised in five minutes. You English, you're so bloody polite. It's a fair question, just complicated. I have English blood in me. Let's leave it at that. So tell me, what are you studying?'

`English. It's not such a high level as yours, of course.'

'I didn't know it was a competition.'

`No. It's just sometimes I feel so daft, going back to college at my age. What about you, how did you decide to do the OU?'

The woman's eyes darted briefly to a faraway past.

`I was at college. It got interrupted. Now I want to finish it.'

Evie was still wary of asking too many questions. `I wish I'd done it all younger, really. Some of the people in my group are the same age as my own son. Can you imagine that?'

She flushed slightly.

`You have a son – what age?'

`Eighteen, just coming up nineteen. He doesn't need me any more.' Evie thought she'd sound rueful when she said that, because that was a habit she'd got into, but for the first time the words came out without emotion. *He doesn't need me any more.* In fact, Evie hardly ever saw him. Just a fact. Mission accomplished. Human being created and reared to be self-sufficient. Just as nature intended. A sense of relief went with this simple realisation that this was just how it was. She was still Evie without Damien needing her; in fact, suddenly more Evie than she'd ever been. The woman looked at Evie closely, astutely. Evie's depths were almost tangible, inviting the young woman to trust her. Evie smiled, spoke frankly.

`For the first time in years, I'm a free woman. I suppose that sounds ridiculous.'

`No. There are some times in your life when freedom is just what you need, and other times when you long for commitment. The trick is to enjoy each phase as it comes.'

`You are so right. Sounds like you've had a bit of a journey yourself, hey. Life can be such a roller coaster. I sometimes feel there's so much for us to know.'

The woman looked at Evie with that direct line eye contact.

`My name's Nikke, like the sports shoes but with two k's. It's nice to meet you. D'you fancy another beer?'

`Yes, that'd be great.'

So they had another beer, and another, talking openly, recognising something in each other, offering little disclosures, generating trust. Then they went to Nikke's apartment, in a large renovated warehouse near the canal, and began something together that was to take on a life of its own.

It was nearly seven o'clock before Evie got back to meet the others. Jeannie was going frantic, while Geri and Fee were just getting stoned. Evie wasn't even sorry.

`I've had,' she declared, `the best time ever. I'll tell you later. Now let's go and eat.'

Twelve
Body and Soul

Card VI – The Lovers

The Lovers card refers to all kinds of getting together – establishing bonds, sympathising with one another, getting closer. It's also all about finding out what you care about, what your moral views are, what your values are. The Lovers represents attraction of people or ideas, looking into pictures and mirrors and wondering what the image stands for. It often means that we need to question what's happening in our life, standing at a bit of a crossroads.

Sometimes it can represent sexual union, of course, or in Evie's case, a bit of a shag: which can also be followed by some difficult choices and decision making.

That afternoon, Evie had told Nikke everything as they'd walked around the canals. It didn't really take long, as much of what she had to say was about what wasn't happening in her life rather than what was. Nikke was easy to talk to, and seemed, curiously, to understand; it seemed that they offered the precious intimacy of strangers who might never meet again. There were times when she looked moved, when she'd flush slightly, all the while nodding and encouraging Evie on. There were other times when they laughed, Evie hearing how plaintive and clichéd she sounded as she outlined her woman's story of lack of fulfilment and redundancy, determination and desires. She hadn't talked so openly to anyone for ages. She suddenly became worried that Nikke would be bored.

`What about you?'

`Don't get me started.' Nikke dismissed herself, her history. `I'd be here all day.'

'I've got all day,' said Evie, and raised an eyebrow.

'Alright, you're on. Let's go to mine.' So they'd taken the short walk down the canal side all the way to Achterburgwahl, near where Evie had seen parts of the University. Nikke opened a small black door, which was sunk back from the street, and they climbed steep stairs to the top door, the door to her apartment.

Evie had never seen a place like it. It was massive, light, and incredibly airy. Everything was in one room, kitchen, sitting room and bedroom, although as Mam would have been the first to point out, it wasn't a bedroom as such. The ceiling was so high, that there was a kind of platform erected half way up which came out over part of the room. It had a ladder leading up, and a large looking bed and some cupboards. The floor space was huge, and it sort of progressed from one end, which was a stainless steel fitted kitchen, past a dining table, towards a comfy sofa and large cushions, and finally, by the window, a desk and some bookshelves. There were rugs and throws everywhere. Evie fell in love with it immediately. Nikke made coffee, the lovely rich Dutch aroma seeping gently from the kitchen corner, and they sat on the sofa. Nikke curled up, shoes off, and Evie felt free to do the same, two bookends.

`So what are you doing here, Nikke?'

Evie sipped the rich tasty drink and waited for Nikke's story with a sense of intrigue, and rightness. She'd shown her hers; it was time for Nikke to reciprocate. And when she did, it didn't surprise, somehow.

Nikke had been born in Canada, the daughter of an Englishwoman and a German man. They had both been professional people and had emigrated to Canada from England, where they had first met. She was a doctor, he a lawyer. There were two children, Nikke and her older brother Kiefer.

`They did their best,' she said, shrugging slightly and lighting up the inevitable Camel light. `We went to good schools, our house was great, the neighbourhood was great, and I can't say I had things tough. Trouble was, they didn't realise about Kiefer.'

She dragged deeply on her cigarette.

`Kiefer was in love with me.' She looked Evie straight in the eye. `And he's three years older than me. So what Kiefer wanted, Kiefer took.'

Evie held her gaze.

`You mean he had sex with you.'

`Yes, that's just what I mean. I've got over that now, and I won't bore you with the details – my parents paid thousands to my therapist so that I could do that. But it changed my life, and that's what's been hard.' She took out another cigarette then, lighting it from the stub of the hard drawn nub of the one before. Outside, a man shouted. A small set of chimes rustled by the window. `Trouble was, he didn't take precautions.' Evie could see that Nikke was looking far away now, to somewhere that she carried deep inside but that in reality was somewhere out there in this big wide world.

`So by the time I was seventeen, I had a son. I called him Art, after Art Garfunkel, of course. I loved Simon and Garfunkel, my mum's favourite, they brought me up on it. I thought I could do it all, have the strength of the rock they sang about, and that Art

129

and I could get on just fine. But it all went wrong when Kiefer told them he was the father. They went apeshit. It was such a mess, and I moved out, ran away with the baby. No money, nobody to help, and I had a kind of breakdown. Art went into care, and then they sent him to England to be adopted. I haven't seen him since he was fifteen months old. I spent three years in a psychiatric hospital. They thought I was mad in the unhinged sense. They didn't realise that I was just mad, period. I'd been violated and robbed for years and years. They said I had to be locked up for my own protection.' She gave a curious smile. `If it happened now, I'd have just played their game, behaved, got out a lot sooner. But then, it was different. So I lost him. He'd be eighteen now, same as your Damien.'

Evie felt guilty. She had her son, Nikke had lost hers. Yet Evie had moaned on about how Damien tied her down, how she couldn't be free until now, how he'd sapped her energy, how boring she'd found it being a wife and mum to a son who didn't seem even to need her any more. She'd recounted her horror when they'd put him in her arms after a two-day labour – harsh reality setting in, how on earth would she cope? She had, of course, and she loved him to bits and enjoyed it all so much when he was a little bairn. But now, now that he was so busy and that he had his girlfriend Susannah, she'd felt as if he was leaving her behind, that she'd become an unnecessary has been in his life. She couldn't remember the last time they'd had a decent conversation.

But she had her son. Nikke didn't. Now, suddenly, Evie felt ashamed.

'I'm sorry,' she said, from her heart.

`Well, you know what they say. Shit happens. Anyway, I got theraped to death, Mum and Dad paying for the best of course, but not until I'd had a pretty wild time. I'd never really slept with anyone who I'd wanted to, only Kiefer and friends he'd kind of lent me to, so it seemed easy to sleep my way around for keep and money. Then suddenly I had to get out, the therapy had helped but I needed to do stuff, to get away, to be independent. So I came to Europe, and ended up in Amsterdam. I've been here for seven years. I go to England twice a year, and that's where I enrolled in the OU.'

She paused.

'And I've traced the adoption agency that placed Art. I suppose that they thought he'd be safe from me in England.' For the first time, a trace of bitterness was revealed in the set of her mouth and her tone. `And I've finally been able to give the agency my contact details so that if he ever wants to find me, he can. And when I've finished this course, and got the cash together, I'm going over there to live for a while and to train in social work.' She looked at Evie.

`Ironic, hey?'

`Nikke, you'll be brilliant, you know you will. You've been through so much, and look at you now, so together, so knowing what you want. Honestly, you put me to shame.'

Evie almost knew the answer to the next question before she asked it. `So what do you do to make a living?'

`Come and see.' Nikke took her to the window, looking down on the little figures below, like an Avercamp scene only without the snow. Evie's dad used to have one of his pictures up in the front room, she'd never thought to ask him why.

`See that window over there?' Nikke pointed. On the ground floor of the building opposite, flanked by deep red curtains, sat a woman in a black and white zebra print bikini. `See that window? Twice a week that window's mine. It used to be every night, but I'm winding down. That's how I got the apartment, that's how I travel to England for study schools, that's how I've escaped. About another six months and I'll finish for good.'

Evie was awestruck. Yes, Nikke was a prostitute. She, Evie, ought to have felt disgust, revulsion. She'd imagined that she didn't approve of prostitutes, `women of the night,' as Beulah would have said. Yet Nikke didn't seem like that, didn't seem disgusting or revolting. She was just a woman, shit had happened, like she said, and she was digging her way out. Not a prostitute *as such.*

131

And Evie was intrigued. Coming to Amsterdam had done something to her, she didn't know what, but something that had allowed her to actually enjoy being on that stage the night before, to not care too much that she hadn't kept her appointment with her friends, trusting that they'd be okay. It was like being off the leash, and she could see things less concretely than she had before. So suddenly, it wasn't even that she could accept Nikke because of mitigating circumstances. Prostitution was just a job to her, and what if she'd said that she did it for fun? Evie couldn't judge her, not while she was standing looking at that window, wondering what it would be like to sell yourself in public, and feeling a surge of energy.

She noticed Nikke looking at her, watching her mind working at speed, looking defiant, daring Evie to try to put her down. Their eyes locked, again.

`Wow,' Evie said. It was the best she could do. Nikke gave a taciturn nod, and led Evie back to the seats.

`I know,' she said.

They refilled the coffee cups, Nikke lit another cigarette.

`So how does it work?' Evie wanted to know. She'd seen the women on the streets in Middlesbrough before of course, and she also knew that the whole thing had changed so much there these last few years – now you got much younger girls much more often, feeding a drug habit as likely as not. Sometimes you saw fighting between them, on one occasion some years before she'd seen a woman being dragged into a car by her hair. Evie had rushed over to help, but it had been her, not the bloke dragging her, who'd told Evie to piss off so she'd stayed out of it. She knew enough to know that it was different over here, snippets she'd heard about the infamous red light district, but she'd never really thought about how it would be to be one of the women.

`It's just like a business.' Nikke was very forthright. `You rent the windows legally and supposedly declare your income. You only have to have a passport and register for tax. You rent the windows straight from the owners, and they set up alarm systems for you just in case. You have access to good health checks. Most of the other girls are alright and we don't have to fight each other for business. Actually, we have quite a good organisation here set up by a woman who used to be a prostitute, so there's all kinds of support if you want it.' She shrugged.

`And then you just do it. For me, that was amazingly easy. There had been so many years with Kiefer where I just felt out of control of it all, it's kind of strangely empowering to be in control. I can't say I like the sex, it's just a matter of getting on with it, but I was well used to that anyway. It's not like real sex, not like with someone you care for. I never kiss. It's mechanical, and a lot of the guys are such easy meat, you can have it over with in five minutes. But at least I'm in charge of it all, I make the rules, I use them more than they use me.' She paused. `But equally, I don't want to be doing it all my life, and I won't be. Once I finish here, I want to switch off from this altogether. It will have served its purpose. And then, the next time I have sex, it will be because I really want to, and it will be with someone I really like, who cares for me –someone dependable, and worthy of me, not someone who just needs me. I won't be having sex; I'll be making love. And until I find that man, or those men, then I'll be happy on my own, in control of my own life.' She said the last bit quietly, slightly wistfully, yet with a real determination.

Evie was rapt. Mechanical sex; how familiar that sounded. Was she as clinical with Stan as Nikke was with her clients? Certainly at times this had been true, times when she was planning something else in her head while he grunted and thrusted and she'd felt totally detached. And times in the past when she'd `let' him have sex just to get him in a good mood when she'd wanted to ask for something. Memories whizzed around in Evie's head.

`Well, Nikke,' she finally said, `let's drink to that time. You are one hell of a woman.'

*

When Evie and Nikke finally parted, late afternoon, it was with phone numbers and addresses exchanged, and a feeling of certainty that they'd have to continue whatever relationship it was that they'd begun. Evie hadn't gone straight back to the others, she'd wandered down the canals, drawn as if in some kind of trance through the uneven streets. She hardly noticed people around her, yet was aware of thousands of faces, masking thousands of lives, unknown, perhaps unshared. She crossed numerous bridges, and eventually noticed that she was near to the Rijksmuseum. On impulse, she crossed the road, paid her money and went in. The building was enormous, and if she had gone in as the Evie of yesterday, she might have panicked.

But that day was different. She bought a guide, and went straightaway to the café, although she felt no thirst. She studied her guide, oriented herself, smelled the musky perfume of the well-groomed woman next to her, and felt a breeze of care between a mother and her young son opposite. Evie decided to go for seventeenth century Dutch. She knew nothing about it other than that one Avercamp picture, but that was just the point. She had a lot to learn.

She made her way up a grandiose staircase, and looked in awe but without appreciation at various sculptures that she knew must have been great works, and yet which struck her as too ornate, too cumbersome. She found the section of the museum that she wanted, and browsed.

It was like being a child in a toyshop. She wanted to take everything in, but couldn't. Some colours she liked, some shapes: some seemed repugnant in their enormity. She found herself drawn to shadows, to subtlety rather than brightness, to shades of light that seduced rather than assaulted. In the middle of her browsing, she was suddenly struck by something she really liked, and she caught her breath.

Later, Evie would know that the picture that got her was a classic, but then she had no idea, and, absorbed in her response, felt like she was totally alone in her discovery. It was the milk that got her, pouring out of that jug like it was real, hanging in mid air forever in a frozen millisecond.

It was only after the milk that Evie noticed, really noticed, the woman. She recognised so much, as if Vermeer's *Kitchen Maid* had been painted especially for her. There she was, sleeves rolled up, slightly flushed, anticipatory, in the early bloom of her life. Evie wanted to touch the swell of her shoulders, the rough texture of her blouse. She wanted to put her arms around her because she saw so much in her expression, the eagerness to please, to do it right, to get the milk into the bowl. Yet as she poured the milk, so Evie fancied that she was pouring away her uniqueness, her potential, honing her skills in the service of others. And Evie saw the tedium, the repetition of the task. How long before some posh git had drunk the milk, before she had to wash the bowls and start it all again. And did she mind being on display? She was just there, exposed. *The Kitchen Maid*. She could have been the Bedroom Maid, the Nurse Maid, like so many other pictures in the gallery.

Somehow, though, she stood out as special. Oh Christ, the silly cow, the gorgeous silly cow, captured forever on canvas, just another young woman getting paid to please whoever it was could pay her. The kitchen scene transformed, the window became a little oblong in a cell. No curtains to protect her; not even a hint of a drape drawn aside. The beauty and the hopelessness hit Evie all at once, and she wanted to cry. She stood for what seemed hours, and when she left, she went to the shop to find out more about the woman in the picture. But there was nothing, just a lot about the painter, the man outside the picture, the voyeur. She read that he used light just to place objects within it. She read a list of what the `objects' were: a picture, a bowl of fruit, a Turkish carpet, a woman. The matter of factness of this statement seemed to be to be so poignant that she could read no more. She looked around at the elegant shoppers, wondering whether they had noticed that something wasn't quite right in the world, but they all looked quite serene and acceptant.

Evie bought a little card of the painting, put it in her bag. She thought if she took the *Kitchen Maid* with her, she could give her more meaning. But instead, she was just reminded of Nikke, of Mam, of the porno actresses, all there as objects to accept or reflect the light.

As she walked back to the hotel, Evie realised that the key to everything was choice. It wasn't okay to be the object; you had to be the subject of your destiny. Then it didn't matter whether you accepted or rejected the opportunities or traps that came your way – you were an active participant. She became aware of the winter sun shining down, and sat outside a café with a coffee. She took the card out of her bag, and studied it closely.

`Alright,' she said to the gorgeous image that wasn't even looking back at her, `what's it to be? Light or dark?' A man on the next table looked across.

`Come on.' Evie was urging the woman in the *Kitchen Maid* to commune with her in some way, to give her a signal. `Back in me handbag or out in the sunshine?' At that precise moment, a lump of bird shit descended from the heavens, right on to the corner of the card so that it moved slightly. Evie laughed, and took it as a sign of good luck. They'd always been grateful for any signs of luck in her neck of the woods, and groped for encouragement in every tiny event. Evie left the Kitchen Maid out on the table when she paid, said goodbye to her.

`You look after yourself,' Evie said, `and don't be letting just any old sod sit here and gawp.' She pressed her fingers against her lips, took the kiss to the face on the postcard. The man at the other table was riveted. Evie flashed a smile his way.

`Don't worry, old English custom,' she said reassuringly. He nodded. `They're all doing it back home in Middlesbrough. Ciao!'

Evie smiled all the way back to the hotel, and when she met up with the others, had a huge appetite to fill. They went out to a Vietnamese restaurant and ordered large quantities of food. She didn't quite tell them about her afternoon, not about Nikke's apartment, or her job, more about food and the Art Museum. The others, in turn, were full of what they'd been doing, and Jeannie was really chuffed with a skirt that she'd bought, quite trendy, much better quality than her usual clothes. They spent the whole evening eating, drinking, laughing, and ending up in yet another bar with late music. By the time they got back to the hotel in the

early hours, Evie was exhausted but really content. It had been a good day, a very good day indeed.
*

When she got home, Stan was waiting. Evie was apprehensive – he would think it was his old Evie coming home. He didn't know about the changes – how could he? He looked sheepish. It seemed an age since Evie had refused to pick up baccy for him. She could tell he'd showered, smelled of soap and clean clothes.
`Evie.' He put his arms round her tentatively.
`Have a good time?' For the first time in ages, Evie felt aroused, stirred by something greater than Stan, yet which allowed her to respond to his masculinity. She felt the seeds of bristle of his beard, so recently chopped down yet always raring to grow, as they rubbed against the skin of her cheeks. She kissed his earlobe, feeling its texture for the first time in a while, felt him stiffen slightly against her.
`Evie.' It was almost a question, a question that he couldn't quite risk.
Evie drew back and looked at him quickly before kissing him. She felt him becoming fully erect then, and enjoyed the power. Prostitute's power.
`Evie.' He spoke in a soft groan.
`Our Damien in?' Stan shook his head, his hands roaming now over Evie's body. She felt naughty as she pushed him away and led him by the hand into the living room. She didn't even bother to undress, just let him lift her skirt up as she ripped opened his fly, surprised him with stockings that she had impulsively worn to come home in. They made love there, right on the settee in the front room. It was over in minutes, but deeply satisfying. Evie even felt tender: she looked at Stan, whose eyes were tightly shut.
'Stan,' she whispered, wanting him to feel the tenderness.
'Eeh, Evie,' he said. `By God, you're gorgeous.'
Warmth filled Evie's soul, the time and space warp of recent months beginning to dissolve, albeit just a little.

`Will I do, then?' she asked saucily, knowing full well that she would. A question she would regret for days and weeks to come. `Will you do? Tell you what, Evie, I bet even Melinda Messenger couldn't turn me on more than you can.'

Typical Stan words, designed to flatter, instead shattering the ambience like a particularly pungent fart. Prickling inside and out, Evie pulled away.

`Well thank you very much,' she stropped. And that was that. No matter how hard they both tried that day, that was it, the end of a fleeting re-acquaintance with closeness. Evie had opened herself up, and Stan hadn't valued the intimacy, the uniqueness. She was just a source of sexual stimulation – in fact, the more she thought about it, he'd hardly even looked at her. She could have been anybody. She could, she realised in that second, have been a prostitute. Skirt up, knickers down, and coming out as good as Melinda Messenger.

Evie slept like a log that night, and whatever angels or devils visited her dreams, she woke the next morning with a real sense that her life was going to take a different road. If she was going to feel like a prostitute, then she might as well feel like a bloody good one. Evie Cutler was not ready to lie down and think of England, and she certainly wasn't going to be constrained by the turgid waters of the Tees for the rest of her life. She'd peeped over the border, and she wasn't going back. Who cared what was on the other side: it had to be more interesting than what she had.

Thirteen
Hell Hath no Fury

A factor that has been of interest to me for some time is the roller fancier who suffers disappointment and how that affects his behaviour.

Graham Dexter, *Winners with Spinners* 1997

Stan walked through the hall clutching his Daily Rag and the post, and tossed paper and letters to the table. He shuffled to the kitchen, loneliness seeping round his feet like a cold wind. Life was shit, it was early December and it was cold. He brewed tea, mentally assessing his birds. The blue hen old bird was rolling well. But they weren't kitting as they should, that mealy was into bad habits, dropping down and taking some of the others with it. If it kept playing up like that, it would have to go.

His team hadn't been right since he'd sent those stars off to Holland. He wondered how they were getting on, what would be bred, whether next year the Dutch fanciers would be admiring a branch of the Cutler family rolling impressively over flat lands and dykes. He'd have to try and get across to see them next year, if he could only make some money. Evie could have made him some on the tobacco, and he couldn't understand why she wouldn't. But then what was new, with Evie? At least she'd come back wanting him, for once. She was still his girl, sometimes at least.

Stan wandered into the kitchen, fancying a toastie: he'd not had a toastie for years. He looked around for the toastie maker, couldn't find it anywhere. He looked in cupboards, noticing that lately they all looked different, and that bloody wind chime hanging over the sink was a pain in the arse. Since Geri had been round that day, Evie kept on changing things. After some minutes, he settled for two pieces of toast and a cup of tea.

He sat down at the old oak table that his dad had picked up second hand so many years ago. The scratches were dirty. It could have been worth a few bob once, but whoever had it before them hadn't looked after it properly. His mum had always covered it with a cloth, and made them put cork mats out on it before eating. She might as well not have bothered, might as well have let him and Jimmy carve their name on it like they used to in the school desks. *Stan was here. School sucks.* He wished that school hadn't sucked, then he might be doing something different now: like Damien and his computer world, alien territory to Stan, a world where Damien, at just turned nineteen,

140

was already bringing more into the house than Stan ever could. Damien never had a school desk to carve on; he'd carried his belongings from class to class round the big comprehensive, like a bloody great burden on his back. It had made him keen to move on, mind, and look at him now. Stan didn't know what he felt most, pride or jealousy.

He opened the paper. *Dwarf Swallowed by Elephant in Circus Fiasco*, it announced. At a circus in Russia, a dwarf mistimed his trampoline jumps and landed in the open mouth of an elephant which swallowed him whole. The audience had gone wild, thinking it was part of the act. What a way to go. He turned the page. Page Three had a double spread. Nice tits, usual toothy smile. The image didn't do much for him today, though; just seemed empty and pointless.

He looked at the mail. No bills, that was good. A circular for Evie from some big store; special preview for *our most valued customers*, 10% off and a free glass of wine. A postcard for Evie from Amsterdam. His heart skipped a beat. Who was she in touch with in Amsterdam, for fuck's sake? It was addressed to Ms Evie Cutler. That wasn't right: she was Mrs Stan Cutler. His mother was always proud to have his father's name. Evie should be the same. He was about to read the card when the phone rang. Stan was keyed up for trouble, but calmed at the sound of Doc's voice, lulled into a false sense of security that all was well with the world.

`Stan. How you doing?'

`I'm alright Doc, I'm alright. How's about yourself?

`Aye, not so bad.' Doc paused. `Stan, have you heard about the pigeons?'

More cardiac somersaults at the tone in Doc's voice.

Someone must have had a flyaway, their birds soaring so high into the blue that they couldn't find their way back. Or a theft. Thieves went to the greatest lengths to steal these birds. One fancier spent a fortune in time and money securing the walls and roof of his loft. One summer morning, he went down the yard to find it empty, not a pigeon in sight. The bastards had jacked up

141

the loft and got in through the floor and got them out that way. Unbelievable.

`What? What's happened?'

Doc's voice growled. `Your pigeons. I've just had an e-mail from a bloke in the USA. Wants to know where they can buy more of our fantastic birds like the ones he bought from Jan.'

`What bloke? Which ones from Jan?'

`This guy's some kind of rich bloke, come into the hobby late. More money than sense. He's just bought some fantastic pigeons, he said, that Jan bought in England. He's just settled them, flown them and he's really impressed. He's bought them to breed from.'

`Jan didn't buy any in England.' Stan was bemused, couldn't understand what Doc was telling him.

`I know.' Doc paused, briefly. `They're the ones you gave him, Stan, they've got to be. The prat's only gone and exported them. I tell you, this bloke wanted to know if he could trade direct with us, to get the price down a bit. Said he didn't mind paying twenty thousand for such brilliant birds, but he wanted to know if we could cut out the middleman for a second kit. Got my e-mail address from the All England Journal. *Twenty thousand,* Stan. He sold them for twenty thousand.'

Stan's brain couldn't compute what he was hearing. `Twenty thousand pounds? Jan sold them? No, Jan wouldn't have done that. This bloke must be having you on. What's his name? Have you talked to him?'

`No, not yet – I've got straight on to you. Has Jan been in touch with you? This bloke, Jim or something, he said it was five weeks ago. He's chuffed to bits.'

`Can't be right, Doc.' Stan's face drained of colour.

`Well, Stan, I think it is. I'm going to try to make some more enquiries, though, see if that mate of his knows anything, or look on their website or something, or ask George, he's just been across there, you know, him from Somerset – he only got back this weekend.'

Silence ticked at both ends of the phone.

142

'I'm thinking it could be true, Stan.'

Then, in a voice he barely recognised, quiet and yet firm, Stan rejoindered.

`Stay there Doc. I'll be right across.'

Stan put down the phone and looked into to the distance. Anger and humiliation were seeping through from the soles of his feet right to his head. He felt slightly dizzy. He didn't know which was most unbelievable, Jan selling the birds, or the sum they fetched. *Twenty thousand pounds.* Words from the past, his and Evie's, began to crowd him. *You're too soft, Stan. If you're going to give the bloody things away, why don't you breed them for sale? They're always after your birds. You don't understand, Evie. It's the spirit of the thing. I like to help them out. They're laughing at you Stan, you're a pushover.*

Twenty thousand. Twenty thousand bloody pounds. It must be a wind up. But what if it wasn't, what if it was real? More voices in his head. *You just have to be clever, Stan, look for the loopholes. There's always a loophole, someone too daft to see what's in front of them.* And that was him, Stan. Stan had been the loophole, his friendly spirit, his pride. Daft, dependable Stan. Seduced by flattery and a fleeting sense of self-importance to give away a whole set of breeders, ten of the very best. Then all the fiddling around to get them vetted, the certificate of health, sorting out the transport, all done with good heart and even a flurry of excitement, as speedily as possible. Only to be taken for a total ride. He was the someone who was too daft to see what was going on in front of his eyes.

Stan locked his hurt pride into a chamber deep within, and, fuelled by a surge of outrage and anger, grabbed his coat. He took his old bike from the back yard, wheeled it through. A cat smarmed around his feet. Stan kicked it, just enough to make it sod off; Doc was so right, vermin. Stan rode the familiar route to Doc's in a trance, through drab streets with dirty nets and dishevelled gardens. Kids still played out in these streets, tatty old cars waiting to be done up lived outside dilapidated front doors, occasional hanging baskets suggesting optimism and cheerfulness against all the odds. Stan cycled right through the estate, onto the main road, turning right into Laburnum Rd through the transition from tatty old Victorian houses made into flats, towards the renovated Victorian houses full of social workers, middle managers, trendy single parents. He turned left on automatic pilot down Oak Avenue, and through into Linthorpe Rd. In three miles, he'd traversed a universe of different worlds.

Doc opened the door even as the red faced sweaty apparition that used to be Stan dismounted from his bicycle and propped it up against the garage door.

'By, you look hot. Come and get a brew.'

'Forget the brew. Make it a whisky, Doc.'

Doc raised his eyebrows: unusual. Inside Stan a lifetime of events rewound and fast forwarded, pausing on a still here and there, memory evoking emotion. The early humiliation of being caned at school, daily, for five years. For being late, for talking in class, for not getting his homework in. For being Stan, vulnerable, inadequate Stan. The mortification of getting beaten up a by a lad half his size because Stan couldn't trust himself to hit back without doing serious damage, over something so stupid and trivial he can't even remember it. The shame of getting sacked, for being told they were sorry, but they had to cut down on forklift truck drivers. He'd worked very hard, but there had to be downsizing.

Downsizing. You can say that again. Stan had walked out of that factory for the last time with two weeks wages in his pocket, and no prospects of another job. The chagrin of that one month when he couldn't make love to Evie, and then the loneliness of her ensuing rejections. The inadequacies of his role as father, of being unable to understand Damien's homework, logarithms, tangents, sines, cosines. All this time, the pigeons had saved him, keeping him sane when life stank. The simple pleasure of a good kit, the camaraderie of the lads, through thick and thin. The generosity – the spirit of the hobby. They'd never let him down.

Until now. Memories and thoughts conspired, reconfiguring the depressed mood of the morning. Good old dependable Stan was metamorphosing, but not, as Evie seemed to think, into a pig – no, something new and far more dangerous. Stan Cutler had had enough. He'd been trodden on, discarded, rejected and he wouldn't be anyone's laughing stock anymore. Finally, Stan's heart was beating the rhythm of rebellion. He would not lie down for this one. He laughed harshly, out loud. He had no job, might not have the house much longer, had virtually lost his gorgeous Evie, now he'd been shat on in the hobby – liberation came with the sudden conviction that there was nothing left to lose.

Stan gripped the glass that had appeared in his hand, and drank greedily, willing the sour taste to relax his constricting throat, letting the heat of the spirit warm him. He breathed deeply, sat down. He was sweating, but the clamminess of anxiety was transforming to the hot release of adrenalin.

`Okay. I'm okay. So, what else do you know?'

Doc had, as Stan had anticipated, set the tom toms pounding. Phone calls had been made between Middlesbrough, the Midlands, and the South West, to and from anyone who was anyone in the hobby. There was no more vital information than Stan had already, just more details.

`Well now.' Doc sipped a beer. `Seemingly this Jim guy is a bit of a geezer. He makes a lot of money from dealing, nobody's sure exactly what in, and he uses the net. Basically, we think it's anything he can get his hands on. Apparently does very well, very flash. He was over in the Midlands for a couple of days last spring, for the World Cup. Come to think of it, I remember Aitch mentioning him – d'you remember, they said he was a right wally, didn't know a thing about rollers, but was loaded – hired a Shogun. For pity's sake, he was only here two days.'

Doc snorted.

Stan had a vague recollection of the Shogun story, but he hadn't made it to the Midlands that year and he couldn't put a face to the name.

145

`Go on.' The warm whisky slipped easily down his throat. `Anyway, it would seem according to Aitch that this guy had told Jan several months ago that he was prepared to pay silly money for a good starter kit or some good breeders, and possibly for a class kit of old birds. Jan just mentioned it when he was here, when we went down to Bromsgrove. Aitch of course had no idea that Jan was going to provide them. Courtesy of us. Well, of you.'

And on a plate, Stan thought, without even having to ask.

'Bastard.' Stan 's eyes blazed.

Doc motioned to his empty glass.

`Might as well.' Stan took the refill easily, drank it in one. `So what are we gonna do?'

Stan suddenly realised that Doc was looking to him for answers, for ideas. Doc, the most educated of the lot, the businessman, him with e-mail, a time-share on the Costa Brava (even though he never got to use it).

`What d'you reckon?'

Stan was woozy, yet felt solidly in his boots.

`I don't know yet, Doc. We'll have another whisky while we think. I'll bloody swing for him.'

Doc poured more whisky, and Stan got up and began to walk towards the conservatory. Doc followed his lead. By unspoken consent they were soon down the garden, and Doc was letting out a kit of pigeons. Stan watched wordlessly, while in his head debates raged.

He wanted to kill Jan van Deuzen. But he didn't want to do time for him. He could arrange to have Jan's birds stolen. No, that would be dishonourable. He could do nothing. Not an option. He could shop Jan to all the pigeon organisations. No. That would only make Stan look more stupid. He could tell Jan how mad he was. Pointless. Then Jan would know he'd won.

Winning. There was something in this concept. Somehow, Stan needed to beat Jan at his own game, to let Jan know that he knew, but not to let him know that he was mad. That would buy Stan time to think, and then he wouldn't stay mad; he'd get even.

By the time the birds were in and Stan and Doc had returned to the house, Stan knew his first move.

`Give me the phone. Have you got Jan's number?'

Doc had, of course, and dialled for Stan, then passed him the handset. It rang for an interminable minute before a woman answered, and there was the sound of a small child in the background.

`Ja?'

`Hello. You speak English?' Stan spoke very slowly and loudly, as if the woman might be very stupid or very hard of hearing.

`Of course. Who is that?' A dog was barking somewhere in the background.

`Is Jan there? It's Stan. Tell him it's Stan from England.'

'Please, one moment.' There was a pause, punctuated by the rustling of clothes and small child chatter. The woman shouted, someone shouted back. Footsteps approached Stan 's ear. A man's voice, deep and confident.

'Hello. This is Jan'

'Jan, it's Stan Cutler, from Middlesbrough.'

'Ah, Stan, my friend. How are all the guys?'

'They're great, Jan, just great. Tell me, how are you getting on with the birds?'

Barely a second's hesitation.

`Ah, the birds. Not so good. Things have changed for me, Stan. Work, the children, you know how it is. I've had to let a lot of them go.'

`Oh. I'm sorry to hear that. So you'll be sending my breeders back, then?' Stan let him sweat for just a second. He could almost hear the ticking of the Dutchman's brain.

`Well, actually, I've shared them around with some of the other guys. You know how it is.' Jan paused. `I have given them away on permanent loan.'

Smooth talking bastard.

`I do.' Stan gulped more whisky. `Only a little bird told me that you'd sold them, Jan. But I was sure you wouldn't do that without talking to me. Am I right?'

147

`Well, some of the guys wanted to buy them, Stan. I took enough to cover my costs.'

Stan's heart pounded, his brain screamed.

Twenty grand, is what I heard, Jan. Twenty grand in English money.

`I am really sorry about that, Jan. I'd wanted them to stick together. You know, the Cutler family. Years of breeding in there.'

`Well, yeah, Stan, to be honest I only split them between two of the guys, and they're going to breed off them, so the family will be really well carried on, and I thought it would be okay because then there will be even more to breed from. I was going to get in touch with you to let you know, but you know, with a bit of domestic crisis it's been difficult. I thought you'd be okay with it, knowing that your family will be all over Holland. In fact, they might even be spread further afield.' He paused very briefly then skilfully interjected, `it's a great compliment, Stan.'

Silence. Stan bided his time. Just enough to be absolutely sure of what he wanted to say. He knew, of course, exactly what he wanted to say. *Do you think I've just fallen off a Christmas tree, just because I'm not very wealthy and not very educated? Do you really think I take this rip off as a compliment? You daft bastard you.*

But Stan was thinking outcomes, and in the warm well of his whisky-comforted soul, he needed Jan not to know that he knew everything. Game on, and for once, Stan was going to win. He would box clever, wait until he had a plan. He'd fall out with Jan van Clevershite when the time was right.

`Well, Jan, I'm a bit surprised to tell you the truth.' Stan gave Jan just a second of uncertainty. `But hey man, I'm sure your judgement's good, and aye, at the end of the day, I suppose it's good to know the birds are okay and that they'll be bred from.' He hesitated before adding, `and I hope things look up for you, mate. You're not giving up the birds altogether, are you?'

Stan winked at Doc, whose jaw was hanging open, then gestured once more to his glass. Doc filled it up again, and Stan was feeling like he'd grown an inch or two. He could see Doc taking in the new Stan tone of voice, the assertiveness.

`No, mate. Actually, I'm going to stop flying so much, and probably won't be entering competition. Or, as I said, breeding.' Jan chuckled amicably. `But I'm looking to keep involved by doing a bit more judging. You know so that I can see the birds but keep things ticking at home, and then I can keep an eye on what everyone's doing as well.'

Stan broke into a slight nervous laugh.

`Sounds good, Jan. Always good to keep an eye on things. And anyway, as long as me mealy cock went to a good home, and is doing alright.' Jan's sigh of relief was just audible as Stan led him onto safe ground, and the Dutchman gave Stan a series of platitudes. Stan let Jan think that he was indeed placated.

`Okay then Jan, better go, Doc's phone bill. We'll be in touch, and take care.'

Stan put down the phone, and looked at Doc, who looked quizzically over at Stan. Big, powerful Doc. Suddenly unsure. Of course. He would be outraged, his sense of justice affronted, his sense of protection to his friend strong: but he wouldn't be incensed like Stan was. Doc had never been a doormat, so he wouldn't understand the same sense of uprising that was coursing through Stan 's veins, or the same sense of certainty that the crime would be avenged. Stan also hadn't clocked this. Doc was slightly thrown by the man he now saw in front of him. After all, Doc didn't yet know that Stan hadn't gone crazy, and might even have been computing how long it would take him to find a syringe and fill it with tranquillizer if need be.

`What did you mean, take care?' Doc was intrigued, almost holding his breath.

`I mean, Doc, watch your back, you wanker.' Stan was grinning now. `I mean we're going to get revenge. He's taken us, we're gonna take him. I don't know how yet, Doc, but I'll think of something.' He slugged some more whisky. `I've had enough, Doc, I've had enough. Now fly us a kit and then I'll see you tonight with Akbar and Frank.'

Stan stood up straighter than usual, losing years in his physiological reshuffle. `Tell you what, Doc, I could get used to this drinking in the morning.' He smiled wider, really grinned, for the first time in ages.

*

Stan sat in the silence of the house and scratched his balls. The wooziness had worn off, and he was deep in thought. There must be a plan, just skirting around his brain, he was sure, but he wasn't yet clear on its content. He'd thought of nothing else all day. He had fantasised, of course, of just having Jan done over, breaking his knees. Plenty in the 'Boro would do that for Stan, and on this occasion, he might even fancy doing it himself. But that would be Stan operating more from emotion than from judgement, and violence wasn't really his style, despite its momentary appeal. There must be another way, and Stan's thinking kept on coming back to the fact that Jan was a crook. A real crook, not only with the pigeon theft. Jan was a crook big time. He also had a penchant for bragging, and that made him vulnerable. The gas fire cast its gentle light on the shadows of his thoughts. The shape of the plan flickered around its edges, an ember nearly ready to ignite.

It had to be to do with the diamonds, he'd got that far. Jan worked in one of the largest diamond factories in Holland. He'd already boasted how he could get through security there, how he was so bloody clever. The words *there's always a loophole* kept on haunting Stan. He'd have to talk to the lads about it. Revenge was most definitely on the cards.

Evie noticed his agitation as soon as she got home, damn her. She pecked him on the cheek, but then drew back, looking at him with concern.

`Stan, you're hot. You alright?'

'Yeah, I'm fine, Evie.' He kissed her again. `Matter of fact, I've not felt so well for ages. Let me make you some tea, love. `Hey'– he suddenly started – `where's that crock dog gone?'

He'd felt something different in this room for a while, yet only just realised what it was.

Evie looked at him again, threw off her coat on to the back of the sofa.

`Stan, it's been gone for months. And if you've only just noticed it, only goes to show you haven't missed it. No, Stan, no tea, I've been drinking coffee in the Union.' Coffee in the Union. She said it so casually, taking to being a student as if she'd done it all her life. Stan envied her. Evie carefully untied the laces of her new leather boots, and put them up against the wall, then flopped loudly to the sofa with a large outtake of air. Stan sat down beside her, and she put her feet up on his lap.

`I've had such a good day.' A smile played at the corner of Evie's lips. `You know that essay I did? Well, it passed. I got a B-. The tutor thought it was interesting and original. Me, Stan, interesting and original. I was really chuffed; he gave me loads of ideas how I could make it better. And, he said, if possible, he'd like it typed out next time. I'll have to ask our Damien to teach me, though God knows when I'll have time to learn it.' She giggled. `Knew I should have done typing in school, instead of hanging out with the riff raff.'

She looked coyly at Stan. The light in her eyes seemed blurred to him, just a touch vague. He felt strange, like he was in the room with Evie, he could feel her feet with his hands and his thighs, see the cheeky look she was giving him, could smell her unique scent and hear her giggle, but at the same time it was like he was outside himself looking in, so that he was in the picture too. Images seemed to pass before him on a second screen, Jan, pigeons, Damien, the computer, Doc's face, Evie, crowds of people together in an imaginary coffee bar, money, loads of it, the computer, there's always a loophole, Stan himself by his loft, handing over his birds with pride.

He shook himself. Must be the whisky.

'Stan?' Evie sounded concerned.

`Sorry, me duck.' Stan zoomed down from the ceiling and felt the strangest sensation of his insides rearranging themselves slightly to fit him better. Was this how a pigeon felt, rolling around up there for ages? He wondered, then smiled, and squeezed Evie's feet. The next sentence seemed to utter itself, without thought.

`Tell you what, Evie, why don't I learn the computer? Then I could type your essays for you, help you out a bit.'

`You, Stan? You, do my typing?'

Evie's incredulity packed the sensitivity of a concrete post, and her face registered her own clumsiness at the tone of her words.

`Why, don't you think I could?' Evie's apparent lack of confidence in him didn't even touch Stan. In his bodily shake up, determination seemed to have ousted, for the moment, vulnerability, so that when she tried to reassure him, Stan could see it all, and felt like he was playing with her.

`Well, yes, I suppose so. It's not that I don't think…' She stumbled slightly, and he watched her try to be encouraging. It was okay: he'd been a long time dormant, you couldn't blame her for not having faith.

`Yeah, well. To be honest with you, Evie, I could do with a bit of doing something. And I've not seen much of our kid lately, so if he'll teach me, I'll learn.' Stan was enjoying the effect he was having. `And anyway, to be honest, I'd quite like to learn to surf the net. There must be all kinds of interesting things on there. Yep, I'll do it.'

It had come to him when he'd been up on the ceiling, looking down. The only way he could get even with someone several hundred miles away was to take a worldview, to see it all from the outside. He needed to be able to find information out, to help himself to find ideas, to make contacts if he needed. Jan worked in a diamond factory. Jan stole from a diamond factory. Somehow, Stan didn't know how yet, diamonds were the key to it all, to Stan's revenge. Stan needed to get sharper, up to date, to know how to find out more about diamonds, to widen his options. And anyway, he would genuinely like to help Evie out, to go up in her esteem, to find some common ground. He patted her on the legs, suddenly eager to move.

'Go on then, let me go for me shower. I'll be going out with the lads tonight.'

'But it's not Thursday.' Evie sounded surprised.

'No, I know, bit of an extra. Doc's arranged it.'

Stan stood up, picked up his teacup from earlier, and strode towards the kitchen. Behind him, Evie was left wondering if she really did just glimpse the man she used to know. When he next looked in to say goodbye, she was curled up and dozing, probably back at college. He blew her a silent kiss.

The lads were early in the Cabbage Club that night. Akbar and Frank were incensed at what had happened, and only too eager to help Stan out. Doc brought a round of drinks to the table and sat down aggressively, placing several packets of pork scratchings on to the table and indicating to the lads that they should help themselves. Akbar regarded all that fat and gristle with disgust, but Doc didn't notice as he ripped open the first pack, savouring hungrily the salty crunch of pig's skin. The way he explained it, at least it wasn't as fattening as eating the whole pig, and was therefore allowed under the Weight Watchers.

`Okay, so how do we get this bastard?' Stan invited his friends to help him out.

`Break his fucking legs, man.' Akbar was his usual forthright self. Stan laughed.

`That's one way, Akbar, but I don't think so. I think we can do better.'

Doc looked thoughtful. `Well, Stan, what d'you want to get out of it? Revenge? Money? You want to be careful, you know, sounds like he's a big player if what he was saying about those diamonds is true.'

Akbar shrugged, adventure gleaming in his eyes.

`So what? That just means he's filthy rich, man, loads of dosh.' He rippled his shoulders through his blue CK shirt. `Just say the word, Stan, me and the lads'll break his bloody legs for him.'

Stan looked steely eyed. `I know, but no. There's got to be something else. Something to do with those diamonds.'

Frank took a long slow measure from his glass, commanding their attention just by the way he reached out for and then replaced the glass.

`I think you're right, Stan. Something about those diamonds. After all, if he really is a bit of a jewel thief, then I think we're

153

right to go after his money, not his bloody bones. I knew they looked a shifty pair of bleeders.' Frank paused slightly. `Although we could give him a bit of a beating as well, to show that he can't mess us around like this.' The group nodded, bravado joining them together. Frank continued. `The way I see it is like this. It's got to be blackmail, and it's got to be good. The man's corrupt. Him and his sleazy little sidekick. They work with diamonds. There's got to be some way of getting a rock from them. The only question is how. We know Jan knows how to get them out of the factory, we've just got to persuade him that we need one to keep quiet.'

'That's it. That's bloody it.' Stan's voice trembled slightly, his eyes flashed bright. `That's the plan. It's blackmail. That is so right, Frank, that's the way to do it.'

This was it, the little bit that had been eluding him all day, as he too knew it had to be to do with the diamonds. They would have to blackmail Jan with their knowledge of his corruption, to use the information somehow. It was easy, a great idea.

The details were more difficult. Stan had never blackmailed anyone before; there were lots of questions. How could they set it up so that Jan could never be sure enough to catch them? How could they apply enough pressure to let him know they were serious? How could they make him go along with it? How could they pick up the ransom money, and how much should they ask for? Key questions for which Stan had no answers as yet.

But he could find out. How many hours had he sat in his chair at home, wishing away his life until Evie walked in the door, until he could turn a kit out, until he could get to the pub? His life was an empty cupboard. Stan's brain cells welcomed the challenge of having to find out something new, of having to set something up, having to do a bit of research. He liked the sound of that; research sounded formal, thorough, and impressive.

`That's how we get the bastard.' Stan swigged from his pint. `But then again I don't want him to know it's us – I mean, he will know, but we never sign our names to it. So we need to threaten him enough for him to take us seriously, and then find a way to do an exchange without blowing our gaff.' He emptied his pint glass.

Doc shuffled.

`Well I think it's a good idea,' he began, in a voice which they knew would introduce a `but' to the proceedings. `But quite honestly, what the heck are we going to blackmail him with? I mean all we know so far is that we think he steals diamonds. But we don't know for sure, we don't know how many, we don't know how often – let's face it, we know bugger all.'

Stan nodded, thoughtful, determined. `Aye, that's true. And we can't exactly threaten him that if we're arrested we'll stand up in court and swear that he told us he steals diamonds. When he was under the influence of alcohol. And so were we. Shite.'

Akbar looked glum, then his eyes brightened. `What about his wife? Or his daughter? We could kidnap them, hold them to ransom.' He looked around the group, while collecting up the glasses to go and fetch a fresh drink.

The lads laughed half-heartedly, and Frank voiced everyone's responses.

`And where do we hide them, Akbar, and how terrified would they be? No, we can't be hurting women and bairns.' Frank got up and went to the toilet, Doc opened another bag of pork scratchings, and Stan sat, frowning, until everyone was back.

`Maybe we have to just accept that you're not gonna get any money for your birds,' said Frank, `maybe this is just it. Shit happens.' He took a sip of his drink and added, morosely, `and then you die.'

`Alright, Eeyore.' Stan laughed at his friend, his face flushed. `Although God knows I could do with some. No, it's what he makes us look like. And anyway,' he paused slightly, `anyway, actually maybe it is the money. Maybe I'm bloody sick of being skint. If anyone gets money out of my birds, it'll be me. If he got twenty thousand, then I want at least fifty thousand off him. Blackmail it is. We just have to find a way to make it stick, so he'll do it, and a way to get the money without getting caught.'

155

Akbar was sarcastic. `Just the details to fill in then Stan. Sounds like a piece of cake.'

The friends looked glum and began to talk pigeons again. The answers, when they came, were obvious. They were talking competitions, how their youngsters were doing, whether or not Doc would judge the World Cup this year if he won it, how much time it would take and how difficult judging can be. Judging. A little light went on in Stan's head. All that Jan wanted to do now was judge, to stay in touch, to keep an eye on things.

`I've got it!' He slammed down his glass with great excitement. `We ask Jan to judge the Invitation Fly – course we do.'

`But he's a wanker.' Akbar looked confused.

`Exactly.' Stan looked triumphant. `Exactly. And I tell you what. It's because he's a wanker that we'll get him. We'll get him drunk. We'll have a tape recorder. We'll ask him, find out more about how he does it, what he's really ripped off. We'll give him a spade and he'll dig himself a hole. What do you think?'

The lads looked interested – they couldn't but respond to Stan's enthusiasm. It was a possibility. They were still looking for a judge, nothing was confirmed with anyone else yet, and anyway they could always double up with a guest judge or a scribe. This was the beauty of the Old Cocks Club – they could do whatever they wanted.

`Okay,' Doc folded the last empty pork-scratching packet into neat quarters and placed it in the ashtray. `This is okay, we can maybe get him back – if he says yes – and we can trap him. That's half the job done. But what about the rest? How do we blackmail him? And how the heck do we get the money without getting caught by the cops, or – even worse – getting our knees cracked by Jan van Clevershite's heavy mates?'

`Your round, I think Doc.' Akbar pushed the glasses over to Doc and the friends sat around thinking while he bought the drinks and brought them back across.

`Swiss bank account?' Stan suggested, half-heartedly.

`Bit complicated,' explained Doc, as if he opened one every day. `You have to have quite a lot of money to deposit to open the account in the first place. Don't think we can do that.'

`What about picking it up through the post – a P.O. Box number?'

Stan shook his head. `Not sure how much that can be traced, and how long it would all take. It's kind of messy.'

Stuck for ideas, the lads turned back to pigeons, to loft design and how the new roof on Frank's shed had got foam rubber underneath the felt so that when the pigeons rolled down onto the top they didn't hurt themselves. The lads were impressed. Then they got silly – and then they struck gold.

It was Frank who started the train of thought. The subject of the loft design led to the story in the paper of the guy whose state of the art security enhanced loft was broken into, and only the corn was taken. They laughed at this clever insult, but nodded despondently at how it only went to show how hard it is to be totally secure. As they finished the last pint, Frank reviewed what else he had seen in the news today.

`Did you see the paper this morning? They've only used a bloody pigeon to smuggle cannabis off a boat. Taped it to its legs, apparently. The paper was calling it a real coo.'

The lads chuckled. Doc started to reply.

`Well, that's not so new you know, d'you remember that pigeon that was used to smuggle from the diamond mines in Namibia...,' and as Stan listened, his brain experienced a blinding flash of the bleeding obvious, and he laughed out loud.

`That's it! That's it, course it is. A pigeon. We use a bloody pigeon. It's been sitting here staring us in the face, we get Jan to smuggle out a diamond worth a lot of money and then we get it sealed in a bag and tied on to a racing pigeon. It's perfect!'

They all looked at him, Frank uncomprehending, Doc on with the breakthrough, Akbar twinkling rapidly. He slapped the table, and leaned forward

`How heavy d'you think a diamond is, then?'

157

`I reckon it weighs just about as much as a pigeon can carry, Akbar.' Stan was grinning from ear to ear now. Brilliant, bloody brilliant.

Frank was struggling, his brain exhibiting the swiftness of a tortoise, and then the lights came on and small smile to begin to spread.

`What's that got to do with – oh, you mean…?'

`Yes, you dozy bleeder, I do mean. I mean exactly that.' Stan was flying now, his arse barely touching the seat of his chair, elbows on the table, eyes bright. `That's it, we've got a bloody plan. First, we get Jan over here to judge the fly, and get him drunk. We find out how he gets these diamonds. Then we find a way to convince Jan that if he doesn't get us a diamond or two, we blow the gaff to his boss. Then we set up a drop off point for him to leave a diamond. In that place, we'll have a racer ready and waiting. And then we're away, he'll never be able to prove it was us. He'll know, but he'll never be able to prove it.'

They all sat round looking wide-eyed. Now they were moving beyond a game, beyond a fantasy, into a possible reality. Wow. Blackmail, diamonds, Amsterdam. Money. Revenge.

`I think,' Doc said gruffly, breaking the four round rule which enabled a certain equality in the group, `I think this calls for another bag of scratchings. Who wants another pint – on me?'

The gang of four acknowledged the gravity and generosity of the situation and acquiesced with grace. While Doc was at the bar, they pondered some details.

`We need a racing man in Holland.' Frank was serious. `Ideally, you would be correct.' Stan stated this evenly.

`But we could use an English racer guy, after all the pigeon would bring it back here okay. And,' he said convincingly, `that could be a lot better. We could be getting it fenced here before they even know it's gone. Let alone where to look for it. We could sort it out in Leeds if need be. Although, Amsterdam's better fur us I suppose, off our turf. So hopefully Amsterdam but Leeds as back up.'

Everyone nodded; they had been in the hobby for years, they could find these contacts without any problem.

'What about setting him up?' Frank contributed, again, that which made them think more carefully.

'Well, I think,' said Stan, 'I think he must have some computer scam going. I mean, he's been a polisher, he knows his stuff, he knows his jewels. But he also knows a loophole, and he works in IT – he virtually let on that there's some computer angle to this. If so, leave it to our Damien – I know he'll sort it out, after all he's bloody brilliant.'

Doc came back with the last pint, and everyone received it gratefully and thirstily, as if the amber nectar would give oomph and clarity to their excited brains. After all, they had a plan, and although there was a load to do yet, it was a plan of the utmost simplicity and it could work.

'Tell you what, Stan, be brilliant to make this work.' Akbar was pink-cheeked beneath his sculpted bronze cheekbones. 'Just imagine what your Evie would say.'

'I know,' Stan chuckled. 'And I tell you what, mate, I've got a feeling that it will work. And I'll surprise our lass yet. But I tell you this' – Stan looked solemn and focused – 'not a word to anyone about this. I mean it, not a single word.'

'Done.' They all nodded solemnly, raised glasses to each other, and downed their drinks quickly so as not to keep Maggie waiting in the car park, where she would be, the paragon of care and control, at precisely eleven o'clock.

When Stan got home, he felt truly inebriated. Evie was already in bed, lamp on and, he knew without looking, coursebook open. He cleaned his teeth thoroughly, found himself grinning at that green eyed man looking back at him, seeing a friend for the first time in months, even a year or two, instead of a fading failure. Even when he turned and banged his head on a hanging basket, he was still smiling. Then he made small cups of tea, and went up the stairs to the bedroom. He was right, Evie was in bed reading, and he took her tea to her side.

'Didn't know if you'd want any, love,' he said, his voice mellow, his face smiling. The gesture was simple, generous, no alternative, sexual motives. He stripped down to his t-shirt and his **I Luv Rollers** logo boxers, the big red heart right around his privates, and walked tall round to his side of the bed. He got in, plumped his pillows, and drank his tea. Then he stretched, still grinning for some reason, and put his arms behind his head. He noticed Evie giving him a curious glance, looked at her and laughed.

`Good night, pet,' he said, and snuggled down into his side of the bed, expecting nothing, just glad to be next to her. As he settled down into his dream, he had the slightest awareness of the paradox that now he was asking nothing of her, Evie seemed to be interested in making some small physical contact with him by wrapping her lower leg around his. He registered the warmth and imagined her with a diamond on her finger, but made no response save a grunt of pleasure before he sprinkled diamond stars into the tunnel of his future, and slept.

Fourteen
Now I've Got You

Another [psychological] game is `now I've got you, you sonovabitch'. This is another classic fanciers play. This is about getting your own back...you simply bide your time and wait until one day either the weather is wrong or the birds aren't right. Now's your chance to get even.

Graham Dexter, *Winners with Spinners* 1997

161

Stan didn't mind admitting that Damien was a gorgeous looking lad. Six feet one, easy growing muscle, slim, and cheery by nature, which showed in his dark brown eyes. Damien might have said that he wasn't so much cheery by nature, more a case of having to be, living in the Cold War that often permeated number fifty-seven. It hadn't escaped Stan 's notice that Damien seemed to prefer to go over to his girlfriend's. Presumably, there he found harmony, humour, and, so Stan imagined, gratification of his sexual needs.

At home, Damien seemed to spend time in his room, a room he had laboured to mould to a personality that was clearly much more modern than that of his dad. He always said he loved his job, painting and decorating some might say, although in reality Damien was something of an artisan, gifted with vision and dexterity. And he was addicted to his computer, the fascination of technology, the ability to make a machine work for him, the development of his own interior design package in full flow. Give or take an hour here and there, as far as Stan could tell, his son loved his life, and would probably soon be off, maybe looking for work down south, even abroad. Stan reckoned that Damien would go far.

On that Monday evening in early winter, Stan surprised Damien with his assertive knock on his son's bedroom door. He stood tall when Damien opened it.

`Hiya, son. Good day?' Stan noted Damien's raised eyebrow, and took the shrug and hand movement as an invitation to enter his son's room.

`Thanks, son.'

Stan stepped in and looked around as if seeing the room for the first time. It was big, surprisingly airy looking. Damien had decorated it last year, grey, silver and white, lots of interesting lighting scattered around at different heights. Probably a room best appreciated from a horizontal position, a seduction room. The room had its own washbasin. Akbar and one of his mates had put it in early last year, and black and white mosaic tiles surrounded it. It looked like a room from another era.

Stan could suddenly see the house as if it were cut in half, like a bombed building that he'd seen photos of, where the inside of the house was exposed for all to see, wallpaper, floor coverings, tables and bits of furniture still standing where they'd serviced their owners' small and soon to be insignificant lives. What would a news reporter make of their house, 57, Wirehill Way? Two different eras rubbing along in the same shell. The new cotton curtains, cheap carpet, and now the red rag rug of Stan and Evie's room, the flowery wallpaper, (tasteful, mind) all contrasted starkly with the track lighting, polished floorboards and minimalist colouring of their son's room. The posters that Stan remembered being in here were gone – no footballers anymore, no Britney. The magazines on the bedside table were *Loaded, Zoo, Men's Health*, and *GQ*, with pictures of space age near nude women with oiled pneumatic breasts on the front. Scary. There was also a copy of *Interior Decorating Today*, and a book called *The Seven Habits of Highly Successful People*. Stan was intrigued.

He could see that Damien was looking a little bewildered too, maybe worried that his dad had come to tell him the facts of life, several years too late. Stan sat down on the bed, and took a breath. He looked at the confident young man in front of him, and reminded himself that he was of his, Stan 's, loins. If Damien could do it, if he could master modern technology and make it work for him, then so could Stan.

`Son, I've been thinking.' He had Damien's attention. `I want to learn how to use the computer, Damien, and I wondered if you'd teach me, and if I could use your machine. When you're out, like, so I wouldn't be in your way.' Stan was faltering slightly. `I mean, I know it's a bit of a cheek, but you know, I could help your Mam out with her college work, and I could learn to surf the net, and well, I just wondered what you thought.'

He could see that Damien was thinking a number of things, probably a mixture of surprise, admiration and embarrassment. Shocked maybe that his old dad was thinking of taking up the net. Maybe he'd be pleased and suspicious at the same time,

163

pleased if they could have common interest, as Stan knew that his son had no interest in the birds. He'd often wondered what it would be like if Damien really made it big time, if he did marry Susannah, good old upper middle class Susannah. Not that class meant much anymore, not unless you were the so called underclass, and even they had no identity, not like when Stan was young.

Sometimes, Stan imagined what Damien and Susannah's wedding might be like. Damien would probably be wearing a right posh suit; Susannah would be resplendent in a designer number, her well sculpted body carrying it beautifully, her green eyes and dark glossy hair belying her Irish origin. The reception would be dead sophisticated, with people who had done well at whatever it was they did, people who had wanted to go further, people with money, with interesting lives.

Not like his.

He'd met Susannah's Uncle Miles from Essex at a family do, a Managing Director who played golf and flew gliders. Damien had introduced him.

`Charmed,' Uncle Miles had said, talked to him for a bit before the dreaded question. `Tell me, Stan, what do you do for a living?'

`On the dole, mate.'

`Oh, how sad.' Uncle Miles sounded like he meant it. `Still, expect that gives you lots of leisure time, what?'

`Oh aye, lots of that, alright. I breed pigeons, you know.'

A look had come over Uncle Miles' face, the one that associated pigeons with lowering the tone of the neighbourhood. `Ah. Fascinating, I'm sure. Do you win many races?'

Stan knew he was probably thinking how absolutely revolting, all that flapping of wings, and nasty pigeon muck. Slightly bevvied, he decided to disavow Uncle Miles of the stereotypes in his head. Not briefly, but over a good half hour or so, explaining how there are as many breeds of pigeons as there are of dogs, how his birds spin with inconceivable rapidity, how it's a myth that they shit on the neighbours' washing and so on and so forth.

Eventually, Uncle Miles had excused himself and went to fetch a drink. He hadn't come back. Was Damien ashamed of him?
`Yeah, okay, dad, why not.' Damien grinned. Stan should have trusted him, and said sod it to all those crazy doubts.
`Bit of a surprise, hey dad?'
Stan was grinning also, sheepishly.
`Aye, well, you know how it is son. 'Bout time I moved on.' Stan indicated the copy of *GQ*, the pneumatic babe pouting out from the cover, hands on the holstered guns strapped low around her naked hips. `By heck, though, I could show her a thing or too.' He chuckled conspiratorially. `Hey?'
Damien nodded to seal the sexual conspiracy, as red-blooded men should.
`So, dad, what d'you want to learn computer for?'
Stan didn't hesitate. He knew, for once, exactly what he wanted.
`Well, two things really, son. First, I'd like to understand these things better. I want to be able to write things, write up the minutes of the club, and help your Mam with her essays. And, I want to get onto that net. I'm told you can get all sort of things, know what I mean?'
Stan wanted Damien to understand, suddenly wished he wasn't wearing the naff t-shirt that said *I'm not an alcoholic, real alcoholics go to meetings* while he was feeling like using his brain. But Damien just nodded and reached for the power switch.
`Coming into the twenty first century then, dad?' he asked. `And why not? Right then, come on, let's have a look. Let's see what we can do.'
Damien pulled up the state of the art stools which he kept neatly stacked by his computer desk (aluminium, with black pads for resting your knees, designed for good posture), and within minutes father and son were positioned side by side, riding the roller coaster of change. Damien showed his dad how to boot up, how to use a mouse, the possibilities of a drop down menu, how to move into a word processing programme through a desktop icon, and how to save a file. Bloody marvellous. The neurons in Stan 's rusty brain were firing, not quite on all cylinders, but

165

firing nevertheless, ignited by adrenaline and powered by determination. Before he knew it, it was half past eleven, and Stan and Damien had been working together for over three hours. Stan could do simple word processing, and had written down the idiot's guide to help him remember. Click on W on the screen. Go to file. Go to open. Type. Go to save. Go to close. Piece of cake, and he began to wonder why it had taken him so long to make himself learn this.

Most exciting of all, though, Stan could get onto the Web. One click of the mouse on that magic *e* symbol, and straight into *Ask Jeeves*, set up by Damien to make it as easy as possible. And already Stan knew how to ask Jeeves for anything, anything at all. He knew how to scroll down the list of suggestions and pull up the things he wanted. He'd found porn, accidentally as it happened by typing in cock birds. He'd found motorbikes, he'd found Asda – he'd even, as it happened, found a website on gas meters. At Damien's suggestion, he'd typed in *Birmingham Rollers*, and he'd only gone and found bloody websites for the birds, including www.nbra.co.uk, the home of the National Fly. There were also several in America, one in South Africa, one in Holland (aha!), and even one in Australia, would you believe. Stan's world was bigger than it had been for years.

After sharing a late night cup of tea with his son, thanking him for the help, Stan took himself to bed. He knew that Evie wasn't asleep, he could tell from her breathing. Desperately wanting to share his animation with her, he put his arm out towards her. He could smell the familiar scent of *Nivea Visage*, the one she kept on the dressing table to keep the wrinkles at bay, and enjoyed the comfort of its familiarity. All he wanted was to touch the woman he loved, to make a sign of affection, begin to build a bridge between their seemingly drifting islands. He would have loved to tell Evie of his plans, but feared her response. He put the adventurous arm around her waist, careful to avoid breast or lower stomach, signalling that it's okay, he'd got the sex message, and anyway that wasn't tonight's agenda. He felt her stiffen slightly, so kissed the nape of her neck, swiftly, pressing and softening his lips on the down between their skin, holding them there just long enough to say *I miss you, Evie, I wish we could talk.* Before she could make any move to spoil the sentiment, he turned away.

Assuming his foetal position, he was recounting in his mind all the steps he'd learned tonight on the computer, and was rehearsing asking Jeeves where he could find information about diamonds. Tomorrow, when Evie would be out at college, and Damien at work, Stan would begin his project. The corners of his mouth turned slightly upwards, and he drifted into the sleep of those who dare dream about a brighter future.

Tuesday morning dawned unusually brightly, with birdsong in the air. Stan leaped out of bed and found himself whistling as he fetched the tea for Evie. He detected a funny look in her eyes, and turned away. He made his way down the stairs, boldly stepping on creaks, no longer prepared to creep around his own home. He didn't shower yet, he was changing the pattern of his day. He took his mug of tea, as usual, to the garden, and let out the old birds.

`Come on you beauties, I've been looking at some of our mates across the water. On the net, yeah, right up there through the airwaves. Away, come on now, away.' He waved the broom handle and bag at the last reluctant fliers.

It didn't surprise him that today they were exceptionally good, kitting well, not a single one out of the group, and some nice deep rolls. He chatted away to them.

`Brilliant, you're fucking brilliant.' `Might get you a new loft when we're rich, hey?' `Oh yes, what a break.' `And you, you beauty, you might have to go in the breeders' pen now. You'll get lots of spreading and treading in there, I can tell you.'

When Evie called him for breakfast, the birds were down and fed. He stepped lightly into the kitchen and boldly pecked her on the cheek.

`Thanks, pet,' he said, and meant it. The paper was on the table as usual. Today, though, Stan was impatient to get on, and had scoured every page within minutes, barely resting on the mammoth mammaries that proliferated throughout the rag. He caught Evie watching him, and looked up.

`You alright?' She quizzed him directly.

`Aye. Why, shouldn't I be?' He felt naughty, carrying his secret plan like a child about to bunk off school.

`Nothing that I know of.' He coloured slightly, as if Evie could see right into his duplicitous head. `Just that you look a bit bright, and you've left your sausage.'

She paused.

`Unusual for you to leave your sausage.'

`Just not very hungry, that's all. It was ever so nice, though, thanks.'

Quickly, he picked up his plate and cutlery and took it to the kitchen, throwing the sausage into the bin and swilling the plate under the tap so that the egg didn't congeal, before stacking it into the washing-up bowl. Evie was just a footfall behind him.

`You could have put that in the fridge, Stan, for later.' Shit. Evie was watching him again.

`I suppose. I never thought.' Stan had never known either of them eat a cold sausage from the fridge, but in these times of hardship, it was at least courteous not to be blatant about waste. Better form to let it linger until it was at the back of the fridge, then you could agree it should be dumped.

Stan whistled some more, made his way past Evie. He cleared the rest of the table and busied himself until she'd gone, feeling the energy inside him as he folded the paper, wiped the table, and vacuumed. He'd put some music on, *Best of the Eagles*, sang along with it over the sound of the motor, almost dancing along as he did the whole of the downstairs. Twenty minutes later, he'd earned a real though curious smile and a kiss on the cheek from Evie.

`See you later, then, don't be working too hard.' He could hear fondness in Evie's voice, and it was paradoxical that just as his wife was feeling warm towards him, Stan couldn't wait for her to get out of the house. The second she had gone, he bounded through to the bathroom, two steps at a time, threw off his

168

clothes and jumped into the invigorating shower, letting the water pour over him like a waterfall from the power showerhead, which Doc gave him, sloughing off the dead cells of his skin, paving the way for renewal and regeneration.

As soon as he was dressed, Stan went into Damien's room. For a second, he wondered if he could remember what to do as he flicked the switch that gave the computer life, but only for a second. Stan moved the mouse to the magic e symbol, double clicked the left button, and there it was, he was on the World Wide Web. Jeeves was on the screen, offering him the oyster of anywhere on his silly little tray. Stan typed in `diamonds,' and when over two thousand possibilities came up, he was away.

Only an hour had to pass for Stan to find just what he was looking for. The website www.adiamondisforever.com had given him a huge amount of information, and he'd printed some out, hoping it was the right stuff. He wanted to know more about diamonds, specifically so he could steal and then fence one. He almost laughed out loud at the thought – he, Stan Cutler, a diamond thief.

Stan went down the stairs wearing the face of a slightly younger man. He spent the next two hours looking through all his notes, comparing sizes, cuts and amounts of money. He easily retained certain amounts of information, and actually found the whole thing fascinating. He'd never known that when diamonds are `rough cut,' they just look like any old stone. He browsed pictures of the biggest rocks you could imagine – the Hope diamond, blue and glittery, the Pearson diamond, round like a little ball, red diamonds, yellow diamonds, stones he never knew existed. None of them looked remotely like the little diamond on Evie's finger that he bought her all those years ago for their engagement, twenty to be exact, from old Arthur Mason's jeweller store, *Good as Gold*, for the princely sum of twenty one guineas. Guineas – way after decimalisation, Arthur had traded in them till the day he died. Evie didn't wear the ring anymore. She said it was too small for her finger.

Stan tried to pick up what he could about types of diamond. He had an idea in his mind of how much money he would like to make. Mustn't be too greedy, though he was still reeling from the huge sum for which his birds had apparently been sold. So maybe he should go for the moon at £100,000, or maybe he should settle for £50,000. He decided that these would be the limits within which he could work.

How would he know that he had the right diamond, then?

He learned that much of the value of the diamond is in the cut, some in the colour and much in the weight, the carats. Coloured diamonds of good quality were rare – best forget that, they might be too easy to trace. The make up of the diamond seemed crucial – a diamond with no flaws inside would fetch the most money. Stan was riveted by diagrams of how the diamonds grew, starting their life as deep as ninety five miles underground, growing in replicated atomic formations, like a series of little cartridges on top of each other until a perfect gem was created.

Then there was the question of weight. A carat is a measure of weight of 0.007 oz. A racer, he knew, could carry about 2oz. So 2 divided by 0.007 – Stan made this about a 300 carat diamond. He wasn't fully sure what this meant, except that this could possibly fetch a lot of money. It would all need some thinking about.

When he was satisfied with his understanding, he nipped down to the pigeon loft and stashed his notes into a plastic folder that he'd borrowed from Evie, which he put into a large box in the far empty compartment of the shed. All that remained was to share the information with his mates, and then to refine the plan. He only wanted enough, and not so much to make it impossible for Jan to smuggle out. Enough to teach Jan a lesson. Enough to change Stan's life; to pay off his twenty thousand pound mortgage, and to buy a little gem for Evie. That would be fine, he reckoned he deserved that.

He went up to the house, opened the cupboard under the stair, and took out the old net curtain that Evie had taken down when her sister did that magic cleansing stuff in the house.

Where was the damn wire – ah, there, in the corner of the cubbyhole. Whistling away, Stan returned to his loft and fitted the curtain over the far window, the one in the empty stock pen. It fitted well, only slightly too long, gave the place a sense of privacy. Stan had the feeling he would need it.

If Stan could master the Web, well, he could probably do all sorts of things. He went back upstairs and rebooted the computer, opened the word processing programme, and began to play with the drop down menus just like Damien had told him. Before he knew it, two hours had passed and he heard Evie's key in the lock. He hurriedly closed everything down, not before printing out his last piece, the one where he got the paragraph indented correctly and the capital letters in place, tore it from the printer and ran down the stairs. He had a new skill, couldn't wait to surprise Evie with it, chuckled – Stan had become a man who can.

Fifteen
Taking it Easy

Card XIV - Temperance

Temperance is all about keeping calm, being moderate and showing self-restraint. Sometimes in life, we need to find a middle ground, a balance. Temperance in the Tarot also suggests a sense of compromise, cooperation, and of bringing people together. In Evie's case, this meant finding middle ground with Stan as well as with Beulah and Geri. We might also think that it meant not to drink too much, and not to get too excited, despite the festivities of the season.

Evie would say that it took her a while to settle after she'd got back from Amsterdam. She didn't really know where she was with Stan: things were shifting, but she wasn't sure where to.

College helped, though. It gave her something to get up for in the morning; it made her think, offered her a sense of achievement. She'd been so terrified she couldn't do it, it had been that long since school, and she'd hated school, but this was just so different. It was like everyone was on your side, helping out, all these people there because one way or another they were picking up their education late. Evie loved the different students, though she didn't know them that well: Mary Murphy, the pensioner from Redcar who thought she'd have a go now that the grandchildren had left home, she'd had coffee with her a couple of times; that punk lad from Whinney Bank, Dan, who'd got fed up of living on the edge and nipping in and out of prison for taking and driving away and god knows what else, she'd stood outside with him while he had fag. There were a few other women maybe a bit like Evie. And then Angie, the lass who'd left school at fifteen to have her baby and come back at nineteen to see if she could get a decent exam result and maybe train to do something with kids, she'd seemed to latch on to Evie a bit – apparently, she looked like she knew what she was doing, and Angie was even more nervous than she was! It was just difficult getting the time to socialise; Evie was always dashing, and so were the others. It had only been a couple of months, and she supposed that would come if it was meant to. The thing they seemed to have in common was that everyone wanted to be there, and they were all bloody terrified, frightened of being the thick one, frightened of being the failure. Now she'd worked all that out, Evie could just get on with it and enjoy.

The third assignment was due early December, and was a bit longer than the other two. Evie's group had been looking at a poem by a bloke called Ted Hughes; apparently, he was really into writing and had set up some centres to help people learn to write. He was also married to Sylvia Plath, that woman in the film, *The Bell Jar*. The poem was called `The Hawk'.

173

Evie didn't know poetry, had only read a little at school. Bits and pieces drifted around her memory banks, something about daffodils, and one about autumn, `season of mist and mellow fruitfulness.' She'd enjoyed them at the time, though she'd never have let on. The Ted Hughes poem was quite different from either of these, less beautiful, but interesting enough.

Evie did her work on Wednesdays, so it was all out of the way if she wanted to go out later in the week. For that last assignment of term, she was stood in the middle room reading the poem out loud, feeling a bit of a prat but doing it anyway, when Stan came in. She jumped, stopped talking straight away, thinking he'd laugh.

`Go on, Evie,' he said, `you sound grand. And anyone who can make a poem about a bleeding hawk sound good has got to be worth listening to.'

She swallowed, carried on, winding the sound of the words round her mouth, her volume increasing with her confidence. Stan seemed to be listening with a kind of loving look on his face, and Evie's slight embarrassment was almost enjoyable, a teenage shyness. As it went on, his face turned to a bit of a sneer, though, especially at the line where the hawk was saying *I kill where I please because it is all mine.*

Of course, she should have known, Akbar had had a real problem with a peregrine a couple of years before, and these days all hawks and falcons were a pigeon fancier's nightmare. Especially one like this one, his point of view immortalised in a poem. Stan snorted and pronounced the poem as biased and unfair to pigeons, which was a different slant to the one the tutor had taken.

Evie detected more than a usual interest from Stan tonight: she knew that he seemed to have come to terms with the threat of her going to college; this was more. Maybe it was since the pigeon fanciers had come – she wasn't sure, and anyway that didn't quite make sense. Then again, maybe they'd just cheered him up. Anyway, he seemed interested in the course and this last couple of weeks, Evie was gobsmacked when he told her that he'd been

174

practising word processing and wanted to type up the next assignment for her. They seemed to be building a bit of a bridge – at least there was something to talk about.

As Evie was trying to understand the questions about the poem, she discerned Stan trying to understand her, probably looking at the same questions, come to think of it. What's the tone? Whose point of view is being expressed? What structure is going down here? What is its form? Maybe Stan was as confused as she was.

`Beyond me, pet,' was Stan 's helpful declaration, so Evie tried to use her common sense, and looked in the notes in the book. What the heck was 'sophistry'?

Even she could see that the poem was written in six verses that had some rhythm, so she guessed that was what they meant by regular stanzas, something she'd already learned about; it didn't take a genius to see that it was from the point of view of the hawk, who was a bit pompous sounding really, and quite arrogant. So there you had it– story of a bird, bit pompous, bit arrogant, and liked a certain rhythm. There you go, Stan, just looking for a bit of rhythm.

Evie found it hard at first to have to pull something apart, but once she'd talked about it a bit with Stan, she found it quite easy to write about, and the plus part of talking to Stan was that he helped her to add in a description about how in reality hawks hover just above their prey and pounce, and some strike from a great height. And he added a bit about pigeons, so it livened it up a bit. She'd got a B for it in the end, her first of the fuller assignments, and was dead chuffed.

And that was the first one that Stan typed up for her on the computer – well impressive. Even though Evie had done it in her neatest handwriting, it looked so much better, so much more professional when he brought it downstairs all tidy looking. She took it into college and handed it in inside a little plastic envelope, and felt so much like a part of the whole college thing it was unreal.

When Evie got home the day she'd given it in, Stan cooked corned beef hash, lovely, and they watched *Hannibal* on video, and of course Stan was pleased to bits because Hannibal talks about Birmingham Roller pigeons in the film, the genetics, the breeding, and how if you're not careful you could breed a pigeon so that it rolled too deep and then just rolled down and killed itself. And how people are like that, so much in the breeding, and Evie wondered about Stan, because behind the man she'd come to be living with who seemed to do nothing but to be obsessed with pigeons, she knew that there was someone else, someone really deep himself. For all that he drove Evie mad at times, she didn't really want him to roll down and injure himself. She snuggled up to him, and for once they made love when they went to bed, in the safety of darkness, but with some tenderness, and for a moment she felt like it would all be okay, they could move on together.

Strangely, though, although at that time Evie felt closer to Stan in some ways, it also seemed like he was keeping something from her. He was much livelier than for ages, and loved playing around with Damien's computer. It was like he was doing something secret, something which excluded Evie altogether, and that was odd. Here she was, glimpsing the bits of him she'd longed for, watching him become more alive and relaxed, and yet most of the time his attention was elsewhere. It jolted Evie, because for so long he'd been very attentive to her, even if she'd found the attention superficial, or misplaced. *Hey you*, she wanted to say, *now you're getting lively, come and play with me*. He still made her cups of tea, kept the house clean, and all that jazz, but he had other things to do now, too.

Maybe it was unfair of Evie to feel that way really, after all, she was well into her course, and college, and hadn't she played her relationship with Nikke close to her chest because she didn't trust what Stan's response would be? She was scared he'd be leery about her job, and not understand what meeting her had meant to Evie, so she said very little. So she wanted her secret life, but wanted let into his. She hadn't felt that way for a long time, and knew it to be unjust, but that was how she felt.

Evie had written to Nikke when she'd got back from Amsterdam, and mid-December Nikke replied. Once again, her words, her very way of being, seemed to have a profound effect.

Dear Evie,

Hi, my friend, so good to hear from you. Sounds like you're having some fun over there in England, your course sounds great. You are one brave woman to be going back to college now and working so hard. How are the assignments - you mention three, you'll probably have done them by now, I do hope it's going well.

I am doing okay. I have to have completed my major piece of work by the 18th of this month, so I'm working hard, researching and so on. I really love the reading, I could spend hours with my head in a book, and it's just wonderful. I've done my major essay on 'the psychological aspects of adoption on mother and child' - no prizes for guessing motivation! Actually, it's been great, and I found out lots of things which have made me feel much better about myself, more normal somehow. I do of course still wonder about Art and how he's doing, and what would happen if he ever tried to find me.

So I've made some decisions, anyway, Evie. I'm going to stay here for another six months, and then I'm going to come to England to live for a while. I'm making enquiries to Brighton for whether they want TEFL teachers at their college next summer, I know they do loads of stuff there, and I've got a TEFL qualification, I did it when I first got here. I've got some money now, and I *think I might have enough for an apartment or even a small house - not quite sure yet, I need to check out a bit more information. If Art wants to find me, I want to be findable and I want to be respectable, at least in some manner of speaking. And anyhow, it's time to move on. I realised when I was talking to you that I don't have to carry my past forever - you don't have to be who you always were, just see the past as having contributed to who you are and who you want to be. Time for a change of direction and college has been a great part of that.*

So if you want to come over again, make it in the next three or four months. I've still got the window until end of May, I've calculated that makes me enough of a cushion for a while. I'd love to see you -think about it.

So how's your Stan, then? Have things got any better?

And she went on to ask things, things about Evie's life, showing how well she understood, but she'd lost Evie's attention, because she knew then that she had to go back: she had to go back and see Nikke while she was still in Amsterdam. The question was how to do that without causing too much fuss.

As it happened, Christmas gave the perfect opportunity. For the first time in years, Geri expressed interest in getting together over Christmas. She phoned to say that she wanted to take Evie and Mam out one Thursday, early December, to discuss plans over lunch. Beulah was suspicious, of course, and phoned Evie.

`What does she want, Evie? We've never been to lunch before.'

Then the sound of a deep inhalation, followed by a wheeze. Not a wheeze *as such*, of course, just a faint strain of the weak wall of her lung.

178

`Mam, she just wants us to get together to plan Christmas.' Evie paused. `She's changed, you know, she's got some time to make up.'

`Aye.' Yes, of course Beulah knew that. If she could be so sensitive to things between Stan and Evie, it must, at some point, have broken her heart to see Geri so unhappy for so long with Henry. She was just having trouble believing that it was really happening, that her first born was coming back. The idea of the prodigal daughter was appealing, but Evie saw that her Mam couldn't trust it.

`What do you wear for lunch?' she followed up. `Should I have to get dressed up?'

`No, Mam, not too posh, but you might like to wear something you feel good in.' Evie smiled down the phone, Beulah reminding her of that first trip to Amsterdam, *what should I wear, what should I wear*. Since then Evie had thrown half her clothes out and lived in the same four or five outfits that she felt right in – a new pair of combat pants the only extravagance added to her wardrobe, a buy which she never regretted.

`What about my grey trews, then, and that red jumper your dad used to like?'

Evie's heart missed a beat. `Yes, Mam, that'd be great.' Then she laughed. `Maybe what we wear shouldn't matter too much. Let's just be grateful that Geri's having lunch.'

Beulah laughed, then, and that was that. Blimey – a meeting with Geri and Mam together.

It was well organized, Geri style of course, at the *Star and Garter*, lounge table reserved for 15th December. Beulah wore her red and grey; Evie felt good in black with bold emerald jewellery and wasn't intimidated by Geri's lovely soft purple cashmere sweater and heavy silk pants, and the usual distinctive bandana.

`Hey,' Geri initiated the hugs, before all sitting down at the little round table, perfect. Christmas decorations hung round like they were going out of fashion, sparkles, paper chains, and Evie breathed a sigh of relief that Geri didn't even clean the seat before sitting down.

179

`Now then,' Geri took charge, `what do you want to drink? I'm going to have a Guinness.'

Yes – Evie could relax, inwardly thanking Geri for her sensitivity, knowing that Mam didn't really go for champagne. That half pint of Guinness did wonders to help her fit in to the pub, and indeed to her family.

`I'll have a stout,' Mam said. One of the waiters came over and took the order, giving out menus. Geri went for scampi, no chips, (couldn't possibly with all that Guinness); Beulah countered such frugality with steak and ale pie, Yorkshire pudding, mash and peas. Evie ordered barbecue chicken with potato wedges. The waiter brought the tray, and Geri led the toast.

`Cheers,' she announced, `here's to us.'

`Cheers.' Beulah took the Victory V tin out of her pocket and put it on the table. She often did this, just had it near like a comforter, needing to know that she could roll a fag if she really wanted to.

`Now then,' Geri began.

`Now then,' said Beulah, fixing Geri with a defensive look. `Our Evie says you're thinking of coming home for Christmas.'

Good old Mam, no beating around the bush, no holding back. She paused only slightly.

`It's been a lot of years since you did that, our Geri.' She took a sip of her stout. `You didn't even come the last year when your Da was still alive.'

The seeds of reproach mingled with the dust motes that were lit up by the rare December sun which shone through the window. Evie swallowed hard. Geri matched Beulah's hard look with a direct one of her own.

`Yes, Mam, I am thinking of coming home.' She mirrored Beulah perfectly, pausing and sipping her Guinness, keeping eye contact over the top of the glass, and swallowing the tiny sip with only a hint of effort. Impressive. `And I'll always be sorry that I didn't spend the last Christmas I could with Dad.' Beulah's eyes softened then, just a touch. Evie shuffled slightly, wondering at the miracle that had reconvened the three women after so long, enjoying the reconfiguration.

`Actually, Mam, there's a lot of things I'm sorry about.' Geri spoke quite softly. `But I can't turn back the clock, you know?' Beulah gave a barely perceptible nod. `So I've got a lot to make up for. And I thought' – she hesitated, unusual for Geri – `I wondered, what about if I came and stayed with you for Christmas and Boxing Day, Mam, and we all got together for Christmas dinner? My treat.'

Beulah's surprise flickered over her eyes. She reached hurriedly for the Victory V tin, and pulled out a Rizla, busying herself. When she spoke, it was gruffly.

'I'd have to clear out the back room a bit.'

Hoorah! Evie smiled inwardly: Beulah was ready to put on fresh sheets and move an ornament or two off the dressing table.

'It's not been slept in for a while.'

'That's okay, Mam, if it's okay with you.' Geri took another minute sip of her Guinness. Fantastic. Evie felt really chuffed for them both.

'What d'you think, Evie?' Geri cleared her throat slightly, lifted her tone.

'I think that's a great idea, Geri. What about you, Mam?' Beulah had rolled the cigarette, now, placed it carefully in the tin for later. She looked up, and this time there really was a tear in her eye, a look of mixed emotion just beneath the watery guard.

`Well, I think that would be grand.' She took another mouthful of stout, emptying about a sixth of the glass down into her thin frame. `And,' she said, caution giving way to a glimmer of excitement, `we'll have a bit of a do on Boxing Day, get the old piano dusted, like we used to, hey?'

And that was that. Christmas would be a family event, not like the previous year when Beulah had come to Evie's, a day just to be got through rather than enjoyed, the stark absence of Evie's dad a great spectre at the feast. Beulah had not been allowed to be alone that first sad festival after his death, but they'd all been alone as they'd sat round the table, Damien doing his dutiful best, all struggling with how happiness and grief could possibly be partners at the same table.

But this year there'd be something to celebrate.

They ate and drank, and planned what they'd do, and on Christmas Day, Evie had Christmas with her family, Beulah, Geri, Stan, and Damien. Her contingent got there at half past eleven, the wreath on the door making her heart skip a beat, reminding her of her dad and yet setting a tone of good cheer, bright red berries amongst the dark green leaves, little light touches of mistletoe woven in, and a large silver bow trimmed with red. Damien knocked at the door, and Geri came to open it, her face bright as a button and a bright red apron on over a nifty black and cream outfit that hung on her like a drape on a clothes horse.

`Merry Christmas,' she beamed, and hugged everyone as they squeezed past in the dim hallway, which had lifted little despite best efforts with silver tinsel. When Evie walked into the living room, though, she could see a few changes here and there, a bright new lampshade allowing light to fill the room much more than the old flutes which had resolutely directed their beams onto the ceiling these past few years. Beulah was grinning from ear to ear, clearly chuffed to bits because she had presents for her girls under a real Christmas tree complete with flashing lights, in her living room, and her face was a picture. Even the feel of the room seemed lighter, maybe because Geri had talked Mam into a new, light, table cloth, and changed two deep wood photo frames for two light porcelain ones (`the energy, darling, was so-o stagnant, I couldn't stand it,' she confided later in the kitchen) and champagne cocktails and beer were out on a tray and ready for the day.

You had to say this for Geri, when she did something, there were no half measures, and she helped Beulah to serve the biggest, best Christmas dinner the house had seen for years. There was vegetable soup, roast turkey stuffed with pork mince and apple, roast potatoes, mashed potatoes, honey glazed roast parsnips, pigs in a blanket, Brussels, sweet corn, bread sauce, cranberry sauce and gravy, yet somehow, there was not too much, so that everyone exclaimed over the perfect taste yet didn't feel stuffed at the end. There was white wine with starters, red wine with dinner, and then Geri pulled out a fantastic sweet, Baileys and Christmas pudding ice cream, rich and light, and served with a Madeira wine, sweet and satisfying. Not only had the prodigal daughter returned: she'd brought the fatted calf.

At some point Evie realised they'd spent three hours together chatting and laughing, and Geri had seemed to make it all go really smoothly – and Beulah had let her, staying at the table for a quick rolly (just the one, dear, still not back on *as such*) between courses. She felt surprisingly satisfied.

Then, Damien and Stan cleared the table and did the first stack of washing up, and Mam made Evie and Geri open their presents. For Geri, some fancy tights, which obviously Mam had made an effort with, yet which were clearly too tacky for dear Geri. To give Geri her due, though, she made all the right noises and stated which outfit she would be able to wear them with. And then, for Evie, an under slip in mock silk, to which Stan gave his approval as he passed by carrying pots, cheeky bugger, always on the look out. And then Beulah gave her girls both another present, each a photograph of them with their dad, just nippers, taken on the beach at Redcar, him in his cap and pipe in his mouth, one little girl in a ruched bathing costume and one in a cossie with a little skirt on – a great photo, and each in a modern silver frame.

`Oh Mam.' A lump rose in Evie's throat, and she hugged Beulah along with Geri, a real precious moment, and it seemed like another step on the road of grief, only a less lonely step than so many others taken over this last year or more. Then Beulah opened her gifts, a mix of bits and bobs, tights, music, underwear, a favourite record. Sadly, this was *The Best of Engelbert Humperdinck*, a classic which she had been on about for ever, since she broke her old long-playing vinyl copy while polishing behind the record cabinet. Damien, bless, had got it for her from Amazon. She was really chuffed, and put it on straight away.

While *Please Release Me* echoed with some resonance for all around the house, Mam opened her present from Geri – the most beautiful little tin box studded with stones and the shape of a Buddha. Inside was a wad of strong smelling tobacco, and a little slice of potato to keep it moist. That little touch must have taken some doing for Geri, she who hated preparing food as much as she hated eating it. There was also a fabulous lighter, silver satin, with *Mam* engraved on it, and the date.

Beulah was impressed by the lighter, but looked bemused at the tobacco tin. `It's nice, pet, but who's this fat bastard on the front?' By the time they were on to *Am I That Easy to Forget*, and another tot of rum had gone down, the tobacco had been tipped into the Victory V tin, and Evie smiled to herself: the stone encrusted tin had now joined the ranks of the Mabel Lucy Attwells on the daily dusting rota.

Damien at this point clearly considered his duty done and had also decided that yes, Engelbert really was that easy to forget, so he said his goodbyes for now and went off to Susannah's house with promises of returning later. Beulah was singing now, and insisted that he waltz her up the hallway as she saw him out, her laughter becoming more and more raucous, her kisses just a little bit wetter than friends and family might have wished for. Once he'd gone, it wasn't long before Beulah and Stan were both snoring along to *The Great Escape*, good old regular English TV Christmas classics. But instead of wanting to tunnel to get out from under on this particular Christmas occasion, Evie was more than happy to accept Geri's suggestion to take a bottle of wine into the front room, where a low fire awaited the evening sing song, and where they could drop into the easy chairs and toast each other. The crisp and tangy Chablis was a far cry from the usual Liebfraumilch that Evie was used to: Geri had done them proud.

`You've done well, Geri. This has meant a lot to Mam.' Evie raised her glass. `Well, to us all really. This was a great idea.'

`I've enjoyed it.' Geri sounded sincere, and she looked great. Did Evie discern the tiniest soupçon of flesh appearing on that

184

skeletal frame – not that Geri would ever be fat, but just a slight layer of softness creeping round her.

`So how's it going?' Evie sipped more wine. `You've had quite a year.' Geri sighed.

`It's okay. It's still a bit strange, being on my own, and although Henry was a right prat, at least he was a prat I knew. So I miss the old life a little bit, have the odd moment when I wake up with a bulldog in the pit of my stomach wondering what on earth is going on.' Momentarily, Geri had a faraway look in her eyes, then blinked, looked straight at her sister. `But you know, Evie, most of the time I feel just great. Just bloody fabulous. I definitely made the right decision there.'

Evie felt a slight tightening in her stomach, a pang of envy, and told Geri about the feeling of being hemmed in and frustrated, and about how much she'd enjoyed Amsterdam and how she'd kept in touch with Nikke and was thinking of going over. Geri got quite excited at this.

`Well why don't we both go?' Evie started to protest, but Geri held her hand up in that authoritative social work manager way of hers, even as Evie bleated about not taking more from her. `No, no, just listen to me. You know I had thought about giving up my job? Well, last week, just before the office party, I handed in my notice. I'm going to do more on the therapeutics side of things, get back to helping people, like I always wanted to. So, I've got my Advanced Diploma now in Feng Shui (*helps me make a buck or two from the middle classes, Dahling, and is tremendously good fun and good karma*), but now I'm going to do some more training in working with addiction. One day, I might even set up my own unit. And guess where there's a really good course???' Geri's eyes twinkled. `Yes, dear old Amsterdam. I'm going there for a two week intensive in May, and then I'm going to use my qualifications and interest to fund a small rehabilitation project – God knows the 'Boro could do with it. So' – she paused slightly for breath – `why don't you come over while I'm there – you can get really cheap flights now you know from Leeds Bradford as well as Teesside, and you could share my hotel room for a couple

185

of nights and stay with your friend as well – what do you think? I mean it's a bit of way away, but something to have in your diary and it will give you chance to really save a bit and have a great time.'

The tightening in Evie's stomach rose to become a mild lump in her throat – was this what it was going to be like now, to have this lovely sister?

'Geri – what a bloody good idea.'

By the time Beulah and Stan woke up, and a dear old Uncle and Aunt arrived and got festooned with paper hats and plied with drinks, and old Frankie B from over the road came over with his son and daughter in law, and Damien and Susannah turned up, looking flushed and hair askew, Evie was in her cups with dates pencilled in for Amsterdam and all too happy to sing along as Frankie played the old Joanna and her family warbled the night away, and could truly say that a good time was had by all. Mam had had her Christmas Day and Boxing Day knees up all in one.

186

Sixteen
A Man with a Plan

To do well, you need to have the ideal in your mind's eye. You may not actually have this when you first start....but you must steadily work towards this. It doesn't come quickly or easily.

Lindsay Oman
Quoted in Graham Dexter, *Winners with Spinners* 1997

The New Year saw Stan enjoying his newfound competence with the computer, and his plan with the lads going from strength to strength. They'd all agreed that the first stage was to lure Jan van Clevershite to Middlesbrough, so they decided to hold their Invitation Roller Club fly in early March, and invite Jan to judge it. In a way, this was the easiest part of the plan, as Stan considered just how much attention to detail he'd have to pay to make this work. The thought of vengeance filled most of his waking hours, a focus both welcome and challenging. He felt good, fancied that he looked good, and had even taken to a daily cycle round the park since that exhilarating morning run to Doc's two months ago. He'd lost a couple of pounds, his stomach felt a little tauter, and although no six pack yet, neither was it a full barrel.

The pigeon loft was looking good too, Stan knew. Stan had nailed up a nameplate which he'd made, on A4 card, landscape, in massive letters saying **Stan's Pigeon Loft**, with a red shadow around the words. He had it laminated, courtesy of the Total garage office services up the road.

The spare pen was now very much an office room. Stan had an old chair in there, the net curtains just heavy enough to lend a certain mystery, an air of privacy, yet light enough for the winter light, such as it was, to shine through. A large cardboard box doubled as a container and temporary table, just until another more permanent desk or table could be had. As Stan walked down the garden in the crisp but windy January weather, he couldn't help but admire his loft, noting that it could be even better with a heater of some kind in it, pondering on what sort.

`What do you think, then?' he enquired of the stock birds as he passed them on the way to the pen which he was coming to think of as the Office. `Paraffin just a bit dodgy, or what? Although I suppose they've come on a bit, I think Doc has one in the hall of the surgery, must ask him about it.' He paused, midstride, smiled in to the breeding pen. `By, look at you my darling, yes, she's laid.'

Stan opened the door to the breeding pen and went to check on the egg which Foxy Lady was patiently sitting: it felt good, hard shelled, and looked strong. She was the first to lay, the first product of the New Moon cycle that Stan had been trying out, learning from Alfie about it at the Cabbage Club. Alfie swore by pairing up the birds at New Moon, and he was no crackpot when it came to livestock. Stan followed his instructions to the letter – why not, he'd no choice but to try some new breeding habits anyway. Exciting stuff. The others should all be producing within twenty-four hours: Stan would have to keep a careful eye on them.

He looked round at the birds, not planning to fly them, definitely too windy and he had a lot to do: a rest wouldn't hurt them. He fed them all in turn, the food mix finely tuned to each kit's needs. The breeders could have as much as they wanted, a real good mix of maples, wheat and small maize, while the old birds and the yearlings had a bit of a mix of wheat and Depurative. He'd have to get some squeaker mix in for the babies, to be ready for them when they fed themselves.

Stan went into the Office, reached inside the temporary table, his hand touching hard plastic, a nest of plastic boxes, designed to keep things dry. From one of these he extricated a folder, on the front of which was written `Invitation Roller Club'. He tucked it under his arm, tidied away the nest, and then exited to the corridor of his haven.

`Okay, let's go and sort that old cheating bastard out.' Stan shared his plans with the birds as he locked up. `And I think I'll see if I can get one of them heaters with the gas bottle, bet Frank'll be able to get one from his brother-in-law's depot.' And on that note, he gave the birds one last look before whistling his way up the garden path.

There were a number of things for Stan to do: he needed to ring Doc and see how he'd got on with Jan, whether the invitation had been accepted. He was also going to have a go at putting the Invitation Roller Fly schedule onto computer – never been done

189

before in the 'Boro, should look tidy. And, he needed to contact Alfie Elliot, to pick his brains about racing men in Amsterdam.

And it was Thursday, night out with the lads. Thursday had become the day that he measured and monitored his success, a kind of review day. He had seen in one of Evie's magazines that the most successful people are those who have a goal in mind. He'd found himself taking Lily the Life Coach's advice and had drawn a little picture of where he wanted to be in six months' time, a picture full of blue skies with Evie beside him wearing a diamond ring. Obviously, he hadn't disclosed this to anybody as they would laugh, but the picture was safely hidden away in a box within the box in the pigeon loft. The more Stan thought about it, the more he really wanted to achieve it, and the more he worked toward it, just as Lily predicted.

Stan had also mapped out the steps to be taken to get him into his future, and knew them in detail. He was absolutely clear as to what needed to be done when, and this day's contact with Alfie and with Doc was crucial. He decided to go from the simple to the complex, the phone call to Doc being today's first step. Not before the usual routine though, although actually Stan's routine was loosening up a little. He still looked at the paper, but it didn't grab him like it used to, and he noted that sometimes the cooked breakfasts were just a little too filling. So on this morning he knew that the headline was *Tarty Tory Transvestite claims Sex with entire Loony Lefty Cabinet*, but to be honest, he hadn't even read the article that accompanied the bold claims. What he always needed, though, was plenty of tea, and Stan filled his large Roller mug with the magic nectar before sitting down to phone Doc.

He timed the call for the surgery coffee break, knowing that Doc's surgery was a busy one, partly because Doc knew many of his patients as long term ones and often sat and let them have a chat before getting down to the business of their health. Doc was actually convinced that by the end of the chat, many of the patients felt much better and seemed not to need a prescription, so it seemed to pay off for him. And anyway, he liked to sound off to them as well about the demon felines and the peregrines. One of his patients even waited forty minutes in his surgery once just to bring in the high frequency alarm system that he'd thought might do the trick in Doc's garden. A nice thought, even though it had failed.

Stan knew that coffee break was routinely scheduled for 10.30 – 10.50, when no patients were booked in. He dialled the familiar number.

`Ey up Doc.'

`Ah, now then Stan.' Doc was sounding positive.

`Well?' Stan felt a tingling of adrenaline in his stomach. `Well, come on Doc, don't keep me in suspenders.'

Doc chuckled, pleased with himself.

`Alright Stan, I phoned him and he's said yes. I've just got to follow it up on paper, keep it all squeaky clean like, and we'll sort out his flight. March 16th, earliest we can make it work.'

`Fantastic, bloody fantastic.' Stan took a huge gulp of tea, nearly burning his throat in the excitement, yelping with pleasure and pain.

`I'll get that off today, so you can go ahead with the schedules for the lads, and we'll be away.'

`Thanks Doc, I'll be seeing you later.'

Stan hung up and realised that he was just sitting grinning. At the same time, he recognised fear in that adrenaline stomach, but in a funny kind of way, it was a welcome fear. He felt so alive, taking risks, feeling excitement. Fan bloody tastic.

Stan went to the CD rack, choosing the latest addition to his collection, *The Best of Roxy Music*, burned for him by Frank, and took it upstairs to Damien's room, alongside the folder from the pigeon loft. He struck up the computer, mesmerized as ever as the screen lit up with so many choices. He clicked on the big blue W, sat comfortably before the screen, took out his folder and withdrew the members' list, the minutes that Doc had given him from the last AGM, and a diary. Then he set to work.

Over the course of the next two hours, Roxy Music revolving relentlessly alongside him, Stan managed to type up the minutes.

191

While he had found typing easy – he was in an experimental equal opportunity school year where all the class had to do typing skills, and all woodwork – he still found difficulty with some of the formatting. Every time he tried to insert numbers to order the points, the damn programme tried to help him out and indented the line too far. Half way through, he lost the whole bloody thing when he tried to block it all out to make his own indent – how the fuck could it just disappear like that? After a pee break and a drop more tea, Stan persevered and was eventually pleased with the result.

Then he mapped out the fly schedule, the bit he'd really been waiting for, the bit where he'd begin to get back at Jan. He perused the final document before saving in c:/stanstuff/invitation, pleased with the draft which he printed out to show the others. He was particularly proud of taking Damien's advice to try out different fonts – the final version was impressive.

This year's Fly will be held over the weekend of 16th and 17th March. We are honoured this year to have a judge all the way from Holland, Mr Jan van Deuzen, and we hope that everyone will do their best to make him welcome and not be too shy to put on the best kits!!!

The **Order of Fly** will let each member fly one or two any age kits, as we are early in the breeding season. Our two guestflyers are Graham Dexter, our friend and Author of *50 Questions Answered for the Less Experienced Roller Flier*, *50 Questions Answered for the More Experienced Roller Flier* as well as the hobby great *Winners with Spinners*, and Gordon Stoneman, whose exports to Holland are well known.

Saturday, 16th March

08.00 Doc
09.30 Akbar
11.00 Snacks at Ak's!
12.00 Frank
13.00 Stan Cutler
14.00 Sarnies at Stan's!
15.00 John Hooper
16.30 Sam Shipston

Sunday, 17th March

09.00 Graham Dexter. 99, Woodbot Rd., Derbyshire. Bacon sandwiches courtesy his lovely wife Fran.
10.30 Gordon 'Gordy' Stoneman
12.00 Finish off drink at the Crew and Harper, Derby.

Saturday night the committee will take Jan out to dinner at 'The Taste of India' and then on to The Bluebell, Acklam. Sunday lunchtime after doing the judging we will take Jan to the Crew and Harper in Swarkestone, Derby. All enquiries to Stan Cutler or Doc, 01632 347821 or 01632 489932.

Stan addressed envelopes to all the members and their two special guests, and then embarked on the hardest yet most exciting job of all – finding someone in Holland who was going to help them, albeit unwittingly, with the getaway plan. He'd decided that old Alfie Ellis was the person to ask, a veteran of the racing fraternity. Alfie knew everything there was to know about racers, plus Alfie had spent enough of his life on enough suitable knife edges for Stan to be confident that he was no security threat – on the contrary.

Stan had already arranged to go to Alfie's for three o'clock. He finally rested Roxy at *Virginia Plane*, put on his bicycle clips and jacket, and cycled the three miles to the allotments. Sure enough, Alfie had his billy tin heating over the calor gas stove and was pouring evaporated milk into two huge tin mugs when Stan arrived. He wore a cap that probably saw the end of the Second World War, and fingerless gloves. All he needed was a whippet to complete the picture, but instead he had a large Rottweiler called Bess who circled Stan before dropping to the floor by her master, eyes never leaving Stan's person.

Alfie gave Stan his tea.

'So, lad.' Alfie looked at Stan quizzically

'Well, Alfie, I paired them up by the moon, like you said.'

'Oh aye.'

'And I've just got my first egg, to Foxy Lady, the others should lay within twenty four hours.'

'Oh aye.'

'So we'll have to wait and see on that one.'

'Oh aye.'

'Heard you cleaned up again last season, Alfie. You'll be giving 'em a good run this season, eh?'

'Oh aye.'

Stan paused, unsure how to proceed. He took a slurp of the sweet strong tea. Bess began to snore gently. Alfie relit his pipe and took one or two pungent puffs. Then he leaned almost imperceptibly toward Stan.

'So what can I do for you, Stan?' he said, watery brown eyes beginning to pierce Stan's countenance. `I don't suppose you're really here to discuss the waxing and waning of the moon, and I know you'll not be wanting to join the racing club.'

This last was delivered as fact, not query. Stan felt briefly shy, and then remembered that he was now a man who gets things done, and cleared his throat.

'Well, Alfie, fact is I need a favour.'

'Figures.'

'It's like this. I need a bird to fly back here from Amsterdam. It's difficult, I need to find someone really reliable.' He coughed. `Not too many questions. Need the bird to bring a message with it. Thought you'd be our man.'

Alfie regarded Stan for a while, Stan regarding Alfie's contemplations. They both knew Alfie's reputation. He was a generous man, a man who had commanded a great respect with a good many fanciers over a significant number of years, like forty. He was a man who wouldn't stand any nonsense. The one time that he had been broken into and his best racers stolen, everyone knew that there were two men in the 'Boro who never walked without limps again. He also organised all the raffles and rallies for multiple sclerosis in the area, raising hundreds of pounds each year. A hard man, Stan knew, but fair.

'No drugs involved.' He looked at Stan again.

'No, sir. Wouldn't touch them with a bargepole.'

Alfie nodded and waited. Stan knew he had to say more, enough but not too much.

'Thing is Alfie, there's a Roller Man been scamming us, and we just want to pay him back a little. No violence, no risks. Just want a bird that's capable of bringing back a small package for us. No questions asked.'

Alfie regarded Stan thoughtfully.

'Is it a package I could get into trouble for?' Stan nodded.

'Yes, Alfie, can't deny that, though we'd take it straight off your hands. Funnily enough, might even take it straight back to Holland, I think, so there'll be no hanging around. And of course, even if anyone knew that the pigeon had the package, they wouldn't know it was coming to you, and they sure as hell wouldn't be able to get here before it.'

Alfie chuckled and nodded in acknowledgement of the shared respect for the speed of his superb pigeons.

'Okay.' Alfie paused, and Stan felt sparks of electricity generating around.

'It's to go back to Holland, you say?'

'Aye, Alfie, that's as likely the plan as any. Just need to pick up here first.'

'I don't think I can do that, Stan.' Stan felt surprise and disappointment mingling with instant acceptance. 'Fact is we don't fly from Holland to England. Always north and south, never east to west. I'd have to train one special, and I'm not sure it can be done.'

Stan's heart slowed – of course, this was obvious information that he should have thought of. Shit. He really should have known. Back to the drawing board.

And then.

'I think I can do better.' Stan started.

'Better?'

Alfie shuffled slightly.

'Aye, Stan, better. Save you a bit of trouble, like.' Stan 's heart rate increased again. Alfie continued.

'Many years ago, when I were a lot younger, I made a trip to visit all the best fanciers in Europe, after I'd topped the Fed from St. Malo for the third year running. 1961 through `63, it was, and I'd not long been in the hobby.' Alfie gave himself a small shake to curtail his tendency to reminisce. `Any road, I met a man in Holland, great bloke, and we've been mates ever since. His name's Franz. And we've had some canny times seeing which of us can be best in bloody Europe. Daft as brushes.'

Alfie chuckled, a faraway look briefly in his eyes, mirth in the crinkles around them. `Good bloke. Anyway, we've done some swaps for breeding over the last twenty years, and I've a hen needs taking back to him. Blue bar, a prize, she was, won him the

Guldensporenvlucht four years on the trot – and that's the most prestigious racing event in Holland. But, she broke one of her legs coming back from Spain year before last. Had to have her ring cut off. Can't compete any more. Seems a shame for her not to do one last job though.'

He looked Stan in the eye.

'I've been breeding from her this season. Spring's about right for someone to take her back to Holland for me. Could probably benefit from a little fly on the way, if something needed picking up and leaving in Holland. Save the trouble of too much to-ing and fro-ing. Long as there was someone at Franz's to pick up straight away, mind, wouldn't want him in any trouble.'

Stan nodded. What a great ideal. A pigeon that's already trained to the area. Brilliant. Almost too good to be true. 'Sounds good to me, Alfie.' He swigged his tea. 'Sounds bloody marvellous, in fact. So you'll need to speak to Franz, then?'

`I will that, son. But leave it with me.'

The interview was over, and both men rose from the packing cases, Alfie glimpsing a younger version of himself in the making, Stan seeing the ghost of his father, with whom Alfie had once worked. They nodded amicably.

Stan walked over to look at Alfie's birds, knowing that the racing man loved to show them off. Stan genuinely enjoyed looking at their fantastic condition and the result of some very careful breeding. Couldn't help comparing them with Rollers though, which he found much more pleasing and elegant than the large racers. But no doubt about it, Alfie knew his stuff and was a master of his field.

Ritual complete, Alfie walked Stan up the allotment to claim his bicycle, when Stan's eye was caught by a piece of porcelain sticking up in the uncultivated allotment next door.

`By heck, what's that then Alfie, a bloody toilet?'

Alfie followed Stan's gaze to the white shiny porcelain piece which was neatly propped up against some kind of stump. He looked around as if unseeing, blinked a couple of times and said to Stan.

`What's what?'

`That.' Stan began walking toward the allotment. `That toilet, that bloody great toilet next door.'

`Ah.' Alfie regained composure. `That. Ah, yes, our Steven was leaving it there.' He coughed. `For the time being, like.'

`But it's bloody brilliant, Alfie.' Stan examined the shiny white object which had tickled his fancy. `Not even a toilet, but a bloody great urinal. And all in one piece. `Where'd he get it then – one of his jobs?'

Alfie nodded in assent. The antics of Alfie's oldest son were well known to be on a very fine line indeed when it came to matters of the law.

`To be honest, Stan, he was supposed to pick it up this morning, but he's just rung me before you came to say he can't find the home he wanted for it. I'm going to get rid of it later, don't quite feel comfortable with it standing there like that.'

`Where's it going, then?' Stan circled the urinal with interest.

`Well, I'm just waiting for our kid to come up with a sledgehammer after he's done his shift. Then I can get rid of the evidence, so to speak.'

`Nah, don't do that.' Stan asserted his interest. `Get him to drop it off at ours. I'll take it. I'll give him a few bob.'

Alfie's eyebrows raised. `For you, lad?'

`Yep. I've got an idea as to where that'll go that will be just right. Yeah, drop it off at mine, it can go straight down the back garden.'

`If you say so, son.' Alfie smiled while shaking his head at the same time.

`Alright then Alfie.' Stan mounted his bicycle. `I'll wait to hear from you. Thanks a lot, mate, thanks a lot.'

Stan cycled home with no awareness of the mechanics of his journey, negotiating traffic and junctions on automatic pilot, his head brimming with daydreams of revenge, riches and refitting of his pigeon loft. Within the shortest time, he was wheeling his bicycle to the back of the house, and whistling as he opened up and let himself into the kitchen.

By the time that Evie was home, Stan was showered and changed, and waiting for the Thursday night lift. Evie looked tired but was high, said she'd been out shopping with Beulah in the sales. She seemed really happy since Geri did Christmas with them, and when Beulah was happy, Evie was happy, and if Evie was happy, so was Stan. Evie declared that she'd be staying in tonight to watch a DVD, that she had a good bottle of wine to drink and would be having a chicken curry take away. Stan went out with a clear conscience, a good day's work complete.

Seventeen
Hanging on In There

Card XI - Strength

Strength comes in many forms, not just muscle. Sometimes it means learning tolerance and forbearance. For Evie, this meant hanging on in there, being able to keep on chipping away, knowing that each week she was getting nearer her goal of opening her horizons and doing something different, reminding her not to give up.

In the Tarot, Strength can also mean being influenced by someone else with courage and fortitude. The Lion on the card is stealthy and solid, and this is the quality that is needed right now for the Querent.

It was hard to follow the best Christmas you've had for ages, and the New Year was a bit of a mixed event for Evie. She'd been invited to a party by a couple of the college kids, but didn't really feel she knew them that well. She was tempted in a way, young blood and all that, but also knew that Stan would be dead uncomfortable in that kind of environment so she'd turned down the invitation.

Beulah of course was going up to the club, and seemed to be looking forward to it, unlike last year. Geri decided to go to a health farm for a long weekend, she said she hated New Year anyway and was as happy to be amongst strangers as friends. Naturally, the health farm was in Thessalonica, so she had a reasonable chance of finding new friends. She'd done her family bit; she'd slummed it, bless her, and now a bit of a treat was needed. Evie didn't blame her.

Jeannie and her family announced that they were going to a New Year's do at *The Phoenix*, the old church built on the traffic island, right underneath the flyover. Middlesbrough County Council had saved it from destruction when all the roads were redesigned, but sadly the church had had to let it go, the A66 being a bit off putting for the parishioners' sense of peace. And anyway, most families took their kids to Asda these days for the Sunday outing – good shopping, and an all-day English breakfast or a Sunday lunch. The church was sold and renamed *The Phoenix*, and turned into a really cheap club. Saturday nights were dance and karaoke, chicken dinner and all the wine or beer you could drink, all for a fiver.

Great.

Evie didn't know what to do really, just felt a bit at sixes and sevens. Damien and Susannah were going down south. They'd been invited to a big party at the parents of some guy that Damien had met through work. They had a mews house, whatever that was. It sounded very posh, and although Evie was pleased for Damien, she felt sort of thrown, a bit left behind. In the end, Stan sorted it all out – they were going to the Akbars' for

201

supper and then on to meet Jeannie at *The Phoenix* – at least that way they'd both be amongst friends.

As usual, Evie felt that the Akbars put them to shame, with fab food and such a lovely house. She looked at Jasmine with that little boy on her lap and could have cried with envy. Were Damien and she ever like that, and if so, why was it all so different now, as if those precious years had disappeared into the oceans of time, as if they'd never happened? She caught herself edging toward that feeling she seemed to get these days, and had to shake herself out of it. She helped herself to beer, and managed to eat another three samosas that Jasmine had left on the serving plate, before she caught Stan's eye and they silently agreed that it was time to leave. He would have stayed there all night for the company, but he liked his drink on New Year, and they never really had a skinful at the Akbars'.

They'd both had over the odds, and Stan took Evie's hand as they tottered down the path way to get into the cab they'd ordered. Once in the back, he put his arm round her and gave her a big hug.

`Tell you what, gal, I think it's gonna be a good night tonight, bit of a bop.' He kissed her cheek. `And I think it's gonna be a real good year for us as well.' Evie felt surprised – usually Stan didn't go in for dancing, and he hadn't danced on New Year for as long as she could remember. As for sounding optimistic about life in general, Evie hadn't heard him say anything positive for months, maybe even years. Anyway, she welcomed his affection; actually, he looked quite handsome, and she thought he'd maybe lost a little weight. She almost told the taxi driver to turn round and take them home, but just at that moment Stan mentioned that he'd just paired up some right good pigeons, and that kind of put the dampers on things. Clearly, his idea of a good year and Evie's revolved around different criteria.

When they got to The Phoenix, it was heaving. They showed their tickets, took their coats to the put up cloakroom, then pressed their way forwards through the crowd. Someone was doing the karaoke to Slade's *Merry Christmas*, and Evie was

202

thinking how stupid it was to have that on after Christmas was over. Her smile felt fixed, till she saw Jeannie waving from a tabletop, and then Evie really did smile. There she was, Evie's good old mate, looking fab in a black beaded halter necked dress that she'd be taking back on Monday, with her hair up and some big shiny earrings on. She looked radiant, and Evie just loved her.

So they'd got in the mood and had some more drinks, danced to *Macarena* and *The Ketchup Song*, and then they all stood on the table and did the countdown to midnight. When Big Ben struck twelve, courtesy of radio transmission through the loudspeakers, everyone leapt to the floor and joined one massive circle for *Auld Lang Syne*. Then there was the usual frenzy of kissing and hugging, and when Stan came over to Evie, he threw his arms round her in a bear hug, and gave her a really wonderful kiss on the lips, the best for ages. Then he held her tight and whispered in her ear, `Happy New Year, Evie. It's gonna be a good one. I'm gonna make sure you get everything you want, my princess.' He smiled as if he was really pleased with himself, and in Evie's drunkenness she thought perhaps he was thinking more than pigeons, after all. The moment was interrupted when suddenly Jeannie's eldest daughter came up and swept Stan away, looking all too old at 17, and for the first time in a very long time Evie felt almost jealous.

Before long they were all back up on the tables dancing, and Evie didn't remember much more except they eventually piled home in a taxi, and although they felt close to each other and Stan was still flirting madly with her, neither had the energy or were sober enough to make love, or at least if they did Evie missed it completely and Stan left no tell-tale signs.

They got back into a regular routine then, Evie working in the chippy and doing her assignments, and Stan seemed a lot happier with himself. He was spending quite a lot of time on Damien's computer, and was doing extra bits to the pigeon loft. He didn't seem to moan so much, and in a way that was good.

203

Evie was learning loads, and loving it. She had to do heaps of exercises about punctuation and sentence structure, and found them quite easy. She also read *Macbeth*, now, and as well as rehearsing it again and again in the shower, she booked to go and see it in York in March.

Now she had two big pieces of work to do for the Spring Term. One was on English language, and it was free composition, designed to give a practice at sentence construction and grammar. The other was to read a passage taken out of a book called *Remains of the Day*, a really nice little story about a man who was chasing a lost love, not realising that he was far too late. Evie had seen the film with Anthony Hopkins, and thought it was really sad.

The first assignment should have been easy. Composition, she'd always loved that at school, they always had to write ones like `What We Did on Our Holidays'. Evie had once got into trouble because she'd written that they'd gone away to a caravan and her Mam had cried a lot, and Beulah had been summoned by the headmistress to see if everything was alright. She'd gone mad afterwards – `what on earth were you thinking of, Evie, we don't write things like that down. And anyway, I wasn't crying *as such*, it was just that it was a bit tough, out there in the rain.' Now Evie had more idea of what might have gone on there, but she pushed those thoughts away. When she told Jeannie about this new assignment, Jeannie laughed and said that someone really had now written a whole book with that title, *What We Did on Our Holidays*, and it was in her shop. Brilliant, Evie would have to get round to reading it one day, see if the author had blown the gaff on his family, or if it was all made up.

This composition was a bit different. It had to be on `A Day in the Life Of' and then you chose who it was, either someone you knew or someone famous, so that you could put together what you imagined to be their life.

Evie wondered about a day in the life of Geri, but remembered too well the pain of exposing too much of family life; it was just that she'd found herself speculating on how things were for Geri at the moment. Then she thought about writing `A Day in the Life of a Sex Show Actress,' but thought that the tutor might be a bit shocked, could be a bit rude. Evie had a word with herself to stop being obsessed with sex, either how much she didn't want it or how much she wanted to be powerful. She also found it hard to talk about with Stan, who was really into helping her with the word processing.

They sat one day after breakfast and talked for about an hour, Stan trying so hard to be helpful.

`What about Chubby Brown?' he said, helpfully. `Wonder how his day would start – probably with a fart and a joke about Jesus nicking a television.'

Evie knew what he meant: Stan and some of the lads had gone to see Chubby Brown when he was signed off in Cleveland, once for telling real bad taste jokes when all the sexual abuse scandal was around, and once for starting a set in a Church Hall which had been recently burgled, by pointing to the big crucifix with Jesus on and saying, `I see you got the bastard who took your television set, then.' And while Cleveland isn't posh, it's still an area where you don't laugh at religion. Especially in the Catholic Club.

Evie decided that Chubby Brown's head was not one to get inside.

`Tom Jones,' Stan came up with next. `Bet he has a good time – get up early, do the stretching exercises – only in his case, they're on his face.' He thought that was really funny.

They went through a whole list, then, of daft ideas. Stan finally came up with `A Day in the Life of a Nurse,' and Evie thought so what, might as well. To be honest, it bored her a little – what a dull routine. Really, the assignment was more about showing she could write accurately, and she drew on what she knew about Doc's practice. She soon got through a thousand words – it seemed such a lot to start with, but then she was surprised that the difficulty wasn't finding enough to write, it was keeping the word count down. Stan word processed it with gusto and thought it was great.

Then, being relentlessly helpful, he word-processed the commentary on *Remains of the Day*. That assignment was interesting. Evie found it quite slow to read at the beginning but was soon seduced into the quaint English ways of Stevens the butler. On a personal or realistic level, his properness and his insensitivity would have driven her mad. But what she really liked about the book was the reminder it gave her, that life is too short, that there is no point in playing with what might have been, or what could have been – all we have left is the present and the future. She enjoyed this lovely bit at the end where the butler is crying, actually crying because things haven't worked out his way, and this guy comes up to him on the park bench where he's sitting and says `it's a mistake to look back too much, for all that we have left is the remains of the day.' And that made Evie think.

Because for all the renewed effort between Evie and Stan, she couldn't say she was happy with him. Yes, fewer rows, yes, they were both doing their own thing, but in a way she was just worried that they were drifting further and further apart. And as for passion – she craved it so much it was almost eating her up.

It was probably that feeling and the next letter from Nikke that made Evie do what she did next. She'd contacted Nikke with Geri's suggestion to go over in May, and loved the response.

Dearest Evie,

Yes, yes, yes - you have made my day. I am so delighted that you are going to come over in May (and yes, you definitely are, I'm sure we were just meant to be.). Stay as long as you like - and I'd love to meet your sister, but only if it's okay with you.

Thanks for your Christmas pressie - the velvet is beautiful, and the violet is my favourite colour - how did you know? It cheered me up, I hate Christmas and to be honest I just got my head

206

down and finished off my work. I can't wait to get this degree and leave here in June to go to the UK, even though I'm scared.

Business is slack just now. Honestly, Evie, I think I'm as bored as you are, though I do feel for you. It's no fun being with someone you're not really in tune with. But then I'm with creeps like that (sorry, I don't mean that Stan is a creep, but you know what I mean) all the time. I've got to go to work tonight, you can't imagine the tedium. I always get showered and dressed here first, the old thong and platform bra always does the trick - I used to go a lot fancier, but can't really be arsed if this works - and it does, men are a pushover. Then I throw on my tracksuit to walk over to The Window and go and get undressed in the little back room. There's just a bed, a heater and a light, and some pretty cheap but fit for purpose furnishings, then there's a toilet and shower room (thank God!)

Anyway, it's on to the chaise longue or the chair till I can get some sucker in, I always make sure my alarm button is switched on, what a way to live my fucking life. Last night I had three punters - one blow job, two shags, I've become quite an expert on making them come quickly, and at least I covered my rental plus some for the savings - and quite a hefty tip from this fat old geezer who ended up crying to me about the state of his life, then felt mortified because he couldn't get it up (thank god again), so it was okay. Maybe too much information, but you'd be surprised what goes on in an average evening.

Anyway, I've probably bored you half to death, so I'm going to go now, but please please make sure you get your cheap flights well in advance and let me know.
In friendship,
Nikke x

And that was that. Decision made. Evie scrapped her day in the life of a nurse, and instead wrote about A Day in the Life of Nikke, only of course she didn't say it was her, and she couldn't believe how easily she created that day in her head. She started when she got up, what she had to eat and drink, and went right through the day. As for the window work, well it was easy. Evie was there, showering, preparing her body, dressing, and parading. Lady Macbeth goes porno. She struggled with the detail – she wanted to write every touch, every movement, but didn't quite know how well that would go down. Anyway, one thing was for sure, the grammar was the easy bit. She hid it from Stan, of course, and when she got her one straight A of the term ('excellent composition' and `insightful creativity'), he was delighted that he'd been able to help so much with the ideas. Evie was amazed at how much she'd got into daydreaming about what it would be like, really be like, to be Nikke. Maybe it was the daydreams that kept her going, those and the college work a breath of fresh air in a stale greasy world of deep fried chips and batter.

But the chippy paid, and every week Evie was putting by at least ten pounds toward her May trip, which was surprisingly easy if she just didn't go out much. It added up really quickly – Geri booked the flights on her credit card, only thirty-four pounds including tax, and Evie paid her back by the first week in February. Then it was just money for spends, and this time she decided not to be so precious about the cigarettes, so had started to collect orders from friends, money up front. Not huge amounts, enough to make an extra hundred so that she could treat both Geri and Nikke at some point.

She was that excited.

Meantime, at the end of March, Stan's pigeon fancier friend from Holland came over, that bloke Jan van something. It seemed such a coincidence that just as Evie was getting into going to Holland the Dutchman had begun to visit. She didn't have much chance to speak to him though, as Stan seemed to be a bit jealous or something – every time Evie tried to catch Jan to swap Amsterdam stories, Stan just happened to come along and interrupt. He was almost an embarrassment, in fact, and came over as very rude beside the more polite and sophisticated behaviour of his Dutch counterpart. Evie couldn't really work out what was going on between them. And then, in April, things came a bit to a head between Evie and Stan, and they both gave each other a few home truths. Evie didn't know which way they were going to go, but one thing was for sure, she couldn't go on much longer with that same old crap.

Eighteen
Team Work Every Time

Just as in corporate working – individuals are only viable long term in an organisation if they can work within team goals, values and specifications. Otherwise their success is random, rather than intentional.

Graham Dexter *The Perfect Team* www.nbra.co.uk
2008

This time round, Spring's light touch in the air, Stan enjoyed the experience of collecting Jan from the airport. So much different from the last time. He knew exactly where to go to in the arrivals lounge, and who to look for, and he walked tall. When he glimpsed his reflection in the newsagent window, he felt good. He was wearing a pair of Tesco jeans, only four pounds a pair, and you'd be really hard pressed to differentiate them from a more expensive brand; a nice light blue colour and a good quality and fit. He had acquired a neat brown leather jacket from Damien's New Year clear out. Stan was still cycling daily, had added some press ups and some sit ups to a little daily routine, had shed another couple of pounds and firmed up the ones that were left.

When he first saw Jan at the barrier, Stan experienced a momentary urge to punch his lights out, but quickly recovered composure and reminded himself of the prize he would be getting in a couple of months' time. He found himself doing a regular visualisation; it was just so easy to imagine Evie's face while he shows her that the mortgage is paid off and gives her a diamond ring – a good one. More than one Life Coach would pay quite some money to know how Stan managed such positive reinforcement at a deeply subconscious level.

When Jan first saw Stan, Stan supposed he might experience a second of disturbance, maybe sense a difference in his English host. Likely Jan would be relying heavily on the belief that Stan was a total fool, probably couldn't believe how easy it had been to take his excellent birds and make money out of them, nor how placid Stan had been about it all. In fact, Stan believed that Jan had sold the birds somewhat hastily, probably intending to keep them a while but then not being able to refuse the offer from the American who wanted them in time for the early breeding season. Stan guessed that it had been easy then to have them transported directly from the port, so that there were no complications with quarantine and very little expense. At the time, Jan probably gave hardly a thought to how Stan would react, maybe had Stan down as a total wuss. And if Jan did have any apprehensions, they would have been allayed by the invitation to come to the UK again. Stan was determined to reassure him, and shook his hand as ever.

It was only seven o'clock when Stan collected Jan. He didn't bother this time making sure that Jan had coffee, just set out toward Doc's house, getting there for twenty past eight. They made polite conversation on the journey, inevitably discussing pigeons in some detail. Jan had an outline of the day's agenda, and they agreed how great it was to be able to fly over the water just for a weekend, arriving Saturday morning and leaving on Sunday afternoon. On the one hand, Jan's departure couldn't come quickly enough for Stan; on the other hand, he was looking forward to the weekend unfolding.

Doc, Akbar and Frank, along with Gordon Stoneman and Graham Dexter, were all waiting in the conservatory, hot tea in their hands. Maggie greeted Jan and took his bag, the lads having agreed that it would be better for Jan to stay there tonight in case Stan had an aberration and lost control if the traitor was bedded at his.

`Are you sure I can't get you breakfast, Jan?' Maggie had already piled a plate with shortbread biscuits and put it on the tray along with the coffeepot and the teapot. `It really won't take a minute, I could do some eggs.'

Graham Dexter spoke for them all.

`No thanks, Mrs Doc. We're okay for breakfast; I see on the fly list that we're having some food at Akbar's, but thank you so much for asking. Marvellous geraniums if I may pass comment. Tell me, what's the secret?'

Jan was ushered down the garden to the loft, where Doc showed him his paper with the ring numbers on it. Gordon joined Jan's side as elected scribe for the day, much to everyone's amusement, and Jan okayed all the paper work. Then with a standing back and a flurry, the loft door was opened and Doc chased out his birds.

The wind was moderate, good for Doc as it was what the birds were used to in this area of the country, and he was an early morning flyer anyway. The birds were fit. Jan was a middle ground judge, and the lads were trying to get his measure as they heard him scoring, `five,' `twelve,' and so on, Gordon marking these figures down. After twenty minutes, Gordon huddled with Jan and took instructions on how many quality and kitting points were to be had. Eventually, Doc made a neat score of one hundred and seventy six, an auspicious start. Stan watched the process carefully.

Then the lads went in convoy to Akbar's, piling out of their cars and arriving looking like the Mafia, all wearing jeans, short jackets and dark glasses. Mrs A was her usual welcoming self, not minding as they trod bits of dirt through the lovely tiled hallway, and ushering them through to the back where she had laid out a neat wooden table with plates, knives, forks, and mugs. As soon as they were through, she took out steaming tin teapots and a tray full of samosas.

`Lamb on the left,' she announced, `vegetarian on the right.'

`Thanks, duck, but I don't think we've got any veggies with us.' Graham Dexter was trying to be helpful.

`I know,' conspired Mrs A, `look.' Graham looked more closely, noticing that there were no samosas on the right – only napkins. He grinned, nodded – this woman knows the men well.

`I'll be mother, then,' he said, and while he poured the requisite amount of teas and sorted out who had sugar and who didn't, Mrs A managed to bring out a tray full of beef sausage sandwiches, onion bhajis and some minced meat kebabs. The lads laid into the food, taking the opportunity to quiz Jan on what it was like to live in Holland.

`Bet it's all sex and drugs over there, eh?' Gordon spittled a flight of pastry crumbs and hot spice as he shared his fantasy of Holland mid food. Jan stepped back a little.

`Not really, my friend. Yes, we have more relaxed rules than you, but you know there is much more to Holland than Amsterdam. And when you get to my station in life, then you have very little need to go – how do you say – slumming it in the city.'

Stan exchanged looks with Frank, who made a quick puke gesture as Jan continued to regale the guest flyers with how he worked in a diamond factory, what car he drove, and so on. Stan felt affirmed in his assessment of the man, and after finishing a sausage sandwich, interrupted the party to suggest that they should fly some pigeons.

Akbar opened up his loft. The wind had dropped slightly, and the sun was now shining through. Perfect flying conditions. Doc began to grumble about how jammy Akbar was and how he always got it right. Akbar grinned cheekily, and chased out the birds in good humour.

They did magnificently for the first fifteen minutes, scoring over seventeen breaks, with eight of those being ten or more. What an impressive kit. Then, suddenly, two of the birds broke away from the kit, and to everyone's surprise, within another minute they were landed. Akbar couldn't believe it, he and his mates willing them to stay up and complete the outstanding performance, so upset to see it come to a disastrous end. Jan looked almost smug as he came over to officially deliver the bad news, which everyone knew was only fair.

`Sorry, my friend, but with two dropping before time, I have no choice but to disqualify you.'

Akbar nodded, cursing inwardly, while outwardly he repeated `unbelievable, unbelievable' over and over again.

Doc shook his head forlornly, and merely commented. `What a waste of good weather.' The company smiled half heartedly, but no one could really muster a laugh.

Next it was Frank's turn, and his birds performed well, although a little on the one wing. Nevertheless, Frank managed to nudge into first place. Jan was particularly impressed with Frank's loft, as were the rest of the company. Frank had a rather suave looking brick built loft which he had lovingly furnished over the years, a deep red padded roof carefully constructed over the felting. It wasn't extravagant, and he'd built it carefully; it looked fabulous. So today he was happy to be admired for both birds and loft, and his gentle manners allowed him to quietly accept the compliments coming his way.

Then it was on to Stan 's and his team flew a blinder, kitting beautifully and making seventeen breaks, but Jan didn't score them all, much to the disgust of Stan and his friends. They noticed that Jan seemed to have changed his preferences from last time. He gave the score paper to Stan, with the comments,

Kitted well, a little short in the roll to really score all the breaks, a team that worked hard. Nice little blue checker hot contender for the nomination bird.

`I'll bet,' thought Stan, wondering what the game plan here might be. Clearly, Jan didn't want to lose faith totally with Stan, but neither did he want to give the birds their due credit. Offering the nomination bird as carrot seemed kind of slimy to Stan; in competition, one bird was picked out as a kind of man of the match, or maybe king of the kit. While Stan's blue checker was indeed excellent, they all knew that it was no better than at least four of Frank's birds. But then there was always some subjectivity in this game. And, from time to time, some sucking up.

Stan asked who'd like sandwiches, and as over an hour and a half had passed since first brunch, Doc was keen to have a little snackette, and was first to say a definite yes. Stan had organised some corned beef and Branston pickle on bread buns, and some cheese and tomato, always a favourite. Evie had kindly plated them up and was putting them out, although she'd cried off dinner tonight, which Stan was pleased about: he'd feel more confident without her while he tried to entrap Jan van Braggart. Happily, she was going out with Geri, another sign of the friendship which was developing within their sisterly relationship. He was still slightly disarmed by how pleased she seemed to see Jan, sitting near him while he had a cup of tea and ate just two sandwiches, commenting on how important it was for him to keep himself in shape.

`So how was your trip, then, Evie? Did it live up to your expectations?'

Evie laughed in response.

`Oh blimey yes, Jan, it was even better than I thought, and I think I'll be going back. I just didn't know it would have such a great atmosphere. And I tell you, I'd never been to an art gallery before, and that was just fascinating.'

Jan laughed.

`So we weren't just good for sex and drugs then?' he teased.

`No, but that was good as well – we had such a laugh at one of your clubs, really opened our eyes, I can tell you. Even ended up on stage at one point.'

Stan overheard this, saw the animation in Evie's eyes, and noticed the appreciation in Jan's. His blood heated a degree. *You've nicked me pigeons, mate, take me fucking wife, why don't you? I don't think so.* He moved nearer, stood next to them.

`So how far out of Amsterdam do you live then, Jan?' he interrupted. Evie shot Stan a quick glance; she stood up and made her excuses, beginning to look for empty plates or cups.

Stan felt uncomfortable, a little guilty, and hoped that he hadn't annoyed her. The temptation to confide in Evie was at times unbearable, but he didn't want her to worry, and desperately wanted to surprise her when the deal was done and dusted.

Once conversation and sandwiches were through, it was on to John Hooper's, whose birds put up a good performance – not a winning one, but they were a promising team. Then finally on to a smallholding just outside of the 'Boro towards Guisborough where Sam Shipston kept a few sheep and some poultry. Naturally, the men always felt obliged to crack sheep and suspender jokes when they went to Sam's loft, but once that was over, they had to admire the beauty of the setting – rolling hills for some miles to the south, blue sky peeping through the grey clouds to lift the view. There were three large lofts, all painted dark green and rising majestically out of the ground.

Sam's birds flew splendidly and, much to everyone's surprise, came in on even pegging with Frank's – a tie at the end of day

216

one. This would make tomorrow even more exciting. The men agreed that they would meet up later for dinner, and once arrangements were made, they went their separate ways for a shave, a shit and a shower before the evening's fun commenced.
*
The Indian meal was as exquisite as ever, and Akbar made sure that the drinks were flowing.

`So I said to him, I said what do you bloody expect, hey?' Jan was in full flow, florid of face and apparently unaware of the slight increase in his volume, and of the fact that two of the company, namely Sam and John were leaving. Indeed, at this point, they were getting their coats and exchanging raised eyebrowed glances.

`Jesus, you could lose the will to live with much more of that,' Stan ventured at the coat hook, sotto voce.

`I mean, if you can't be bothered to put in the time, then don't moan when the birds don't perform.' Stan noted that Jan stopped talking only to down another swig of Cobra. Sam and John called over.

`Right then Jan, we'll see you in the morning, thanks a lot.' The pigeon men prided themselves on decent manners, at least when sober enough to remember, and were keen to get away to the club where they could have a bit more of a laugh. Jan said cheerio, burped and excused himself to the lavatory. Stan gave the nod. Akbar's eyes gleamed; this was their chance. Quick as a flash, he whipped out a bottle of vodka from his inside pocket and poured a hefty slug into the Cobra, while Stan went over to the counter and distracted the staff by ordering another round of three Cobras and two Cokes. The staff were delighted, as they now had their new alcohol license, and were doing well tonight. Akbar made the ultimate sacrifice in pretending that his religion didn't allow him to drink, while Doc had volunteered to drive so that he could stay sober. This way, at least two of them were guaranteed to stay in a fit state to orchestrate the rest of the evening's jiggery pokery. Stan felt pretty sure that he would stay sharp as a tack even with a few drinks inside him, but they were

217

going for belt and braces, and the sacrifices of Akbar and Doc were welcomed. Someone had to egg Jan on, so it was down to Stan and Frank to be the willing drinkers. Doc was compensating by attempting to get through every Indian sweet in the restaurant, but had got stuck on kulfi and was now on his third portion. Knowing Doc, he'd figure that it was good for him, all that calcium, and after all, it was only light.

When Jan returned, Doc had his Dictaphone secreted up his sleeve. Akbar had a slightly more elaborate plan going. He had made a point all evening of using his mobile with a hands-free set, and had the set on the table for most of the night, drawing attention to it and being the butt of various jokes. Now the mobile and the hands-free set were still visible; the hands-free was now connected to an i-Pod underneath the table.

`More beer – fantastic – I'll be seeing double of these birds in the morning if I'm not careful!' Jan lifted his glass and took a swig from his topped up glass, let out a satisfied sigh.

`Ah, you'll be fine, man.' Stan exuded bonhomie. `Still, beats working, eh? Not that I'd mind your job, though, sounds right cushy.'

`Well, can't say I've done badly.' Jan took another self-satisfied slurp of vodka-laced beer. `Reckon I should be able to retire in about five years' time. And then it's just fun, fun, fun all the way.'

Akbar and Doc nodded, and Frank spoke next.

`What, you'll only be what, forty-two, forty-three by then? They must give good pensions at your place, mate. Unless there's any more of them little perks you were telling us about last time.'

Jan looked around, changed his voice to what he imagined was a softer tone.

`Shush, can't remember what I told you last time, but you can never be too careful.'

`Sorry, mate,' Frank took another glug of beer. `But seriously, it must be a good pension?'

Jan rambled for five more minutes, the lads all pretending to look interested while they encouraged him to drink more and more.

`So what exactly is it that you do, then Jan? Can't quite work out from what you've said – is it security, or management, or what?'

`Well, it's a bit of both, my friends, as it happens. Actually, for the last two years, I've been in charge of the IT side of the security. I knew a long time ago that that was the direction to go into.'

`Fantastic.' Stan was right on cue. `I've just started learning computers meself. Nothing like you do, I don't suppose, but I'm dead chuffed. What do you have to do then, Jan?'

`I develop systems for tracking the diamonds as they go through the factory, then I monitor them.'

`Wow. Bet that's good. So what do you have to track?' Stan gauged correctly that Jan was well enjoying the attention now, and was happy to respond.

`When diamonds come into our factory, they are all logged as what grade of diamond they are, which we can usually tell on first examination. Then they go through the polishing system. We used to do that by hand, and now we do a mix, mostly laser polishing but we have some exclusivity because we also still have some artisans who do it the old way. But every time anyone handles them, we have to log them out of the system and then back into it when the stone is returned to the lock up. Too much temptation otherwise.' He chuckled, took another swig of his drink.

`So how would anyone steal them, then Jan?' Akbar leaned forward in a conspiratorial manner. `If they're that tightly regulated?'

`Ah, now you're asking. As far as I know, we've only had three attempted thefts at the factory, which resulted in two dismissals.' Jan gave a smug wink.

`What about the other one?' Akbar kept up the pressure. Doc took charge of another plate of sweets, and Frank ordered more beer.

`Well that, my friend, was the triumph of the decade.'

Stan leaned forward and spoke in hushed tones.

`So how did you do it, Jan?'

219

Akbar was checking the volume of his recording, and Doc was moving his arm nearer and nearer to Jan, until Frank gave him a warning look, as the lump of the Dictaphone threatened to slip further down his arm into the kulfi which he had mashed up for ease of ingesting.

`Well, between you and me, it turned out to be surprisingly easy. You remember my good friend Allan?'

Four heads nodded enthusiastically.

`Well, he's in charge of collecting the diamonds in at close of play and checking them into the system. Last February, when we decided it was time for a bit of a bonus, he simply chose one which didn't get put back into the safe, gave me its identification, and I eradicated all trace of it from beginning to end.'

`Wow. That sounds so easy.'

`I know.' Jan smirked again. `It sort of was and it wasn't. There were a lot of numbers to sort out, from the purchase order all the way through to the final statistics, which I had to make up on other stones. But that wasn't too bad, as we made sure that we took a stone from a batch. We could never take one which was really exclusive, or specially ordered, for example.'

`By, man, you've got some nerve. I've fiddled the odd gas meter, but never anything like this. Well done, my man, you're impressive.' Stan led the lads in raising their glasses to Jan who was redder than ever.

`Well thank you. And let me say how impressive your birds – and your astounding ability to drink are. Is it just me, or are we all very drunk here?'

`No, it's all of us, we've had a lot tonight.' Stan answered swiftly and took a large slug of his beer. `Come on though, Jan, you're in Middlesbrough now, got to keep the end up.' And so saying, Stan clinked his glass on Jan's, encouraging them both to take another swig.

Jan nodded, his red face shining now, his eyes becoming pinker and piggier as he took more beer and vodka. Stan was watching him carefully: bet he thought the English were so stupid, for him to come here, rip them off, and then have them wine and dine him and find out how clever he really is. He was grinning. Stan grinned back; *just you wait, mate, just you wait.* Akbar went in for the kill.

`So don't you get searched when you go in and out of the factory, though? I'd have thought with all them diamonds they'd have been body checking you where the sun don't shine, hey?'

`I should be so lucky.' Jan chuckled a smutty chuckle. `No, these days it's done by x-ray. We do searches, but they're spot searches so that no one ever knows when it's going to be them.'

`So how do you get the stones out, then Jan?'

`Aha. That would be telling.'

`Come on man, how can we believe that you're that clever if you won't tell us that bit – could all be bullshit for all we know.'

Jan couldn't resist the challenge.

`Well, you know the people who don't get searched and x-rayed are the tourist parties who come round the factory. They never get to go near to a diamond, you see, not in the usual course of events. So we used them to get it out.'

`But how, if they don't get to handle the diamonds?' Stan was genuinely intrigued.

`Well, once I'd got all the technical side seen to, Allan arranged for someone we know to come round in a party. He hid the diamond – you'll like this, lads – he hid it wrapped up in tissue paper in the Ladies' toilet, in the sanitary bin. Then we got our plant to pick it up. And the daft bloody factory never knew a flaming thing.' He looked up at the faces. `Brilliant, hey? Bloody brilliant. We were brilliant.'

Doc leaned forward and made his one intervention, a skilful one at that.

`So you're really asking us to believe, Jan, that last February you managed to eradicate all signs of a diamond in the system in your factory and that you and Allan then smuggled it out, right under their noses, broad daylight?'

`Yep, Doc, we did. Just before February 14th, a great Valentine's Day present for someone, hey? We just got rid of all traces of it –

under my supervision, of course, being security – and sent it out in a party of tourists.'

Stan could hardly believe the crispness of this confession, pushed it further.

`So how much was it worth?' He was almost holding his breath now.

`Not a lot.' Jan was playing with them now, the pleasure of boasting mixing with the arrogance of the drunk. `Just about 100,000 I suppose.'

Akbar's eyes were popping. `What, euros?'

`No man, pounds. I was converting it for you to make it easier for you to understand.'

`But that's massive.' Stan was genuinely gobsmacked.

`Well yes, but not when you work in millions, my friend. You're probably just not used to that, hey?'

`So how did you get rid of it?' Questions were easy now as the fascination was real, and for Stan the possibilities were changing all the time.

`There's always a market for diamonds, my friend. Ten per cent of all the diamonds in the world are illegally traded. We have a contact in the city that had a customer lined up. He bought it for a discount, and we were all happy.'

`So would you do that again then, Jan, really, now you've got away with it once?'

Jan almost guffawed, his head wobbling on his neck as if he were some kind of bendy toy.

`It so happens we've just had an order in where we think we can afford to lose one. I mean use. I mean either use or lose.' Jan grimaced in the general direction of the lads. `First for over a year. Should be ready to go out month after next. So, yes, we'll be doing it again – second week of May. All fixed up.'

`You clever shite.' Frank spoke with a mix of genuine admiration and loathing. `You clever little shite.'

Stan was delighted. So much information down on record. And now he knew what he needed to ask Jan to do. Although even in his elation he could see one final problem – how to get rid of the diamond. But he could afford to be optimistic; something would turn up.

The waiter's presence took them by surprise and Stan was suddenly aware that it was time to go. To go with what they came for.

While Doc was paying the bill, Jan staggered to the toilets, and Akbar made sure that his i-Pod was safely in his inside pocket. It was lucky that Jan was in the toilet, for Doc was so excited he'd forgotten that his Dictaphone was up his sleeve, and as he raised his arm to take out his credit card, it clattered to the floor. Stan had it picked up within seconds, giving Doc a scowl.

`For God's sakes man, be careful.' The waiter looked with interest at the shenanigans, but he knew the lads well, no need to ask any questions.

When Jan reappeared, now looking totally befuddled, Doc put his arm around his shoulders, led him out of the restaurant toward a taxi rank.

`So tell me, how do you get rid of cats in your neck of the woods?'

The other three followed gleefully, Akbar giving his i-Pod to Stan on the quiet. When taxis arrived, Doc poured Jan into the first one with himself and Akbar. Frank and Stan said an enthusiastic farewell.

`Cheerio all, thanks for a good night.' Then they exchanged a handshake before taking the next cab together, and the cab driver dropped Frank off on the way to Stan 's.

When he got home, tired and elated, Stan 's adrenaline was pumping well. All the lights in the house were off, and he unlocked the door very carefully. He couldn't wait till morning; knew he had to check the recording now. He crept to the living room and rewound the Dictaphone. For a moment, he was appalled to hear nothing but a faint crackle, before realising that he had pressed pause instead of play, and when he made the adjustment, he heard Jan's voice, a little slurred in tone, but coming through clear as a bell. Now all he needed was to get the i-Pod into the computer tomorrow, and the next stage would be set to go. Fantastic.

The next day's fly went well, despite Jan being bleary eyed and complaining endlessly of a headache. Everyone drove down to Derbyshire, and the weather was kind for the lads down there. As it happened, no one could nudge Frank and Sam out of first place, and Frank got it on the toss of a coin. Graham Dexter came a close third, and of course all the men were impressed by his strong stock and good company.

Jan ate only a light lunch at the Crewe and Harper pub, but everyone was polite to him, thanked him profusely.

`You've been a great help to us,' said Stan, `more than you can ever imagine.'

Jan nodded acceptingly, as if to say, *yes, I am good, aren't I, you morons*. Stan saw in his eyes his belief that the British lads really benefited from his expertise. Got your number, mate, Stan thought. He was glad when Jan talked little on the journey back to the airport, and indeed when he fell asleep. By the time Stan left him at the airport, Jan was apparently starting to feel a little better and embraced his hosts warmly.

`You must come over to Holland, some time,' he smarmed.

`Aye, that'd be good. You never know, it might be sooner than expected.' And with that, Stan and the lads turned and left Jan to check in, sharing a little smile with each other, and looking forward to that trip.

Looking forward to it very much indeed.

Nineteen
The Devil May Care

Card XV – The Devil

When you see the Devil in a Tarot reading, take caution. It can indicate that you feel somewhat trapped, that you're not seeing the whole picture, operating from not knowing what others are doing. In Evie's case, this meant a touch of despair when she realised that it was her and Stan on their own now, and was not immediately filled with deep joy. Unfortunately, the devil also drives us to excess. In Evie's case this meant losing her sense of the spiritual and going instead for the spirit – a silly mistake that could happen to any of us.
Playing straight into the Devil's hands.

The row was inevitable, really. Coming together over an essay from time to time was far from enough for Evie. Life was really, really routine – cooked breakfast, Thursday nights out, and, for Stan, bloody pigeon flies. While college and Amsterdam were great, Evie still felt that Stan didn't see her for who she was, and there remained an element of boredom so great that Evie could easily have lost the will to live. So to say that the row was inevitable and that Evie would regret it later wasn't quite right: rather, she regretted that it was necessary.

It was a Tuesday night. Evie had had a hell of a day, the chippie had been run off its feet, and Beulah had been off colour, a touch of bronchitis they thought, so Evie had been in to see her on the way home. She was knackered. To top it all Damien had dropped a bombshell. He'd got a job in Surrey, courtesy of one of Susannah's uncles, and the two of them were going to be moving down there in a month's time. He was chuffed to bits.

Evie was shocked at her own reaction. While she'd known this day would come, believing it was another matter. Since talking to Nikke in Amsterdam, she'd seen a bit more of Damien, was enjoying it. When she was first back, they'd been out for dinner one night when Stan was with the lads and Susannah was away on a course. It was Evie's idea, and at first he'd just looked at her like she was way off – going out with his mum? But then he'd grinned and said yes, why not, and they went to the big Chinese in town.

They talked about all kinds of things, and he told her then his plans, his hopes, and how eventually he wanted to start his own business. Evie encouraged him; she was always keen for him to do well at school and knew she didn't want him being another deadbeat in Middlesbrough. And she laughed.

'So when you're the boss of a big corporation, will you have a good job for your old Mam then, son?'

He looked her straight in the eye.

'Not so much of the old. You look great you know.' Evie was taken aback. She'd just stopped having her hair bleached and she'd kept it shorter since her long weekend away. Overall she

226

thought it worked well, but still wasn't totally sure about her new image. She welcomed his reassurance.

`And I tell you what, Mam, this college stuff seems to be doing you good. Maybe you should be looking for a new job, you know?'

That made Evie think. And then thinking about jobs, she'd thought about Stan, and before she knew it, a great sigh escaped her lips.

`What's up?' Damien looked at her quizzically.

`Eeh, nothing really, just I wish Stan could get a job. To be honest, he seems to have stopped looking. It's so tight, Damien, always so bloody tight.' Evie had surprised herself talking like this to Damien, but he seemed okay to listen. He considered for a minute.

`I suppose he has, Mum, although I don't really see him much so it's hard to know. But he seems to like the computer – at least he knows how to use one, and you never know, that might help him find some work eventually?'

`Suppose. All it seems to me at the moment is that he's found another hobby. And it's almost like he's up to something, like he's somewhere else a lot of the time. D'you think he's okay?'

`Don't know, but you two don't seem to argue as much, I'll say that.'

Evie felt a bit of a pang of guilt at that, and there was much more she wanted to say, but thought better of it. She just let Damien be reassuring, and it was good to leave it at that so she didn't get him too involved. Poor lad, he'd certainly seen his parents at their worst over the years, must have been difficult.

So after that night he went back to being very busy and mostly at Susannah's. Evie was pleased that he and Susannah came for Christmas at Beulah's, and the two of them had Sunday lunch at home a couple of times. Evie had felt that little bit closer to Damien. And then he dropped the bombshell, and she was completely taken aback when the reality of it hit home.

He told them both together, to be fair and he was looking so pleased and yet so nervous, Evie didn't want her own horror to

227

overshadow his pleasure. Because in that moment, when he stood before the fire and said he was going, Evie's heart quickened. Stan beamed at his son, then he turned to Evie and boasted `so that'll just be the two of us then Evie, you and me.' He turned back to Damien.

`Congratulations, son, we're proud of you.'

Well of course Evie was proud of Damien, but suddenly she really didn't want him to go. She felt a lump in her throat at the anticipation of how much she would miss him. And she couldn't get past the `just the two of us.' Because although it was more or less like that already, at least Damien popped in, stayed there sometimes, and she felt like she was just starting to know him more again. And now it was hitting her that `just the two of us' was going to be forever. And Stan was excited about that.

Oh. My. God.

Evie gave Damien a big hug and mustered up from deep inside herself the response she knew he needed from his Mam.

`I'm really pleased for you, son. Well done.'

And then they talked about where he'd be going, what he'd be doing, and the prospects he was going to have. He'd be running a small team of people doing painting and decorating, but he'd also be going on a course on interior design software technology, taking him to a more advanced level than he was already at. This was his dream, and it was going to come true for him. How could Evie be so selfish as not to be pleased?

She phoned both Jeannie and Geri the next day to tell them the news. Jeannie was well impressed.

`Oh my God, Evie, he's done so well. Brilliant.' Then she paused slightly before asking. `So how does that feel for you, Evie? Are you alright?'

Geri was more direct.

`Just what he needs, to get out of this dump and set his sights on something better. But my God, Evie, this will be a big change won't it, just you and Stan.'

They all arranged to meet, and the following Thursday saw them necking the beer in the Italian restaurant where Evie had met Geri on that night several months before.

`Eeh, this is a bit posh, eh?' Jeannie gawped at the modern interior. She soon relaxed into it though, once she'd had a beer and Geri had sipped a cold white wine. Geri was definitely mellowing – it was a joy.

They all complimented each other on their looks. Geri had started working out at a gym, and while she was no fatter, she looked really fit, and was waxing lyrical about Pilates. She was beautifully turned out as ever, in slightly more pastel shades than she sometimes wore, a kind of light mauve with silky grey, almost silver, and it suited her.

Jeannie was delighted because she'd lost a stone in weight, and just couldn't stop enthusing about how easy it was to do this since working in the bookshop.

`I used to be so bored in the newsagent, I'd just nab meself a Mars Bar or a Flake or something, but now I don't even think about food unless I'm hungry.' She eyed Geri with interest.

`And maybe I might even join a gym – fancy meself in a bit of a leotard.' Evie laughed; good old Jeannie never took herself too seriously.

And they both thought that Evie's shorter and more natural dark brown hairstyle was looking good.

`Comes a certain age, dahling, where blonde can look brassy. I think that really suits you – you could even take a bit more off to the top of the cheekbones, and have a deep plum woven in – you'd look fantastic.'

It was food for thought.

They'd eaten and then Evie started talking about Damien going. It was now only two weeks until he was going down to Surrey, then he was going to come back the following weekend to finish off a job he was midway through. The rest of the work he had lined up he was going to give to someone else, supervising by exchanging photos on the net and coming back up at some point in the next month. Then that was that, he'd be gone for good.

`Jesus, I can't wait for mine to start going.' Jeannie laughed, and Evie knew she didn't mean it – Jeannie was maternal in a way that Evie had never quite been.

Until now, apparently.

`You don't mean that, Jeannie,' Evie laughed.

`Well yes and no, I mean, I can't really imagine it. But you know I've started to see things I could do as they get older, and I must say it'd be great not to have to find quite so much money.' Evie felt selfish then, always on about herself and there was Jeannie juggling so many balls in the air.

Geri looked slightly uncertain.

`I don't know what to say, Evie, because I've never had children, even though I'd have loved to.' She looked slightly wistful, provoking another slight twitch of guilt in Evie. `But I think when I look at you that this is going to be really tough. I mean, where are you and Stan really going? What do you want in the next few years?'

And of course, she'd hit the nail right on the head. Where the fuck were they going, and what the heck did they want? Evie had been reading some books on personal development from the college library, and could see that she needed something to move towards. Not that she didn't know that anyway, but they helped her to focus, and then she got scared.

Because what she wanted was freedom. She wanted enough money not to work in a chip shop. She wanted to have the option to do more at college next year if she wanted. She wanted to travel. She wanted a man who was witty and interesting, or no man at all. She wanted someone she could really talk to about her new found passions, not someone who just nodded and only got excited if a poem included a bird. She wanted to be swept off her feet.

And when she said all that out loud, she realized she wasn't just dissatisfied, she was really scared of spending more and more years in her and Stan 's little house with their little debts and their little life and their Thursday nights out. And although there was nothing that new in this, the conversation seemed to throw

230

into sharp relief how desperate it was all becoming, now that Damien was going.

Jeannie just looked at Evie when she'd finished, at the tears in her eyes which seemed to become more prolific with every glass of beer, and put her arm around her friend.

`Don't worry pet, it'll be alright. Really it will.' Geri looked her sister in the eye.

`You, my girl, are in trouble,' she said. `Something's got to give, Evie, I don't know what yet, but you need to start thinking hard.' Then she did a typical Geri.

`But for now, we're going to have some fun.' She summoned the waiter. `A bottle of champagne for this table please. And make it your best.'

So by the time Evie got home, the three of them being the last to leave the restaurant after being the first to arrive, she was much more drunk than usual. And that's when Stan got it in the neck.

He'd been out too, but seemed reasonably sober.

`Good night, love?' He made to kiss her, but Evie withdrew at the sound of his boring old voice.

`Yeah, it was great. It was really great, actually, the best I've had for ages.'

He raised an eyebrow, and then he grinned. Evie could see a glint in his eye. The tedious old twat, he thought his luck was in.

`But now I'm tired,' she said, `good night.'

`We don't have to go up yet,' he said, and put his arms around her. `And Damien's not here.'

So predictable. So very predictable.

`Fancy a shag then, Stan?' Evie heard her voice come out louder than she'd intended, and Stan looked surprised, and then delighted.

`Fancied one for weeks, love.'

He thought it was an offer.

`Well then you'd better go and get one.' He flinched. `I'm not just a shag, I'm me, Evie, and I'm bloody sick of you.'

231

With hindsight, she couldn't blame him for being a bit surprised – Evie hadn't really said much to him for weeks, and now had revved up from bottom to top gear without any in-between.

`Eeh, steady on, Evie,' he said. `No need for that.'

No, there wouldn't be. Stan didn't do confrontation; no wonder it all welled up.

`Actually, Stan, there is. I can't remember the last time you said you wanted me, or had any idea of when I wanted to have sex with you. It's always about when you fancy a shag.'

He looked like he'd been slapped.

`Maybe we'd better talk about this in the morning,' he managed.

`No, Stan, let's talk about it now, because that's the trouble, we never do talk in the morning, we never bloody well talk at all.'

He moved toward the door.

`I think you're a bit drunk, Evie love. Come on, I'm going to bed.'

`Why, Stan, been a tiring day looking for jobs again, has it?' The knife went straight in.

`Or is it looking after the pigeons that gets you down? All that walking up and down the garden, all that looking up at the sky? Or is it playing on the computer – is that what does you in?'

He looked at Evie askance, the flickers of his eyes reflecting shock, hurt and finally anger.

`You know I want a job, Evie, but you bloody well tell me where a man of my age and with my qualifications can get anything more than a minimum wage round here?'

`I don't know, Stan, but I go out to work every day to that smelly shithole of a chippy, and the wages aren't great you know, but at least I do it and it's something extra to the dole and at least I have some self-respect.'

He'd gone pale by now, and somewhere Evie thought perhaps she should stop, but the champagne had loosened her tongue, which wasn't about to tighten up.

`Well, Evie, I'm doing my best, you know.' He looked like he was going to tell her something, but then suddenly his mood changed and Evie could see the glint of anger in his eyes dominate every other emotion. `And there's a lot of things you don't know, you know. D'you think I feel good having no sodding money, not being able to buy things for you, take you out in the style you seem to want these days? After all, you're not really happy with the club any more are you, not since you've been at *college.*'

He almost spat the word out.

`That's not what I mean, Stan, you don't get it, do you? It's not just about the money. It's everything. We don't talk, we have crap sex, you have no idea of my emotional or sexual needs at all. You make me feel like a stuffed dummy, there for your entertainment, but where am I in all this, Stan, where for Christ's sake am I? Bored bloody shitless, that's where, and now that Damien's going what the sodding hell is it all about? If I didn't have college, I'd be bloody brain dead. After all, there's sod all to keep it alive around here.'

There. It was out. All of it, filling the room with a silent low pressure, Stan registering more hurt, then a kind of confusion, and then again some more anger.

`Alright, Evie, I might not be the world's most exciting bloke. But do you think I like the way things are, Evie? And yes, you're right, where the fuck are you? You're certainly not here with me. You're away with your dreams, your college work, your assignments, and your new fancy friends, I suppose. We can't all be like you, Evie, I can't talk books and ideas with you like you'd like to. And you never wanted me to before, so don't be blaming me if you're not happy.'

Evie reeled slightly, waited for him to stop, but could see there was more to come: when it came it wasn't quite what she expected. Stan 's voice was low and steady now.

`You never have time for me, Evie, you never listen to me, so you have no idea what I'm doing or what I'm capable of. And as for sex – well, you never have time for that either. You're right, you might as well be a stuffed dummy for all the good our sex life does, but that's not for lack of trying on my part, Evie, not for lack of trying.'

That shocked her, that she could have some part to play in what was going wrong. Evie knew there was some truth in what he was saying and now her head was in turmoil. For a second, she thought this her opportunity to explain to him what she meant, to get him to see her point of view, that there was sex and there was really seeing her sexually, that this was about her essence, her core.

`But you don't try hard enough, Stan. Not like with your pigeons, all that time you spend with them, all that looking after. You feed them, fly them, bathe them – Christ, you even talk to the bloody things.' She hiccoughed. `I want you to see me sexually like you see your sodding pigeons, Stan. I want you to see me like a pigeon – I want you to treat me like a pigeon.'

Stan looked at her incredulously at that, and then, to her chagrin, he started to laugh, almost hysterically, just repeating now and then `she wants me to see her like a sodding pigeon,' and Evie began to cry. Eventually he stopped laughing and got up, looking at her with a slightly pitying expression.

`Evie, I love you, but I don't know what the fuck you're on about. I'm sorry I'm not the man you want me to be, but I think for now you've had too much to drink and you'd best go to bed.' And with that, he went into the kitchen to get himself a mug of tea, and she could hear him muttering now and then `a sodding pigeon,' with this strange sort of chuckle, and then she staggered up the stairs, got undressed, and fell into more of a coma than a sleep.

When Evie woke up, the events of the previous night came back to her slowly and with alarming clarity, and when Stan brought her the usual cup of tea, not looking straight at her, she didn't know whether to try and explain herself soberly or what. Stan made the choice for her, leaving the bedroom and going straight into the usual routine. Her head throbbed, and she felt tearful and stupid. She took paracetamol, drank the hot tea, and gingerly got out of bed. Once showered, she made breakfast and left for work. None of the issues had been spoken of since.

They rubbed along, and Evie could see Stan making an effort, poor bloke, but he was right, he was never going to be interested in Ishiguro and maybe Evie shouldn't expect him to be. And he

234

hadn't made any sexual overtures at all for the last month and she didn't know whether that was better or worse than before.

By the second weekend after that row, Damien had packed up his room. Evie found herself starting to go into it more than she had for a year or two, noticing as if for the first time the different bits of décor that he'd done, and just how smart it was. He'd decided to leave his computer and desk for now, as he had himself a fancy laptop that came with the job. Stan was going to carry on using the old one, but everything else, all the personal stuff, disappeared.

Damien left on a Saturday, and they hired a transit van for both his and Susannah's things. Stan helped him load it up; the two of them looked really close together, harmonizing their bodies to lift and place, creating spaces, a real team, and they had the odd laugh. Evie just made tea. When it came for Damien to go, he gave her a big hug.

`Don't worry, mum, I'll be alright. And anyway, I'm back in a fortnight, so don't be moving into me room just yet!'

She felt tearful then, but didn't want him to see, so she hid her face in her son's shoulder for a few seconds and then bounced up with a relentlessly positive smile.

`You enjoy yourself, son.' She touched his face. `I'm proud of you.' And with that, she gave him a kiss on the cheek and ushered him off to the van. `You take care, now, and phone me when you get there.'

`Okay, Mam, you too!'

Evie stood outside her home beside her husband, and they both watched their Damien until the van was out of sight. They should have felt great, like they do in the movies. Evie should have cried and Stan should have put his arms around her and comforted her. But it wasn't like that, not at all. The fallout from the row hovered between them, and really, they were just two sad individuals standing on a pavement watching an episode of their lives together disappear in a small white van.

Damien came back, as promised, for a weekend, but Evie even felt miffed then, as when he wasn't working Stan wanted him to

235

show him something on the computer, and it was clear that she wasn't welcome in that particular little twosome. She knew she should have been pleased for them but instead she just felt excluded and pissed off. So it hadn't been brilliant, and one way or another, Evie had the feeling that something else had to happen to enable her and Stan to move on.

Twenty
Bringing the Team In

The fancier who has the ability to see what is going on in the team, to be able to recognise the signs of excellence and also the individuals who are disturbing the team is the one most likely to succeed. The fancier, of whom I know too many, that watches the team for only a few moments then turn their attention to the tea break is sadly not going to make it. This type of fancier, when they are in another fancier's territory, tends to study the construction of the loft, the breeding boxes, the kit boxes, the feed bin – while the birds are in the air. These fanciers will never learn what they need to learn about a team of birds from these efforts, although they might be hot on office furniture and Feng Shui – which are valuable – but should be attended to after the kit has landed or at least flown some time. The fanciers that don't pay attention to the team in the air are seldom likely to become the astute observers that they need to be for success.

Graham Dexter, *The Perfect Team* www.nbra.co.uk
2008

Jan van Deuzen had had a splendid weekend, and was both recalling it and listening to his favourite classical music programme on the radio as he drove speedily yet carefully towards the outskirts of the city. He enjoyed combining his pleasures, had become extremely good at it – this was how he became so rich. He knew when to play and when to work, when to do both, when to give and, especially, when and how to take. So he'd spent Saturday on a pigeon fly with the lads. He'd heard that the American had already bred some stunning youngsters from Stan 's breeders, and hoped that Jan would be able to get across and see them one day. So the quality of Stan 's birds had matched their reputation. Good. Those stupid English – easy meat or what!

And on Saturday night, he had a great night with Anja, out for dinner and then she'd been unusually assertive in bed, which suited him fine. He'd felt a vague disquiet at first – why was she so unusually aroused? But then he had shut out the disquiet, after all, he was a good-looking man with a finely tuned body. His body was a temple – he chuckled at the memory of those English fanciers, most of whom had let themselves go – if their bodies were temples of anything, it would be the temples of doom. So yes, no wonder that Anja wanted him. He felt a twinge of pleasure at the memory of the sex, a frisson of blood engorging his veins. A car beeped its horn at him; lights had turned to green and his responses were slack. He waved in acknowledgement, accelerated away.

And then on Sunday, he'd taken the boys out to the lake and thrilled them with the new model boat that he bought last week through Pieter at work – they had loved it of course, and had then all gone home to a full dinner table and the warmth of a comfortable sitting room. Jan was replete; he lifted one cheek off his cream leather seat and broke wind with the self-satisfied smirk of a man whose life was bursting with good luck. And as Gary Player noted when congratulated on his good luck in golfing, `the more you practise, the luckier you get'. Well, Jan was practising at every opportunity, and boy was he getting good at it. Thus he basked in the blissful ignorance of not yet knowing that today's wind would be an ill one for him.

So when he pulled up into his parking space in the Gassan diamond factory, he was feeling energised. He leaped up the stairs, their light purple metallic rails embodying sleekness and success, showed his pass at the top, and nodded at the guard who allowed him through the heavy reinforced glass doors. He said good morning to all the staff he met, women in smart uniforms and immaculate make up, men in suits looking cool, as they began the week's business in the diamond market. He passed workrooms where men in overalls sat hunched over machinery, hamsters on a wheel, their furrowed brows etched onto wizened faces, deep lines about their eyes, as they ground away at the big stones to begin the refinement process. Jan passed the bust of Gassan himself, taking pride of place in the hall. Eighty years, the old bugger lived for, so he must have done something right. Jan saw the treasured bust as something to respect and to admire. Self-made men – that's what the world was all about. He saw Allan, but was careful not to spend any more or less time with him than usual. This was the big week, and he'd already put some time aside today for making some adjustments to the purchase orders. This was a delicate phase of the operation, and he wouldn't like to mess it up now.

Jan entered his office, the office of a senior manager on the up, and sat enthusiastically on the well-upholstered chair. A photograph of Anja and the boys adorned his desk; alongside a new porn DVD – *Spitroast Special* – courtesy of Albert the media technician, which he put in his drawer for later viewing. He switched on the coffee maker, booted up his computer.

He scanned his list of e-mails, mostly predictable, mostly recognisable. When his coffee was brewed, he opened the known ones, the mundanities of business; plus one from Heine, one from Colin, both pleased with the birds that they saw over the weekend. Then he opened the new ones which were mostly business. The most intriguing, he saved for last. Its sender was a new one for him, entitled Ivor Deeltocut, and he knew as he

239

opened it that it was going to be either very good or very bad. It had got through the spam filter, through the firewall, but the significance of the name only fully filtered as his fingers were already pressing computer keys to open it. He read it and a slight shiver hit his spine, which he ignored just as he'd ignored his slight disquiet at Anja's sexual overtures. The e-mail was brief and to the point.

```
Hello Jan, ripped off any good pigeon fanciers
lately? Well prepare to rip off more - a little
gem of an assignment coming up for you.
Watch this space - we'll be back. Just Men.
```

At first Jan was confused. Was this someone's idea of a joke? Then he was alarmed: this was his work e-mail and whoever had got access to it was putting his job in jeopardy. He was also intrigued – what the heck was this all about? And a flush of guilt threatened his neck and cheeks, because it must be someone who knew about the birds. But surely not Stan, poor, semi illiterate Stan? No it didn't make sense. As quick as a flash, Jan deleted the mail and emptied his recycle bin. Then he lifted his coffee and scalded his lips. The day was changing.
*
Meanwhile, Stan was enjoying his usual routine, tea taken up to Evie, and now the pigeons were aloft, and the smell of a good bacon breakfast was wafting through the mild May air to his nostrils. His weekend had been a great one. He spent Saturday daytime with Akbar, ringing young birds and generally messing about. On Saturday night he watched TV with Evie, and although he hadn't got a shag, as usual, he'd felt she was being really nice to him for the first time in ages for some reason, and he was in the mood to be grateful for small mercies. Since their argument, he hadn't really expected any sex from her and had distanced himself more than ever in this department, taking solace in solitary sexual activity whenever he felt the need.

240

Which, curiously enough, was less and less now that he was so preoccupied with plans of vengeance.

He'd had Sunday dinner up The Blue Lagoon with Evie and Beulah, then a drink with some of the lads over the match on the TV. It would have been great to be down the Riverside Stadium to see the 'Boro playing live, but at the prices they charged, he could have bought a hundred Sunday dinners and still have change for some ale, so stuff it.

Although, if things worked out, then maybe a season ticket next year?

And then, last night, after a good old snooze in front of the gas fire, while Evie was poring over some course work and some magazines, travel magazines he thought, Stan had gone upstairs to the computer and finally done the deed. He had sent the first e-mail. He didn't know what response it would get, but by, did he feel good. He'd thought long and hard about the words to use and he liked his `little gem' pun – Stan was grinning just thinking about it. He'd also put a little flag beside the message, just like Damien had told him, so that he would be able to see if it had been opened even if there wasn't a reply. Remembering, Stan felt a flutter of excitement as he watched the birds lift on the wing and score a break of seven for him –fanblooditastic. Stan put his hands in his pockets and grinned.

Evie's voice cut into his reveries.

`Stan, your breakfast's ready.'

He waved an acknowledgement and spent another five minutes waiting for the birds to drop, shaking the corn tin and calling to them. When he got into the house, Evie was already finishing her meagre plate of one rasher of bacon and one fried egg. She was still on the Atkins diet. Wouldn't do for Stan though, not with no bread, but he must admit she was looking good on it. Slimmer than ever and bright eyed. He thanked her for the breakfast, and opened the paper. Exclusive – *Britney Secret Surrogate Mother to Friend's Quins* it blared, and he engrossed himself, enjoying the sensation of biding his time until he could go upstairs and check the computer.

`Stan, I'm off.' Evie sounded a touch impatient. Stan looked up.
`Sorry, pet, miles away.' He put down his special mug and got up, giving Evie a kiss on the cheek.
`See you later, then,' she said, and she gave his arm a quick squeeze.

Stan swilled out his Roller mug and made himself more tea, brewing it to the right strength and putting in two sugars and another one for luck. He then took the tea upstairs, over the creaky step and into Damien's bedroom. He placed the tea carefully on a mat on the pristine black desk, all that was left in the room now, and pressed the power button with a little flourish of his hand. On came Windows, followed by a new screensaver, which Damien must have put on when he'd come up to check on his decorating job, and it was a new photo of Susannah. He must have taken it recently with that fabulous little camera he'd got. Which reminded Stan, he'd like to get some of the birds with that, it's great, you could just erase the ones you don't like and then play around with the ones you like.

Stan logged on to ForJustMen@yahoo.com, the address that he'd proudly set up the week before. There it was – the little message that told him that his e-mail to Jan van dirty Deuzen had been read. His heart missed a beat, and he gulped at his tea, almost burning his mouth in his excitement. There was no message, which was no surprise. Stan couldn't imagine what Jan would be thinking, but knew that he would be agitated. Stan also felt agitated, yet kind of satisfied. He took out his notepad from his top pocket and read the content of message number two that would now be going Jan's way, and carefully typed it in.

Dear Jan. So pleased that we have the right
address. Please watch this space carefully as we
will soon be making a request. We know you can
oblige us. Back soon. Stay in touch.

Stan flagged the message, and sent it off. He printed it out, folded it carefully into four, sharp creases at the edges, and switched off the machine. His energy level felt like it was through the roof. He went downstairs and rang Akbar. He got Mrs Akbar, and became his old slightly stumbling self as he heard the familiar warm smile in the tone of her voice.

`Yes, Stan, what can I do for you?'

`Can you just tell Akbar that the flag's gone down?' He hesitated – he didn't want to make her suspicious. `It's the pigeons,' he added quickly. `I've got a bit of a bet on some of the racers. It's the starting flag.'

Silence.

`You know, like in a car race. Only it's not a car race, `cos you know, we're not really into the car races.'

Stan heard a strange muffled sound, almost like Mrs Akbar was trying to stifle a giggle or something. Stan supposed he should know by now that she was quite happy to know as little as possible about the lads' shenanigans, undoubtedly suspecting many of them to be illegal, but not really minding as long as they didn't bring trouble home or hurt anyone.

`Which is probably a good thing, because otherwise we'd be even busier, and then you know, you'd have even more time without him, and then where would you be, hey, you'd be right out the back of black stump.'

Mrs Akbar delivered a considered response.

`Well that's right Stan, so I will tell him that the flag is down. But Stan, if I may ask, what is it, this black stump?'

Stan paused: it was a good question. He thought for a few seconds.

`D'you know, Mrs A, I couldn't tell you. It's just one of those things that we say, `the back of black stump,' and I imagine that it's just an expression which means a long way away.'

He drew breath and launched firmly on. `It's bit like `Guy Flip,' I suppose.'

Damn, he didn't know where this came from either, it was an expression his Gran used to use and he hadn't heard it for ages. Suddenly Stan felt about five years old. He coughed, embarrassed, and said quickly, `Anyway, great to talk to you, and I'll talk to Akbar later. Bye.'

`Bye, Stan.' He could hear Mrs A smiling down the phone.

Next Stan phoned Doc, got the answer phone, and left the message – `the flag is down.' No point contacting Frank yet, he wouldn't be in, didn't have a mobile and didn't use an answer phone.

Feeling chipper, Stan moseyed off down the garden into his loft. He opened the outer door and made his way toward the Office. `Looks like we're in business, chaps,' he chortled as he passed the kit boxes. `Good, eh?'

Obviously, their heavy cooing was a sign of the birds' agreement. Stan opened the door to the Office, which was well swept out. He'd put some wood on one side to make a small table. He had also put in a chair that he found for a fiver in a second hand shop.

He picked up the clipboard which was stashed inside the box within the filing box. It was already stacked with sheets of paper, and he added his print out. Then he turned on the old Roberts radio which he had taken to keeping there too, the only keepsake he had from his dad, the back taped over with some masking tape to hold the battery in. He listened to Radio Two, Bruce someone followed by the Jeremy Vine show. He went into the shed and got out his tools, whistling along to that golden oldie *Satisfaction*, even finding a certain little wiggle in his hip and a bit of a pout going on as he walked back down the path, pausing to admire the blossom in the gardens around. He set up the workbench, and over the next couple of hours, he knocked up a tidy little table with runners for a drawer, and gave it the first sanding.

Then he went to the kitchen, made a mug of tea and a cheese sandwich, two thick slices, mature cheddar, and a liberal sprinkling of Branston pickle, (one item that he and Evie agreed you could never get the cheaper brand of), and came back down. By now, Jeremy Vine was debating proportional representation, and whether that should be measured on the basis of constituencies or votes. Stan found himself agreeing that it should be the latter, although he would never vote for the only party who argued for this because they would never get in. Not without proportional representation.

Stan ate one half of his sandwich, then took out one of the sheets of paper from his clipboard and studied it closely. It was a chart with the dates of the month on, and the phases of the moon. He checked that it was the end of the full moon that night.

Yep, as he thought.

Then he made complicated signs on a second sheet of paper, which held the details of his stock birds. If he paired them up in two days' time, then, that meant they should lay around the time of the New Moon. He was surprised how much he was enjoying his new breeding experiment. That conversation he'd had at the Cabbage Club with old Alfie Elliot had triggered it off, and he'd also done a bit of research on the web into this full moon business. He'd come across an article by some old American geezer who swore by it, so Stan had been having a good go, and the experiment seemed to be paying off. He paired the red mealy, Foxy Lady, to that blue bald cock, Top Gun. Then the speckled hen he'd loved for ages, Starry Night (should bode well), was put with Big Bad Bill, the old black cock. Probably his last breeding round, as he was getting on a bit now, but never mind.

Then he had another eight pairs to sort out, some on loan from Akbar and Frank to help out after he'd given so many good ones away. The dilemma he'd had with them all along was making his mind up what to do about foster parents; if he wanted more eggs out of the hen, then they couldn't all be born on the night of the new moon, but then again it should all come round again at the right time for the next lot. In the end, he'd used sitters, and that seemed to have worked okay. But would it have been better some other way? Stan chewed the second half of the sandwich, washed it down with tea while he puzzled over the conundrum.

Before Stan knew it, Jeremy Vine had been replaced by Steve Wright, and that lovely Jamie Lee Grace, voice like liquid sex. But there were things to do, and so when he'd eaten and drank, he

245

locked up the Office, took his crocks into the kitchen, washed them up. Then, as agreed in the plan he'd made with the lads, it was up the stairs and into Damien's eerily empty room, and then Stan was smiling as once again he signed into his e-mail account.
*

As Monday drew to a close, Jan was aware that he had resisted examining his e-mails for the last few hours, in the hope that whatever problem he was about to walk into would have gone away. Finally, he had to look, knowing that he couldn't avoid them. Amongst the business mail, he saw to his horror, though not to his surprise, that there were another two from `For Just Men.' He was pretty sure now that this must be the stupid Englishmen, and he had a slight sweat on his brow as he read them – especially the second one, because this was very specific.

```
Dear Jan,
Well well well. Bet you thought you were safe,
hey? Well no. Now then Jan, we know that you are
acquiring a tasty new `pigeon' this week, and
thought it would be great if you gave it to us
to   replace   those   that   you   unfortunately
accidentally gave away for no profit – what do
you reckon, Jan, have we got the right timing?
```

This time Jan replied in frustration.

```
You can't e-mail me here. You've got the wrong
end of the stick. If you want to talk about
pigeons you've got to use my personal address –
jan.666@agw.com Then we'll talk. But you must
realise that I can't discuss my hobbies at work.
```

Then Jan printed out the e-mails before eliminating all traces of them from his computer. He slotted the print outs into an envelope, and gave Allan a quick ring.
`Fancy coffee, Allan?'

Allan began to desist, his inclination being to keep a low profile between himself and Jan just now, but something in Jan's tone made him change his mind. Jan was sounding tight.

`Pigeon stuff,' Allan heard as the justification. It was well known round the factory that both men enjoyed the same hobby. Allan also knew that they had already agreed to meet tomorrow night, so this could only mean that there was something wrong.

`Okay. Café Noir. Six o'clock. Cheerio.'

An hour later, the two Dutchmen were well away from the factory and had coffees in their hand.

`So what's up?' Allan was straight to the point.

`I've had these.' Jan gave him the printed out e-mails. Allan perused them.

`So what the fuck…'

`I think it's the Englishmen, stupid Stan and his mates.'

`But what are they on about, Jan? Surely it can't be anything to do with the pigeon egg?' Jan knew that Allan was cautious, would never have spoken of the diamond in any other terms than code when they were in a public place.

`I think it is.' Jan scalded his mouth for the second time that day as he drank his black coffee just a little too soon, his hand shaking slightly as he replaced the cup on its saucer. He was shuffling slightly on his chair and avoiding eye contact with his erstwhile friend.

`But how can it be, Jan, no one knows about it,' Allan was hissing now. `Unless…' Jan saw the growing horror in his eyes, his discomfort intensifying.

`Oh no, tell me you didn't Jan, tell me you didn't.' Jan was nearly whispering.

`The night I went out. When I was judging their ridiculous competition. I might have said something then.'

`What do you mean, you might have?' Allan's anger was audible, almost palpable. `For God's sake, man, I need to know what's what here. We've already started to log the bloody egg out of the system!'

247

`I know, I know, I've done the purchase order today.' Jan spoke quietly and took a deep breath. `Okay, I had a few drinks and they asked me how I'd managed to beat the system. I think I might have told them too much.'

Allan was wide-eyed and furious.

`I can't believe this. You talked to four thick as shit English men about our scheme? Of all the people in the world! What the fuck did you tell them, Jan, come on, I need to know.'

Jan recounted what he could remember about the night in the Indian restaurant. He was a little vague: he remembered how fascinated they were at his prowess and how good it felt to impress them, and he knew he told them how he and Allan had got the last diamond. But he couldn't remember what he said about another one.

Jan watched Allan digest this information with scorn.

`I can't believe you've done this, Jan. Ripping those guys off was easy – and so was selling the pigeons on the net. They should never have been able to do anything about it. And now, you moron, look at you. For Christ's sake, you might have spoiled everything.'

He put his hands to his forehead. `Let me think, let me think.'

Jan's hand was shaking more now, his arrogance replaced by pure fear, and a strange feeling that he thought might be guilt, although this latter was not something that came easily or naturally to him. They sat in silence for a little while.

`Okay, so you blabbed, you drunken idiot. But let's be calm. You told them too much, like I warned you not to. But there's no evidence.'

`I thought they'd be safe because they don't really know us.' Jan was whining now, not an attractive sound, and his round face was red.

`Unbelievable.' Allan turned briefly away from the livid spectacle of his partner in crime. When he turned back, he spoke firmly, so that Jan would listen well.

`There's no evidence. They're trying it on. They're mad at you because they know what you did with their birds, but there's nothing they can do. You need to e-mail them back that you don't know what they're on about, have their e-mail address identified as SPAM, and we'll just carry on as we are. That should be problem sorted. We bluff it out. This is all set up for Thursday, and we can't stop it now, so just keep your head down and your wits about you.'

Jan nodded.

`I'll meet you tomorrow, here, and for goodness sakes keep calm.'

Allan strode away, and Jan was left to pay for the coffee and to wend his miserable way home.

Once there, he went through the motions of being a good dad and a caring husband, and encouraged his wife out of the door on one of her increasingly frequent nights out. Anja told him that her best friend was having a tough time and she was going out to support her. She was dressed up to the nines, and Jan thought how lucky he was to have such an attractive wife. Tonight he was glad to see her go out so that he could get out his laptop and check it once the children were in bed.

Sure enough, a message.

So here's the deal, then, Jan. We won't disturb you at work as long as you play ball with us. We know that this week you will be collecting something very important from your factory. You know that you owe us money. So let's just say it will be a fair exchange for you to follow instructions and make sure it gets to us. Otherwise, you're shopped. Reply within twelve hours to let us know you've got this, or you're shopped anyway.

Jan was suddenly furious. The stupid arses. Did they really think they could get him, did they, intimidate him into falling for their stupid ill thought out trap? Allan was right. There was no evidence. He was safe. So the `for just men,' such a sad pun that they probably thought was clever, would get their stupid reply

249

within twelve hours, in fact they could have it straight away. He typed fast and furious.

```
I don't know what you think you know, but you
must be mistaken. I just go about my business
like anyone else. And if you continue to harass
me then I will have to take serious action. Go
back to your petty little lives and get off my
back.
```

Jan felt better when he pressed the `send' button, went downstairs and poured himself a small whisky. Just the one, as he needed to sleep well to be on the ball. By eleven o'clock he was in bed, though he tossed and turned until his wife came in, around midnight. Once she was in, he began to relax as he heard her pottering around downstairs. Odd, he thought he heard the sound of a shower running; it was probably just the dishwasher. He fell into a fitful and unsatisfying sleep. Monday night was finishing very differently from how it began, and Jan was not a happy chap.
*

Jan wasn't the only one checking his e-mails regularly. Stan left Evie downstairs working on her last assignment of the year, or revising, he wasn't sure which, and there seemed little point in asking her about it. Since the night they'd had the row, he'd kept a safe distance. Once this adventure was over, he planned to present her with the fait accompli of a paid off mortgage, and, with luck, a small diamond. Or maybe a holiday; he'd have to see when he and the lads had sorted the money between them. Anyway, he felt free to go to Damien's room knowing that she wouldn't be bothering him, and was well excited as he opened up.

As he suspected, Jan as yet had no idea who or what he was dealing with. He thought they were idiots. A grin spread across Stan 's face – no, mate, I will not be going back to my petty little life. In fact, he would now be giving Jan the pièce de resistance.

He composed the shortest of e-mails.

```
See what you think when you've listened to this
then. Be in touch tomorrow. Will want to be
collecting on Friday night.
```

Then he went to Attach Files and attached the clip, the edited clip, of Jan in his cups. He replayed it just once more, for his own pleasure.

`diamonds... surprisingly easy... my good friend Allan... Last February... didn't get put back... eradicated all trace... searches... tourist parties who come round the factory... someone we know... hid the diamond... sanitary bin... factory never knew a thing... brilliant... Jan... you and Allan... broad daylight... under my supervision, of course... 100,000 pounds... contact in the city... we'll be doing it again... second week of May.'

This was brilliant. Stan just kept on impressing himself at every turn. He had even muffled Doc's voice so that it was not easily identifiable, just in case. And then Stan guffawed, closed up the computer, went downstairs, and brewed up for him and Evie. She was in a good mood, as she would be leaving for Amsterdam on the coming Wednesday, for a long weekend, and would be back on Sunday night. This had bothered Stan slightly at first, realising that they would both be there at the same time, but he had already talked to her about it, the kinds of things she would be doing and the kinds of places she would be going, and it seemed impossible that they would meet there. Anyway, if they did, it would be after Stan was rich. And then he'd be quite happy to tell her that he had been doing some business there, although he wasn't sure yet whether he would ever say exactly what it was.

So after a pleasant enough half an hour sitting with Evie while she read, it was early to bed. With a book that he just couldn't help reading at the moment, *Diamonds are Forever*, only he kept on changing the `forever' to `for Evie' in his head, and by the time she came up, he was fast asleep, a smile at the edge of his lips.

Tuesday morning dawned bright and sunny on both sides of the Channel, and Stan was up early on the computer. He made sure that there would be two mails waiting for Jan when he got to work, the one with the recording, and the next one, very, very simple.

We will want our package at close of play on
Friday. You'll hear from us where it should be
taken to. I think you know what happens if you
don't play.

*

Jan van Deuzen read his mails first thing, and was horrified to hear the recording. A cold sweat broke on his brow, an unwelcome cramp gripped his bowel. Then he contacted Allan, and they confirmed that they would meet later for coffee. Then he explored his system; could he and Allan undo what they had started, but he knew that this was useless because the purchase order ledger, so brilliantly doctored, had been copied to his senior and throughout the whole system. A task that had taken some stealth and brilliance on his part, and one that meant there was no turning back.

And anyway, the English arses had recorded his voice. So when Jan and Allan met after a tense day, and Jan broke this latest bit of bad news, they decided that they would have to go along with it, although Allan was furious.

`You daft bloody bastard. You big mouthed shite. What a stupid thing to do. Well I tell you what, mate, if we go down, they're coming with us.'

Jan was slightly trembly.

`But they can't, Allan, we've got nothing on them, other than that this will show on their computer records, but how the heck do we get anybody to those. By then we'd only be telling the authorities because we'd be about to go down. And I'm not going down. Not for anybody.'

Allan glared. Jan knew he knew that this was right, and that that was infuriating Allan even more.

'Well in that case, man, when we do the exchange, I tell you what, I'm going to be breaking some bloody legs. They'll have to pick the egg up at some point, and if that's what I have to do, then so be it. They can take the bloody thing, but they're not going without some damage.'

The men parted in anger and fear, Jan knowing that he had messed up badly, and also knowing that Allan could do bad things with a baseball bat. His drive home was not a comfortable one, and neither was his night. Anja declared that she was taking a break at the weekend, going to some hen party, so would he have the children. She had a suitcase out and was already packing some things. Jan assented: of course he'd have the children, but he knew already that he would be sending them to his mother's. This was going to be one hell of a week. If Anja was to be away, a piece of information which had left him surprisingly niggled, then at the very least he was going to need to go out and get himself drunk.

Twenty One
By the Light of the Silver Moon

Card XVIII – The Moon

The Moon is often associated with Lunacy, and carries warnings of the dark side. Sometimes it can mean operating on illusion and we are told to beware having an unreal idea of what is going on.

But the moon also governs the tides, shines out light in the dark, and when I see the Moon in a reading, I see possibilities for stepping outside of the box, incredible creativity. Which in Evie's case, meant getting good with the face paint and stepping inside the box – the like of which she'd never done before.

The trip to Amsterdam couldn't come soon enough for Evie. The fallout from that argument had been hanging heavily for a while now, slightly dissipated but leaving dust beneath their footsteps. And Stan had really got on her tits trying desperately to show an interest in everything she was doing – what essay was it, what was she revising, kind of nice of him but they seemed like pointless conversations, because when she told him it didn't seem to make a lot of sense to him. And as for Amsterdam – Evie couldn't work out whether he was jealous or what, but in the week before she was going, he went on and on about what places had she been to before, where would she be going, was it right in the centre of town or what, did she tend to stay out late at night. He was driving her nuts. Which was a shame really, because he was more energetic and looking better than he had for years – seemed even to be getting a bit of a six pack where once there was a barrel threatening. In the end, Evie told him she'd be spending one night out and one night in the hotel with Geri, would probably go out on the town on Friday night and then have dinner at Nikke's on Saturday night and stay in. He seemed satisfied with that, and stopped the interrogation.

She was taken aback by what came next.

`You know, Evie,' he said, `I've been thinking about some of the things you said. Maybe we should go out for dinner when you come back, and we'll talk. See what we can do to make things a bit better. You're right; we can't go on like this forever. Neither of us has been very happy lately.'

Evie felt stunned. He went on.

`I might have a bit of a surprise for you when you're back, anyway. Might make life a bit easier.'

Now she was intrigued, but really didn't want to get into it right then. Had he got a job or what? It seemed all too heavy to even think about. Evie nodded, and said 'yes, we'll talk.'

When she got back.

As it happened, she'd planned carefully what she was going to be doing over the long weekend. Geri's course was running over unusual hours. She was going to be free on the Wednesday night

255

and all day Thursday, and then working on Friday and Saturday. Evie was going to stay with her for two nights, and Geri would probably only want to go out late on the first one so that she could be alert on Friday morning. Then Evie would be at Nikke's for the other two nights. Brilliant. Except on the Saturday night she was supposed to be working. And Evie wanted to see what she did, to watch her, to see how it all worked. She was hoping Nikke would let her, somehow, learn more about what she did. Evie was fascinated, though she also didn't want Nikke to be embarrassed. She'd have to see how the land lay.

On the Tuesday before her trip, Evie went round to Beulah's after work. She was looking good, and Evie was hopeful that her Mam had turned a corner on her health. Colds and bad chests had been prevalent during her first year of grieving. She'd definitely been brighter since Christmas though, and now that it was May, she was doing a bit of work in the garden. Once she'd made Evie the obligatory cup of tea and had a roll up, Beulah took her daughter out to the back. It was a smallish garden, but Evie's Dad had structured it well with some stone edged flower beds, some tidy lawns, and various big pots all over the place. Last year it had been neglected, but Beulah had mown the lawn, done some weeding and had bought some plants.

`Look at this one, Evie.' She proudly showed off a vibrant geranium. `This is the last one that I've got that your Da planted. I thought it had died, but I've cut it back, and re-potted it and fed it, and look at it now.' Evie felt a lump in her throat at her Mam's pride and her Dad's memory.

`I loved him so much, you know,' Beulah confided, `and nothing really changed that. You mustn't think it ever did.'

Evie hugged her then, and both women laughed at themselves to cover their slight embarrassment. Beulah showed off the other flowers she'd put in, pansies and begonias, and the colour in the beds was mirrored by the flush on her sun-kissed face. Her wrinkles looked more like laughter lines now, and less like wear and tear.

They sat down on two little wooden chairs that were out back, and Beulah gave one of her looks.

`So have you decided where you're going, Evie?'

Evie started to reiterate that it was Amsterdam and prepared to tell about all the places and sights she wanted to visit, but Beulah interrupted.

`No, Evie, you and Stan. Where you're going.'

Evie talked to her then about the whole lot, and for once felt her Mam really listened carefully. She finished by letting Beulah know that Stan and she were going to discuss things when she got back.

`Ah. So you've not decided that it's over as such,' Beulah concluded. `Good. He's a decent man, you know, and he can't really be blamed for everything. Give it your best shot, Evie, and look after yourself.'

She left feeling lighter somehow, and went home to pack. Stan took Evie to the airport on the Wednesday morning for the early flight, and gave her a big hug when he dropped her off.

`Have fun,' he said, `and give my love to your mad-arsed sister.'

Once Evie got through to departures, she felt as free as a bird, and went and treated herself to a new lipstick, really dark red, vampish. She'd carried on saving her ten pounds a week and hardly been out for ages. She still had a bit of the money Geri had given her in the November, as well, as she hadn't spent it all on the last trip, so she felt unusually flush. It was great.

Evie felt a bit nervous about flying on her own, but decided that it was either her day to die or not, and since she wasn't going to pull out now, she might as well relax. Of course, the flight was fine; by the time she'd had a cup of tea and been to the loo, they were landing. She got the train from Schipfol airport to Amsterdam, then a taxi to Geri's hotel. She was proud of herself, so chuffed when she got to the hotel. Geri had said it would be a good one, and Evie wasn't disappointed. She didn't know what it cost, because this was the one part of the trip that Geri had insisted on paying, but it was even more up market than the last one.

257

Geri was on her course when Evie arrived, so she checked herself into the room. The sisters had decided to share, and there were two double beds, as well as a large sofa, writing desk, and fantastic bathroom. Evie unpacked swiftly, and then looked through the hotel facilities. On a whim, she rang the hairdressers that was located in the beauty salon and booked a cut and colour. Then she ran a bath, and switched on the Jacuzzi function. She had to laugh at herself, she'd put some bubble bath in and of course within minutes there were so many bubbles that they overflowed onto the bathroom floor. And Evie didn't give a toss, they were soon mopped up with towels that someone else was going to wash.

Once bathed, Evie lay on the bed, all wrapped up in another hotel dressing gown, this time deep blue velour, and slept for over an hour. She'd set the alarm as the hair appointment was at one o'clock. On waking, she ordered coffee and a toastie to eat in her room. This was luxury.

The beauty salon was like something off the pages of a magazine, all clever lighting and plants everywhere, yet lots of space. Evie told the stylist to shape up her hair around her cheekbones, and then between them they picked out a real bold plum colour that Evie thought she could get away with. The stylist suggested full lowlights in two almost identical shades, to add `texture and depth', which Evie went for. While the colour was taking, she was invited to have a manicure and pedicure at a special price. *What the hell*, she thought, *what the hell, sales pitch accepted.*

By three o'clock, Evie was done. A mass of deep plum highlights in her short sharp hairstyle, fingernails and toe nails to match. She felt fabulous, thought it money well spent. She went upstairs and settled on the sofa with her book. She was reading Janice Russell's *Algarve Affair*, purely for pleasure now that she was at the end of her course, and was engrossed. When Geri arrived in the early evening, the sound of the door made Evie start.

Geri was full of warmth and enthusiasm.

`Evie – oh my God, you look fantastic!' She hugged Evie, then held her at arm's length, making her do a twirl to show off back and front.

`It's great – I knew it would suit you like that. Oh darling, this calls for champagne.'

Good old Geri. She went to the fridge and took out a bottle which she'd obviously brought with her specially, bless her, Moet et Chandon, and the sisters toasted each other. Then Geri went and got ready and Evie rang Stan, briefly, just to let him know she had arrived safely.

Geri and Evie went out for dinner and just talked and talked. They hadn't really seen each other much since Christmas, and not at all since the night out with Jeannie. Evie realised just how much she'd been looking forward to this visit, not only for Amsterdam, but to have Geri's company. Geri had been really busy, setting up her own consultancy, and she was bubbling about this course that she was doing.

`They know so much here, Evie, about the drug scene, and they're really starting to make a difference. I've only done the first day, and it's just superb, the attitude, the facilities, and the approach they have. They don't see drug users as criminals, just as people, people from all walks of life, people who need a wide variety of support and help. Just like any of us do.'

She sounded full of both passion and compassion, and Evie could see in her the depths of her own experiences. Now, she couldn't believe that she'd been taken in by her sister's outward appearances for so long, and wondered why she hadn't tried to help her in the days when she'd known that Geri was bulimic. She felt ashamed that she'd somehow seen the eating disorder as some kind of posh hobby; clearly, Evie had been guilty of being a lot shallower than Geri. While her older sister's life had looked so great from the outside, Evie knew now that she'd endured a lot of emptiness, a lot of guilt and feelings of failure. And now she was inspired, wanting to use her knowledge and her compassion to make a difference where she could while enjoying her own life to the full. Totally admirable.

`And Evie,' Geri grinned almost coquettishly, `I've met a man. And,' she said with real pleasure in her voice, `I think it might be going somewhere. He's an architect. Self-employed, wealthy of course, and is really interested in my Feng Shui. He thinks we might be able to work on our projects together, you know, he designs the brickwork but I can advise on some of the energy and help with the interiors. Might even result in some work for your Damien – who knows.'

`Wow, Geri, that's great.' Evie was touched that Geri would think of Damien. `What's he like, then?'

Geri grinned and produced a photograph. He looked about thirty-six, dark hair and strong features, brown eyes and a long lean body.

`Wow,' Evie said again. `So has he got a twin brother by any chance?'

`Now now, Evie, you're a married woman.' Geri twinkled. `Anyway, we're going on a sailing holiday in September around the Greek islands. He's based in London so we only get to see each other at weekends, and it's fab. I feel I want my space, and yet he's becoming a regular part of my life. And if it doesn't work out, well fine, it's been a lot of fun.' She sipped her cold white wine. `Although it would be nice if it does. But we'll see.'

Evie raised her glass.

`Here's to fun, then. And here's to you – you're a great sister and a great woman.' She could swear she saw a tear in Geri's eye at that, but was proud to let her know how much she appreciated and admired her. Geri deserved that, she really did.

Then Geri gave the social work look.

`Anyway, Evie, enough of me. How's that man of yours, then? Things any better?'

Evie brought Geri up to speed on the row that had occurred after their last meeting, and the despondency that still seemed to linger on. Geri was encouraged though by news of the heart-to-heart that was planned for Evie's return.

`You've at least got to do that, Evie. Then you'll be in a better position to know what you need to do.'

She was right of course. They talked some more about how difficult relationships could be, about what they each thought they both wanted. It was so great to be able to get it all out and to bounce thoughts off someone who cared. They finished their meal and had coffee and brandy, and then went on to the good old Piano Bar, where they listened to music and eventually danced the night away. When they threw off their shoes at three in the morning in the hotel room, they were both knackered but giggly with it.

On Thursday they went to the Rijksmuseum. Geri knew a bit about art, and she was fun to be with as she could explain some of the symbolism in the paintings. Evie was amazed at this, how a skull on the floor could mean so much, or a stick in the background. Then lunch, followed by the van Gogh museum, which Evie really liked. It was very different from the styles of painting she'd seen so far, and it was great to see sketches as well as painting. Then they walked up to the Vondelspark, and walked until they were tired, when they sank down on the grass and drank bottled water. It was lovely, warm and open, and so easy to be in. They ate in the hotel that night, and on parting on Friday morning, they hugged tight, definitely closer now than ever before, and Evie liked it that way.

She took breakfast slowly, lingered in the hotel for a while, taking a slow bath, taking time with her make up, packing her few clothes carefully. She had arranged to meet Nikke at one o'clock in the café in which they'd first met. When the time came, she took a taxi, and made the driver stop off on the way so that she could buy flowers. When Evie walked into the café, Nikke was waiting, at that same table in the window, the big open window, as she had been when they'd first met six months before. On sighting her friend, Nikke jumped to her feet and rushed to hug her.

`Evie! Fantastic! You look brilliant!' And it was just as if no time had passed since they'd met before. Evie gave her the flowers.

`Oh Evie. Those are lovely. All the flowers that there are in Holland, and no one ever bought me any. They're beautiful.'

They ordered lunch, and couldn't stop smiling at each other.

`It is so good to be here, you can't imagine. You look great, Nikke, really great. Come on then, how's it all going?'

Nikke looked proud, and laughed.

`Well, for one thing, you are now looking at Nikke Amber, Bachelor of Science –with honours.'

`Oh wow, you did it. Brilliant. Nikke, I'm so pleased.' Nikke's face was a picture, so chuffed and proud, just as she should have been. This woman was becoming Evie's inspiration, in more ways than one.

`Yep, I passed those final exams and even got a high two one.' She saw that this meant nothing, and explained. `That's the second highest degree you can get – they grade them one to three, with two sections in the second. I only just missed a first.'

`I'm impressed. You deserve it, Nikke, you really do.'

`Well, I worked hard enough, that's for sure. And – even better – guess what?'

Evie was all ears.

`They've accepted me on a social work course in England.'

`Fantastic!' Nikke was coming to England. Evie was almost as pleased for herself as for her friend. Now she would have someone on her wavelength, within at least train ride distance. `Whereabouts?'

`Birmingham. The University of Birmingham. I don't know the place at all, but I'm sure from what I hear that there'll be plenty for me to practise on.' Nikke looked radiant. `It starts in September. So I'm going to carry on working for another month, and then I'm coming over to find accommodation and then that's it – all this will be behind me.'

`And there's something else.' She looked straight at her friend. The radiance was obviously for other reasons as well. `The agency. The adoption agency. They've had an enquiry.'

Evie caught her breath. `From Art?'

`From someone called Simon. Simon Welks.'

Evie began to giggle. It was inappropriate, she knew, but what a surname to get saddled with. Fortunately, Nikke giggled too.

`I know. Gross. But it's Art, he's made a preliminary enquiry. The agency says not to get my hopes up. Lots of adopted children make a first enquiry then they choose not to take it any further. But I've got a feeling it might go further. And if it does, I'll be settled as a respectable mum, doing something worthwhile.'

Evie looked at her friend with affection, this woman who had worked so hard to make things change for her, to recover from so much in her past, to take charge of her life. If she could bounce back from where she had been, then there had to be hope for Evie too.

`Nikke, you so deserve this. I've never met anyone like you, and I hope to God that it works out. You're already respectable, you daft tart, everything you've done these last few years.' She nodded gently.

`Thanks, Evie. I don't want to get false hopes up, but at least I now know that I've done everything I can. The rest is up to him.'

Evie shook herself, fought down her emotions, and did a Geri.

`This calls for champagne,' she said, and ordered a bottle of the best in the house, which wasn't a Moet standard, of course, but it was cold and it was bubbly, and it was just right for the occasion. When the bartender came over and poured it out, Evie raised her glass.

`To a great woman, Ms Bachelor Nikke,' she said, and downed the champagne.

When they'd finished the bottle, they took a taxi to Nikke's apartment, which was just as stunning as Evie remembered. Now that it was May, window boxes were flowering, a mass of vibrant colour adding even more character to the building. The Amsterdam spring air created a freshness, an energy. This was fab.

They talked then, as before, for the whole afternoon, just catch up stuff. Nikke listened carefully despite her level of inebriation, and was sympathetic to what now seemed like petty moans. They had a steady refill of beer, and Evie suddenly noticed that something was different. Nikke wasn't smoking Camel Lights like there was no tomorrow.

`Nikke, you've stopped smoking.' She stated the obvious as a question. Nikke smiled, smugly.

`Yep. I decided that it really was time to look after my health. It's been over a month now. Actually, one month, one week and two days.' She laughed. `And eleven hours. Actually, after the first week, it hasn't been as difficult as I thought.'

Wow. Was there no end to this woman's abilities to transform? Well, if she could do it, so could Evie. She was feeling really relaxed and a bit squiffy, so she went on.

`I tell you what, Nikke, you're making all these changes and doing all this stuff. I think I want to have a go at some new things.'

`Like what?'

`Well, I tell you what, I've been thinking about your window. What it's like to be in there.'

`What? You're joking. It's just a job, Evie, just a job.'

`Yes I know that's what it is to you, but for me it's intriguing. I wanted to know if I could watch you, you know, get a feel for what it's like.'

Nikke laughed.

`You mean you want to be a perv, hide in a cupboard and watch me?'

Evie supposed it must have sounded strange.

`I don't know really. I just know I've been thinking about it, what it must be like to have all those blokes looking at you, feeling sexy, and powerful.'

Evie saw Nikke look at her, saw the idea forming in Nikke's head at the same time as it was forming in her own.

`So why don't you have a go, then, if you're serious? Take the window tomorrow night. Dress up in some of my clothes. Be me for a night, Evie, if you really want to.'

It was like someone had thrown down a gauntlet. `You're not serious?'

Both women were deadly serious: both started to laugh, almost hysterically.

264

`What about your money?' Evie managed to say at last. `You'd lose out on a night's income.'

`No I wouldn't. You'd be earning it for me.' Just for a second Evie thought she meant it..

`Sod the money, Evie. I've saved up loads, I'm only really working out the lease on this apartment. If you want to you can go and parade in my window tomorrow night. The owner is never around on a Saturday night, and by the time he hears anything from the other girls – if he ever does – I'll be gone or going anyway.'

Evie's head buzzed. Here it was, the opportunity to step right into her fantasy. Her heart raced. They say to be careful what you wish for: in that moment, Evie knew why they said that.

`Wow.'

`Come on Evie, let's go walkabout and you can take a look at some of the girls. We need to eat anyway, I don't know about you but I'm starving. Then you can see if you think you can really do it.'

`But Stan would go mad,' Evie protested, and then heard herself copping out, using Stan who she had systematically pulled apart all afternoon for his weaknesses and imperfections. The idea of selling her body, of having sex with someone else, had sent Evie running back in her head to the safety of her old pair of comfy slippers husband.

`Evie, you don't have to do anything. You can just disappear into the back room whenever you like, you know. Then the punters will think you're busy.'

Once Evie knew that could be an option, her fantasies changed direction. What if she really did fancy someone, what would it be like to feel a new pair of hands on her body, to have sex that she was in control of? Now that really was scary, in the most exhilarating way.

So they went out and walked the Achterburgwahl, and Evie looked at all the women of different ages, different sizes, all strutting their stuff, and at the end of half an hour she had decided. Yes, she too could do that. And she would.

They ate curry in a nearby restaurant. Evie asked Nikke about what to wear. They were around the same size, maybe Nikke was a little shorter, but similar bust and hips, the important clothes would fit for purpose. Most of the women in the windows just wore bras and thongs, fairly unimaginative really. One or two were more flash, stockings here or a basque there. Evie realised that she wanted the whole caboodle. She was going to do it properly or not at all, and properly meant full theatrical dress.

They got home tired but elated, and agreed that next day Evie would go through Nikke's outfits and try on what she wanted. She would have done it then and there, but wanted to wait until after a shower, and it was far too late for that now. Instead, they talked about the etiquette of window prostitution. Nikke was, as ever, very forthright.

`Well, I don't really think you'll do anything, Evie. And you're in complete control of that door, remember. And if you do fancy anyone, you negotiate first, through the intercom. You tell them what you will or won't do, and how much it will be. And if you do let them in, you take the money first.'

Evie took all this in, but was tired; she needed to sleep on everything. She couldn't believe she was going to go through with this. She dropped onto the bed settee gratefully, and it wasn't long before she drifted off into a sleep full of erotic and mysterious dreams.

After sleeping late and then taking that lovely warm shower, Evie went through Nikke's working outfits. Platform bras, half-cup bras, basques, stockings, thongs, cami knickers, crotchless panties, robes, scarves – you name it, she had it, a co-ordinated collection of tart's outfits. Fantastic. If Evie's English tutor could have seen her now – now there was a sexy thought. Nikke gave advice, and between them, she and Evie chose what Evie would wear. The newly manicured and pedicured nails looked great, and augmented everything beautifully.

Evie had been planning to go and explore more of Amsterdam, but in the event, she and Nikke just went out for lunch. It was

266

another glorious day. Walking up the Achterburgwahl in the daytime was so different. All the windows were empty, and the streets almost deserted. You'd never guess it was the same place as last night. They walked the whole length, and then stopped for a light lunch, goat's cheese and honey on toast – Evie so enjoyed that. Then they bought wine. Evie decided that she would have to have a little tonight, not too much, just enough to shore up the confidence.

At about nine o'clock Evie began to get ready. She cleaned and oiled her body, and draped herself in luxurious underwear. Then she put on a loose tracksuit of Nikke's for going over the road. She put a silky gown into a bag, along with a bottle of wine and an opener. Then she made herself up. The new dark lipstick looked a treat. When Nikke saw her friend, she squealed.

`Evie, do you look the part or what! Amazing. You could earn us a fortune.'

`Yeah well, we'll see about that.'

The idea was that Evie would start at ten and `work' till one o'clock. Then they would go out for late supper. At a quarter to ten, Nikke got up.

`Right then, let's go.'

They made their way across the street, Evie a little nervous and Nikke highly amused. Nikke used her own set of keys to get into the building and then into her window room. It was great – a lovely chaise longue, a chair, a footstool, fabulous rug, big gilt mirror, and a small table, Evie thought it an occasional table, although that phrase didn't quite make sense to her. Either there's always a table or no table, surely? Anyway, out back there was the bedroom and large bassinette with cupboard. The bed was double sized, and covered in a patterned silky sheet. At the side was a bedside cabinet with drawers.

`Condoms, lubricant, vibrators,' Nikke detailed cheerfully. Then she opened the doors of the bassinette cupboard. It held liquid soap and various massage oils. She pointed to two cardboard boxes with top dispensers.

`Tissues on the left,' she said, `rubber gloves on the right.' Yuk. Evie just knew that she wouldn't be using rubber gloves, whatever else happened tonight.

`The safe's on the wall behind that picture,' Nikke said, pointing to a small elegant picture of a nude. `If you make any money, it goes straight in there. Combination is 69690.' She laughed. `The 0 is to confuse them.'

Evie nodded at everything. Okay, she told herself, this will be fine. Then Nikke pointed to two old bell pushes in the bedroom, one by the door and one by the bed.

`These are real,' she said. `If you have any trouble, give them a press, they go straight to the owner and he has direct access to the police. They'll know where you are.'

`Have you ever had to use them?' Evie looked at Nikke quizzically.

`No,' she said, `nearly, but I've always managed to sort any possible trouble out. It's only usually if a punter's a bit drunk. The real pervs know where to go for their action.'

`Okay.' Evie felt reassured.

So then they opened the wine and Evie poured herself a glass, and Nikke made to leave.

`I tell you what, I'll walk by now and then, see if you're alright,' she said. `Although I know you will be. So I'll come and meet you at one. For late supper. Have fun, Evie,' and she chuckled as she left her friend to it.

Twenty Two
Top Team Earns Rewards

You are the kit master. You will have learned what an excellent team is through seeing one in action or having exceptional vision of exactly what you want to achieve as an end result. It is well known that a writer who starts a story without knowing the end page will nearly always fail to achieve a good result. It is only when you are able to recognise what you want, or visualise the finished product that you will be able to move forward towards your personal end result.

Graham Dexter *The Perfect Team* www.nbra.co.uk
2008

Stan had little else to do that week save to quietly organise himself to pack, which he did when Evie was out. He washed and ironed a few clothes, and bought spare toothpaste and some after shave. He busied himself with his pigeons, who were flying a treat, and finally finished plumbing his urinal into the loft. He had put it on the outside, of course, to deter nasty smells. This had meant quite some work, as he'd extended the roof to cover it over, and then erected some close spaced lattice fencing over which he carefully retrained the Russian vine. He plumbed it quite easily, as there was already a water supply to the loft. As the urinal would only be occasionally actually in use, he wasn't too worried about the distribution of urine. He managed to pipe it in so that the urine would go underground and just out of their back garden to the mud path on the playing field beyond. He reasoned that this would be as healthy as the occasional piss on the grass that happened anyway.

On Wednesday, he drove Evie to Leeds/Bradford airport and gave her a big hug.

`Have fun,' he said, trying to hold her to him. `And give my love to that mad-arsed sister of yours.'

She gave him a kiss on the cheek and walked away. He had a second of fear, then reason reasserted. They would talk soon, only he would have something to really talk about. He'd be able to offer her some treats, some declaration of his love for her. And he'd be able to stop being secretive, like on that night of the row when he really wanted to tell her what he'd been doing – learning computers, researching the lie of the land in Amsterdam, making contacts, getting paperwork from a vet and from the Ministry of Fishing and Agriculture for the racer, learning about how to set up a small business. He just hadn't been able to tell her, that's all.

He walked hurriedly back to his car, drove back to Middlesbrough on the now familiar route from the airport, and once in the house went straight upstairs to check on the e-mails. Yesterday Jan had mailed,

```
Ok, you bastards.
```

So today Stan mailed back.

```
The recording is backed up and in a safe place
in case you think of doing anything stupid. You
will need to drop the package in Amsterdam.
We'll tell you where tomorrow.
```

Stan smiled as he then walked down to the pigeon loft. `You'll never guess what, my beauties,' he said to the birds as he looked through the bars of each door before going into the office. `I think it's gonna work. We're gonna be rich. Yes, bloody rich, and we're gonna show 'em all. And,' as he put his keys into the final lock, `I'm going to get my Evie back. Oh yes.'

He went to the makeshift desk and removed one of the plastic folders stashed carefully within, and then whistled a `cheerio' as he left the loft and went up the path to the house. Once there, it was into the kitchen, a brew on, the usual cheese and Branston sandwich, and into the front room with the folder. He emptied it out on to the sofa, and then arranged it so that he could see each sheet of paper, each document. As he ate the sandwich, he perused them to make sure that everything was in place.

Export licence for one racing pigeon. Ferry confirmations.

Green card for Doc's car.

Telephone numbers: Jan, Franz, and the man they know only as `D.M.', the fence.

Addresses for Franz and for D.M.

A map of Holland.

A street map of Amsterdam.

One small leather pouch with fine leather straps for looping over the pigeon's neck and tail.

He couldn't think of anything else he might want, save his passport, which he'd secretly acquired and had posted to Frank's. And that was with his wallet, inside the inside zip of the lovely leather jacket. Waiting and ready to go. He washed down his sandwich with his tea. Then it was down to the loft to fly the young birds, and to sort out the hoppers that he created with Frank's help, so that there'd be plenty of food and water for the birds while he was away. Then he settled for a quiet night of TV and a takeaway Chinese – why not be extravagant, after all. Evie rang at about eight o'clock to say that she was there, the hotel was fab, she'd had a rest, and told him to `take care.' He took the advice, and surprisingly, he slept that night like a log.

Thursday was a key day, and although Stan was aware that there was much to do, he was taking everything at a steady pace. He got up at eight o'clock and showered, drank tea and checked on the birds. Good. The hoppers were working. Then it was straight away over to Alfie's loft to pick up the racer in a specially made pigeon box. Alfie was full of encouragement to him, and Stan noted that he would see the old man alright when everything was sorted.

`Good luck,' said Alfie, `whatever it is man, good luck and go steady.' They shook hands and Stan went back home. He packed a small plastic cup for water, and a small-lidded plastic storage box with corn in – just a little, he didn't want the bird to be too well fed to fly tomorrow night. Then he packed his clothes into a neat rucksack – he didn't need much – and put all the paperwork into its outside zip pocket.

Then he went to the computer.

Vondelspark. Amsterdam. Tomorrow night – Friday – 6 p.m. Be on time. Carry your mobile.

Stan sent the e-mail with a flourish, before closing up the computer. He went downstairs and rang the mobile number that he had for Jan, taking care to programme the phone so that his own number stayed anonymous. Jan picked up on the third ring, his thieving voice instantly recognisable. Stan hung up, smiling, and pleased that everything was in order. Then he simply waited for Doc to come at a quarter past eleven to catch the one o'clock ferry from Hull. So far so good.

*

Jan van Deuzen was sweating. It was twelve o'clock Holland time. He had held the diamond and it was a beauty. Allan intercepted it at the point when he should have been putting the laser identification mark on it, which of course he neglected to do. He brought it to Jan yesterday, at close of play. This morning Jan had to find a way to get into the Ladies' toilets without anyone seeing. This part was easy – there were toilets for the public, and toilets for the workers. As a head of security, Jan was entitled to check any of them on a random basis, and knew where there were cameras. It was a piece of cake to check each cubicle on pretence of looking for things and then to casually drop the package into a sanitary bin as he blocked the camera view.

Now he was watching the tourist party through the reinforced window between his office and the part of the building where the tourists walked around, oozing and aching at the diamonds on display, reading about the history, and watching through glass some of the hand polishers. Maria was there, one of the many women with whom Allan had once had a brief affair, although reading between the lines, it seemed that Allan was in a more settled relationship with someone now. Maria was trustworthy because of her own shady past and her need to earn some money. She had no idea of the worth of what she would be carrying, and would be delighted to pick up her two hundred euros. Jan turned away at the sound of his mobile ringing. He answered it, but the line went immediately dead and the phone indicated that the call was from an unknown number. He didn't watch the exit of the group – he knew that the chances of a search were slim, but they existed nevertheless. It was like this last time, but Thursdays were busy because there was a delivery, and the factory on the look-out for bigger heists than this one. He had read the latest e-mail, and his sense of helplessness had grown by the minute. What the hell would happen if the lift went pear shaped? The rest he had some control of, but for this part he was dependent on Maria and the security team. It was too much.

*

The ferry port was medium busy. There was the usual security to go through, but the lads had nothing to hide. They had to open their boot, to declare the purpose of their visit, but everything was in order. Stan showed them the papers for the pigeon, which the lads had named Ruby, and had to pay twenty quid for it as if it were a family pet, because they hadn't declared the pigeon on their ticket request.

`Didn't know it wanted a bloody seat!' Frank was unusually incensed.

They were on a sea cat and so the crossing was only a few hours. Once the car was locked up with the pigeon safely in the boot, watered and lightly fed, they went for some lunch. One beer each, but no one wanted much as they needed to be fresh for the drive from Rotterdam to Amsterdam. Once they'd eaten, they went on deck. Stan relished the brisk winds, which whipped across the lovely blue-skied day, and enjoyed the sense of openness all around him.

The arrival at Rotterdam generated an air of excitement. Akbar was to be first driver. Stan sat in the front next to him, navigating from his well-studied Auto route map. They reckoned on about a two-hour drive, and once out of the mêlée of the port exit roads, began to relax and enjoy the sights around them, commenting on the flatness, the way that all the houses had lofts, the intermittent tulip and tomato greenhouses.

`It's awesome. It's so different.' Stan was riveted. Doc munched a sandwich which he bought on the ferry, and Frank was lightly snoring, his long legs curled up to one side and his head lolling. One pink and one red sock were visible below his trouser hems.

It seemed like no time till they got to the outskirts of the city, and dusk was just falling. They stopped once for fuel and Frank woke up to take over the driving. Stan had made step-by-step directions of how to reach their hotel, and they had a smooth ride of it right until the very end when they missed the street and had to drive around a block to relocate it. But this was nothing, and when they reached their hotel, they were delighted with themselves. They had chosen to be near the Vondelspark, overlooking it in fact, and were more than satisfied with its price and its proximity to bars and restaurants. Stan made it clear that they wouldn't go right into town tonight – for one thing, they needed to keep their wits about them, and for another, Evie might see them. Unlikely, but it would be silly to blow things now.

They showered and went to the small hotel bar, where they could loosen up and have a few beers. Then they nipped out to the nearest restaurant, a small cosmopolitan affair where they opted for ribs and chips. Then they turned in for the night, after checking that Ruby was okay in her box in the boot, and that she had enough water. All the men were happy to be in their beds, and particularly excited at the range of adult programmes available on TV. In reality, though, once he had flicked through, Stan was asleep in seconds.

*

At seven o'clock on that Thursday evening, Jan and Allan met in a bar in Utrecht. Allan was still furious. He had got the diamond from Maria, but there was no joy, just a claustrophobic feeling of frustration.

`What a bloody travesty,' Allan shouted, then lowered his voice to a whisper. `Well I tell you what, you may be on your own tomorrow for the meet, but I'll be very bloody near you, and the minute those tossers are out of public view, I'll bloody show them.'

`D'you really think that's such a good idea, Allan?'

`Well I might not get my money back, but they're not exactly going to go to the police, man, are they? Not while they stand to get the egg.' Allan was hissing now.

Jan's heart rate was up, and he felt those unwelcome stomach gripes again. Jan had never been in a fight, although he had had others do dirty work for him before. He was turning as yellow as he felt.

`Where's your bloody loud mouth now?' snarled Allan. `Come on, let's get this sorted.' He knocked back his beer in one, and the

275

two men made their way to the toilet. There Allan handed over the beautiful diamond, protected in the toilet tissue and now inside a little velvet bag. `You wait till tomorrow,' hissed Allan, `I'll show them, believe me, those bastards will be nursing bruises tomorrow night. And they won't know what hit them, because they'll never know it was me.' The men left the Gents' toilet and went their separate ways.

Jan got home earlier than expected. He called for his wife, hoping for some solace; she was upstairs and he ran up to find her. She was in the bedroom, and Jan was surprised to find her going through her clothes upstairs yet again. What was the matter with her? She'd already packed once, how much stuff did she need for a girls' weekend? Anja started at Jan's entrance.

`You're earlier than I thought,' she said, and quickly came to brush his cheek with her lips. `Supper's in the oven.' Then, almost as an afterthought, `I just can't make my mind up what to take. I don't want to be too overdressed, or too underdressed. So I thought I'd better take a bigger case and cater for everything.' She smiled at him, and something was not quite right in her demeanour, but Jan had no energy to find out what was wrong at this moment. He went downstairs, grunted at his children, and put out his supper, only to find that he had no appetite. Then he poured a large whisky and went into his study to ring his mother.

`Yes, darling,' she said, `of course the children can stay. Shall I pick them up from school and then you can bring some clothes round later?' Jan could do better than that: he told his mother that he had a late meeting, so it would be great if she could use her spare key and come back with the boys to pick up what they wanted to on their way to her house. She was a keen grandmother, and so said yes. Good. At least Jan wouldn't have to worry about any of that until Sunday.

He sat and drank his whisky, and stared out at the darkening sky for what seemed like a very long time. A very long time indeed.

*

276

Friday morning dawned bright and clear, and by ten o'clock, Stan, Frank, Akbar and Doc had had breakfast and were out and about in the Vondelspark. They took a good walk around, looking for park benches, trees, any place that seemed like it might be suitable for the drop. The park was beautiful. By midday, it was filled with people enjoying the May sunshine. There were mothers with children, women on their own with books, old men walking dogs, couples lolling lazily on the grass, groups of people sitting round, some smoking big fat cigarettes. There were skaters and cyclists, and the hum of relaxed activity made for an atmosphere of pleasures and friendliness. The lads found two possible positions where they could leave the pigeon. One was in a hollow in a tree, and the other wedged under a bin by a park bench. It seemed that both were visible from the hotel bedroom. Frank was sent to check this out, and when he was back in the hotel, he rang Doc's mobile to confirm. He considered the tree to be a better bet. It could be seen from the bedroom, but was just off the path and so offered a little cover. It was important that no one find the boxed pigeon before Jan, and that he could tie the bag on in seclusion. Good. Stan committed it to memory, noting the landmarks around it, and counted the paces between the tree and the park gates as he left. This needed to be a smooth operation.

At two o'clock, Frank rang Jan and spoke in the heaviest whisper he could muster, while the others sat around him, watching and listening.

`Hello?' Jan's voice sounded edgy.

`Jan. You have a package for us.'

`Ah. Yes.'

`Okay. Listen carefully. Be at the west gate of the Vondelspark. Tonight. Six o'clock. Have your phone with you. Come alone.'

Before Jan could reply, Frank hung up. The tension was palpable, and the lads were each mentally running through the rest of the day's plan, rehearsing their part thoroughly, imagining what could go wrong, willing everything to go right. This was the biggest gamble that any of them had ever taken.

277

They played cards to while away the afternoon, and drank tea and coffee. At five o'clock, they were too twitchy to play anymore, itching to be doing things, to be ready to move. Each man packed his bag, double-checking for forgotten belongings, and Akbar and Frank took the bags down to the car. When they came back up, they brought the boxed pigeon. Doc held it while Stan fitted the leather straps to its leg and around its neck; they were attached to the small leather pouch which had a zip and a tiny lock, and which now rested neatly on Ruby's chest. Then they put the pigeon back in the box, and the box in a plastic bag with holes dotted in. Then they put an empty plastic bottle on the top and a scrumpled up chocolate wrapper, so that it would look like rubbish. As soon as it was five thirty, Stan made to leave the room. The others were looking at him expectantly, and Akbar nodded. Stan needed to get the pigeon in place in case Jan van Clevershite arrived early. They knew that it wasn't impossible that he'd have heavies with him, and were keen to avoid that. When they got back to England, assuming all was successful, they would be sending one final e-mail with a warning that if violence befell any of them, the recording would be exposed. For now, they would just be careful.

Stan went down the stairs, and the other three watched in fascination as he came into view and walked to the West Gate of the park. He sauntered casually along the path until he passed the first bench, and then went left to the large oak tree. He was just in view as he sat down for a minute or two, his back against the trunk. When he stood up, the bag was no longer with him, and he walked back the way he went as casually as he could. He was back in the hotel room by a quarter to six. Then they waited, on tenterhooks.

They saw nothing of significance for ten minutes, but then Doc shouted out.

`Bloody hell, that's that Allan, isn't it?'

Sure enough, Allan was walking through the gate and turned to the right, walking along swinging a baseball bat, wearing a baseball hat as if he was out for a game in the park. He moved to

278

the first cluster of trees on the right and leaned against one, then lit up a cigarette. This must mean that Jan was close behind. Stan raised his eyebrows at the others. They were so tense that they could hardly talk. At one minute to six, Jan arrived and stood at the West Gate, looking anxiously all around him.

`Okay,' said Stan, `let's go.' He took out his mobile phone and dialled the preset number.

`Jan.' said the voice on the other end.

`Okay. Now start walking into the park on the central path. That's it. Keep walking till you've passed the bench.' Jan was obeying instructions, looking nervously from left to right, whether for them or for Allan the lads couldn't tell. He was clearly very uncomfortable. Good.

`Okay, now go over the grass to that big oak tree. No, the oak tree. Yes, that's it. Go behind it and you'll see a plastic bag.'

`Look,' said Akbar, `that Allan guy is moving across.' There he was, trying to hide under the baseball cap, scouring the area around him, doubtless wondering where they were. What a clod; even if they were going to pick up the diamond in person, he should at least have stayed out of sight. Jan meanwhile had hit the spot and seen the plastic bag.

`Okay, now look in the plastic bag.' They saw Jan taking out the rubbish, and then his manner changing. He had found the pigeon. Stan continued to speak, very calmly yet with a hoarseness to his voice so that it didn't quite sound like his, and was very clear about the instructions. `Open the box with care, and put the pigeon egg in the pouch. Be careful, and be very quick.' Another few seconds passed, while they watched Jan manoeuvring. When he raised his head, Stan continued.

`Let it go. Now.' Jan looked shocked. `Now, Jan, unless you want to be in prison for a very long time.' Jan shook himself, then he threw the pigeon into the air, and up it flew, soaring away, sluggish at first, then gaining lift and speed, and before they knew it, she was out of sight. Then they saw Jan moving back toward the path, still saying nothing into his mouthpiece, but looking disturbed as Allan began to run up to him. Time to sign off.

'Cheers, Jan, and remember – no hanky panky.' And with that Stan pressed the red button on Doc's phone to end the call, and all four of them moved swiftly to the stairs, downstairs to the car park, and before they knew it, Frank was driving them away and Stan was sitting in the front seat with his map and directions, and suddenly they were laughing.

'Jesus wept,' said Doc.

'Can you bloody believe it? Fantastic!' Akbar was almost whooping.

'Brill. Let's hope that the pouch stays on and that the pigeon gets to Franz, hey?' Stan was excited yet couldn't count his chickens yet. The lads subdued themselves a little as they rushed on into the evening, each minute taking them further away from the scene of the crime.

*

Jan was totally bewildered. He was surprised at how shaken up he felt. He had been nervous as to what Allan might do to the English fanciers. He had no idea where they were, but had assumed that he would be dropping the diamond off, and they would pick it up. Now he was gobsmacked at what had happened. They had made a total fool out of him, using a pigeon. The bastards.

Allan was catching up with him now near the path, his face red, his brow sweaty.

`What the fuck is going on?' he demanded. `Where were they?'

`They're not here.' Jan sounded defeated.

`What do you mean, they're not here? They must be here. Where's the diamond?'

`The diamond's gone. They left a pigeon. I had to put it in a pouch they had attached to it. A bloody racing pigeon. It's on its way home.'

Allan was incredulous.

`You can't be serious? You put it in a pouch on a pigeon? Surely you at least got the ring number?'

Jan shook his head miserably. `It didn't have a ring on.'

`It must have had a ring on. All the racers have rings on, they have to.'

`Well, it didn't. I'm telling you, it didn't.'

Allan stared at Jan, not knowing what to do next. He couldn't believe that they had been outsmarted by the English lads. He had been so looking forward to venting his anger on them, maybe even taking the diamond back, although he hadn't let Jan know this last. He raised his baseball bat and smacked it against a tree.

`Stop it.' Jan was starting to sound angry now. `People will look.'

`So let them.' But Allan knew that Jan was right. He needed to be calm. And even in his fury, he was beginning to admire the way that this had been pulled off. The English lads have outsmarted them.

Just as he outsmarted Jan. For Allan had smuggled not one diamond out of the factory, but two, the second a tiny affair for which Jan, not he, will have to account. Jan may have been head of security, but Allan was pretty nifty with IT himself, and he had covered himself with a small insurance. Not a big rock that will be immediately missed, just one that will net him fifty thousand Euros, and he had his buyer lined up for next week. When he would be some way away from here with his lover. And Jan didn't know this either. When Allan remembered these facts, he calmed down surprisingly quickly. The English were not the only ones to make a fool out of Jan, and this was more than a little compensation.

`What a farce.' He gave one great, last sigh.

Jan looked at Allan, and saw that the peak of his anger was past. Jan himself was not so much angry as crestfallen. He needed a drink.

`Come on, let's go. How about I meet you in the club at home. I could do with going out. Maybe pick up some skirt.'

The two men were walking out of the park now, towards their cars. Allan shook his head.

`No, man, I've got plans for the weekend. I'm already late.'

281

Jan nodded. It would be some woman, the woman whom Allan has been seeing for a while. Good luck to him. Their mood pacified, so by the time that they were at their cars they were sharing what Jan imagined to be a companionable silence. He turned to Allan.

`Okay, mate. Look,' he began sheepishly, `I'll make this up to you. There'll be another chance. And I won't let you down again.'

Allan grunted, and the men shook hands, a somewhat diffident handshake, but a handshake nonetheless.

`I'll see you on Monday then.' Jan was beginning to settle down.

`No, I'll not be in. I've got some leave. Booked it a while ago. Thought it would be a good time to get away. You know.' Allan was finding it difficult to look Jan in the eye.

`Okay. Have a great time.'

`Sure I will. And Jan -' Allan finally raised his eyes - `take care.'

And with that, the two men parted company. On the drive home, Jan was thinking that this last was decent of Allan, given how much he, Jan van Deuzen, mastermind extraordinaire, had messed up the plan this time. He would make it up to Allan, and before long they would be able to find another gem, maybe in a few months' time, and this time there would be no bragging. No sir, Jan would not be fooled again.

By the time he got home, he began to anticipate that the weekend might be fine after all. He had in some good whisky, he had new DVDs to watch. That was all he could cope with tonight. He reached his comfortable home and drove through the electronically controlled doors into the garage. He was glad that Anja was away, he didn't need any questions or sympathy tonight.

Once in he went straight to the bathroom and with each garment that he took off, he felt the layers of humiliation, frustration and despondency lifting. By the time he was scrubbed up, he felt almost energetic. So it was even more of a shock when he went into the bedroom to dress and there, on the bed, was a letter from Anja. How unusual.

He had to read it twice, for he was incredulous. No. This couldn't be true. She has left. She won't be back for two weeks, when they could talk practicalities. She was so sorry. Yes, there was someone else. And she was so sorry about that too, and that it should be someone whom he has regarded as a friend for all these years. But she was sure that it will work out, and that, in time, they can all be friends.

Jan van Deuzen was sitting on his best quality king sized satin dressed bed and suddenly, from within the flood of rage which was coursing through his veins, he realised that he was howling like a baby..

*

It was quite late when the lads reached Franz's house, and the sky was just dark. It took longer than they thought to get there, due to heavy traffic leaving Amsterdam and then one wrong turning. Franz lived out in the sticks, his small holding a large white building, surrounded by various outbuildings. He was expecting the lads and made them welcome. The pigeon was home, and they all heaved a sigh of relief.

`Yours, I think,' said Franz, and handed the unopened pouch to Stan. Then he fetched brandy, and each of the men took a small glass. They raised them in unison, and the hot liquid was welcome and reviving. It had been a heck of an afternoon.

The lads didn't stay long at Franz's. He was more than helpful, and when they offered him money by means of thanks, he declined.

`No my friends, not necessary. As far as I am concerned, I just wanted to thank you for bringing back my pigeon. Alfie told me you're alright. I am not involved in your reasons for being here.'

And that was that, their business was concluded and the lads didn't linger. The drive back to town was smooth, and remarkably subdued. Not until they were checked into their next hotel, a sight more up market than their last, and secure in a locked room, did Stan take out the pouch. They were all holding their breath as he removed the package within it, still wrapped in tissue paper. And there it was. One diamond, bigger than they had imagined, shinier than they could have ever thought. It was almost time for celebration. But only almost. One more step to go, and it could be the most dangerous yet. Stan locked the precious gemstone in his hotel safe, and the four men took to their beds, exhausted yet excited, for as much night's sleep as they could get.

Saturday dawned before they know it. By ten o'clock, they were back out on the streets and driving to the outskirts of town to the address provided for them by Alfie's son Steven. It wasn't hard to find, and they were there in good time for their appointment. They decided that only Stan and Frank would go to make the exchange. When they rang the bell of the forbidding looking door, it was opened by a man of about fifty, fit looking with silver hair and gold rimmed glasses.

`D.M.?' Stan asked.

`Ah. Come on in. You have something for me, I believe.' Stan nodded, and they followed the man inside. They didn't know his full name, they didn't need to.

Stan handed over the pouch.

`One moment please. Take a seat. I will be back.' There was no option but to trust him, and Stan and Frank sat. They waited for five, maybe seven minutes. Then the man came back, a large smile on his face.

`Congratulations. You have a beauty here. I have a customer waiting. He will not be disappointed.'

Stan's heart raced.

`How much?' he asked, his throat surprisingly dry.

`Your share? I can give you ninety thousand English pounds. This is after my cut.'

Ninety thousand pounds. Stan and Frank looked at each other with disbelief.

`Oh aye. Oh aye, mate, that'll do fine.'

The next moments were hazy for Stan; the man went to a back room and returned in minutes with a huge envelope stuffed with notes.

`It is all there. You can check.'

`You're alright mate, you were highly recommended.' Frank did the talking, and Stan nodded assent. No point distrusting now: they'd either done it or they hadn't.

`So that is all.' The man nodded at them. This was not a good place to hang around, not for any of them. As soon as the lads were gone, a courier would take the diamond straight off these premises and on to its next stop. And soon, everyone would be happy.

Frank put the envelope into a canvas rucksack which he'd brought with him specially, looped it over his shoulder and hung on to the strap with his hand, so that the bag was near his front. He and Stan left quickly, got into their waiting car and Akbar was instantly speeding back to the hotel. Once again, nothing was opened until they were safely ensconced in Stan's room, and at that point, when they opened the bag and took out the cash, they began to believe that they'd pulled this off.

`Holy Moses.' Akbar was wide eyed.

`Bloody Norah.' Doc was grinning from ear to ear.

`Fuck me sideways.' Frank was unusually profane.

`Blimey. We did it.' Stan was still dazed, although daring now to breathe more fully, to let a huge grin begin to cross his face. `We only went and bloody did it. We're fucking rich, lads, we're fucking rich.' He took a wad of the cash and raised it to his lips. This was the fruit of the deed that will change his life forever.

`We need to divvy up.' He looked round excitedly.

`Hang on a sec. Let's get some beers.' They all nodded at Akbar's suggestion.

`And some sandwiches.' Doc was hungry.

By the time room service arrived, the bag of money was in the wardrobe. Akbar poured the beers, and Doc started on the sandwiches.

`Bloody marvellous,' he pronounced, his mouth full of beef and horseradish on malted brown. Frank raised his glass.

`To us,' he said, and all followed suit.

Once the first beer and plateful of sandwiches was gone, Stan took the bag out again, marvelling at its contents, and at all that had happened. Perhaps now he and Evie could get back on track. `So, let's see then. Ninety thousand between four of us. I make that just over twenty two thousand each. And all our expenses. Fantastic.'

Doc coughed and he, Akbar and Frank exchanged glances. 'Well, not necessarily, Stan. The lads and I have been talking.'

Stan looked up, without comprehension.

`Well, the way we see it is this. You've done all the leg work for this, it's your baby.' Stan began to protest, but Doc held his hand up and silenced him. `Think about it, Stan. It was your pigeons that were stolen. You did all the masterminding.' Stan's chest swelled. `You learned the computer, you set it all up with Alfie and Steven, sorted out the maps, everything really. All we've done is come along for the ride. We think the money should be yours.'

Stan was totally taken aback. He might have done most of the work, but he couldn't have done any of it if he didn't have the support of his friends.

`No, Doc, I can't do that. I couldn't have done this without you. We share it. That was always the deal.'

`No, it wasn't, Stan, ' asserted Frank. `We never worked out what the deal was. And Doc's right. We don't need this as much as you do. We're just glad to see you alright. I don't want any money. I mean it.' Frank set a particularly stubborn look in his eyes and directed it to Stan.

`To be honest, Stan, I'm alright for money,' Doc went on. `I've a good income, a house that's paid for and worth a bloody fortune, I should think. And I've got money in the bank, and a good pension. I don't really spend what I've got already, not with Maggie being as she is.' He flushed slightly. `The truth is, and I'm ashamed to say this, the truth is that if I take any of this, it will just go into an account and stay there till I die. I don't want that. I want it to make a difference.'

Stan nodded, overwhelmed. He didn't know what to say. `And I'd have to hide it, Stan,' said Akbar. `Jazz knows I'm a bit of a lad, but I can't take twenty grand home. She'd have a fit. And anyway, Jazz's family are wealthy, and that will all come to us one day. You have it, mate, do the things you want to. That's what I want.'

Frank assented.

`Listen to them, Stan. It's all true.'

In the end, Stan insisted that Akbar have five thousand to invest for his children. He could put it in some account and reveal it later in his life and pretend he'd saved it up. He insisted also that Frank take five thousand for the family that he keeps so private. Doc insisted on nothing. Stan was choked.

And he was better off than he had ever been. He had, give or take, the princely sum of eighty thousand pounds. His life was on the turn. His thoughts pleased him. The small mortgage would be paid off, cash. There would be a holiday. And he'd start a business, maybe transporting small livestock. Stan gave all of his friends an uncharacteristic hug. He was rich in more ways than one.

Then it was more beer, and suddenly they were all tired, worn out with the excitement of it all, and agreed that they'd rest and meet at seven o'clock in the bar. Tonight, they'd go out on the town, and on this occasion, it would definitely be Stan's treat. He just had one errand to do first, and when the others left his room, he went to the safe, pocketed five thousand to change to Euros, and went shopping.

*

Once showered, the four men met in the hotel bar, and had one beer each. Electricity tingled in the air, on edge with something unknown and vibrant.

`Come on then, lads.' Doc stood up. `Let's get going, let's go and give them girls a thrill.'

Doc's paunch had been gently cajoled into his smartest jeans. The others stood to join him, precious money secreted in tight pockets, anticipation running wild.

`Whoa hey! Look out girls, the lads are here. I dunno what yours'll be like, Frank, but mine'll be gorgeous.'

Stan laughed at Akbar's exuberance, while Doc grumped and Frank smiled, those keen eyes missing nothing. A young Dutchman walked past and gave them a bored look; more Englishmen abroad. They made their way to the Leidse Plein, eyes darting, brains processing to take it all in. Stan was transfixed. He'd never seen anything like this city, with so much buzz. People hanging out on the streets, but not like hanging out in Middlesbrough, or Redcar. These were young people, middle-aged people, all sorts of people in designer gear, well thought out combats and matching hair-dos, buskers in carefully torn dungarees and jeans, with pierced noses and ears, studs in their eyebrows. So many sights, everyone here seeming to have one sole common aim, to have a good time. Lively, laughing, relaxed. No one looking aggressive or threatening. Two entertainers with shaved heads were throwing burning juggle sticks to each other, talking to the crowd in cheeky English. Everyone looked confident. A woman walked past, in the shortest yellow skirt that Stan had ever seen. He let out an involuntary breath of lust, in tandem with the others.

`Phwoar.' Frank was uncommonly vocal.

Akbar groaned. `Oh aye, I could definitely manage that.' Almost unconsciously, the four men formed a hungry pack and followed the woman for twenty yards before they became aware that their tongues were hanging out, like dogs after a rabbit. They laughed, and Doc stopped the troop.

`So are we gonna find this wacky baccy shop, then?'

`Aye. I'm on.' Akbar took out his information guide complete with map, and looked at signs on streets. `We'll go to that one where they do ready rolled joints, see what it's like.'

They walked up the little street to the right. The early evening sun was warm, and appropriate to the gaiety outside every restaurant. There was Indonesian food, Mexican food, Indian food, American, Greek, Italian, setting out their tempting wares and smells. Akbar shouted excitedly.

`It's there, look, Rookies.' He pointed to a modest looking café with a blue and pink sign outside, with a seemingly unlikely picture of cherubim, a celestial vision in clouds. Two women were sitting outside, giggling. Stan felt excited and a bit nervous. He sat down near the café window.

`Who's going?'

`I will, Doc, you come and help me with the beers.'

Doc and Akbar disappeared into the dark of the café, and Stan looked around at the constant stream of people, families, couples, individuals, all conveying certain vibrancy. He was captivated by the two women in front of him, who were sitting at an angle so that he caught their side view. One was strawberry blonde, longhaired, looking very mellow. She was gazing at the street, and gently caressing one arm with her other hand, softly, tenderly to herself. The other woman looked taller, bright copper hair, a half smile playing around her lips. She sipped her beer and said something to her friend. They both laughed, the sound of their humour and good spirits tinkling in the balmy evening. They looked relaxed, attractive in an unusual sort of way. Stan felt a stir of curiosity and desire. Then he thought of Evie. Has she ever been here? Where was she right now, having dinner with this mysterious friend of hers? He felt regret that they couldn't be here together, yet excited that soon he would be able to take her somewhere really wonderful. Doc and Akbar emerged from the café, beers in hand.

`Whoa hey.' Akbar was exuberant, and when he sat down, they looked at him expectantly.

`They've only got a fucking menu in there, for Christ's sake. Thai grass, Columbian grass, hash, ready rolled joints. I think this one said skunk, it's the house speciality. Or is it white widow? Can't remember now. Who wants to go first?'

Stan had never smoked dope before, and it seemed strange to be doing it in public. Doc surprised them all by being first to reach for the spliff.

`Give it here,' he said and took the little green canister in his hand. He undid the top and shook out a perfectly rolled joint,

289

which he lit up in the cup of his hand. He took three deep drags, and passed it on. Frank took just one and spluttered in an ungainly fashion. Stan was next – three drags like Doc, and managed to keep it down. Then Akbar, smoking as if it was his usual habit, drawing long and deep. And that was more or less it, just one more small drag for Doc and Stan, Frank waving it past. Akbar looked at him with concern.

`You know this is brilliant for your sex life, don't you?'

Frank looked back, steady gaze.

`So I'm told. I tried it one night you know at home, one of the lads down the pub gave me one. I was with a lovely lass, Hazel her name was. I sent her upstairs for a bath – get your bath, Hazel, I said, I'm coming up – and so I smoked this joint with a nice can of John Smiths. Then I had another can `cos the joint had made my mouth dry, and anyway I was enjoying the anticipation, so I finished that can and then had a third. By then I felt really relaxed, so I closed my eyes for five minutes. Next thing I know, it's two o'clock in the morning and I'm waking up with a hangover. I go up to Hazel, and she's lying across the bed in a short black satin nightie and hold up stockings, only she's flat out with her jaw on her chest and snoring. It wasn't the most sexual night of my life, I can tell you. So I don't think I'm too fussed to try it again.'

Stan laughed, and thought again of Evie, while looking at the two women beside them. He felt entranced, and suddenly wondered if he was staring. Nothing much seemed to matter to him now.

`I can see why people use this for pain control,' he said.

`There's a bloke comes in the club, old Arthur Glen, his missus has got MS. Swears by this stuff, you know, gets it off Jimmy Reid. Shame they can't have it like over here, really.' He caught Akbar's eye and they started to laugh.

`What's so funny?' Doc looked grumpy. Stan laughed more, setting Akbar off. The two women looked at each other and began to giggle too. One of them, the strawberry blonde, turned around, catching Stan's eye for a nano second, causing them both to laugh more. Akbar nudged Stan, Doc looked slightly less grumpy than usual, and Frank smiled largely and benignly all round.

'Yes, this should definitely be available on the NHS. If ever you were ill, this would certainly chill you out.'

The two women got up, the copper haired one stumbling slightly. They were both still giggling and hanging onto each other's arms. They turned and looked at the men.

'Enjoy yourself, don't be smoking too much now.'

They sauntered off down the street, teetering and tittering. Stan felt wistful. What would it take to get up and follow them, ask them for a drink, chat to them? He didn't even have to get off with them, it was just an urge to know them, to have the company of women. They looked so cool, so carefree. Stan sighed. Akbar interrupted as usual.

'Phwoar, look at the arse on that one. Couldn't 'arf, eh?'

Stan assented, because yes, he could. He was genuinely tempted by the company, but then no way would he have turned down the chance of sex as well. Except of course he already had, through passivity. And anyway, the women were only being friendly, they hadn't really offered anything. He was ahead of himself.

'Give 'em the best two minutes of their lives, hey?' Stan said the right thing, and they laughed conspiratorially. As they relaxed, so the full impact of their day's work began to sink in. Frank allowed himself a chuckle. The others looked expectantly. His eyes swept their faces.

'Ninety thousand quid. Ninety thousand blooming quid. Give or take.'

Stan laughed, thought yet again about Evie – he'd give her such a surprise. He ran through it again. Pay off the last fifteen thousand on the mortgage. Some cash in the bank for him to set up a little business, yes, importing and exporting small scale livestock – there must be a lot of demand for that kind of carriage – and then the holiday of their dreams. If it isn't too late. The Seychelles, she'd love something like that, or Goa, he's heard

291

that's nice, or even Florida or something. He was on top of the world. At last, he's made a success of something.

And he'd got the diamond ring that he bought earlier, stashed now in the hotel. Just one, elegant, pristine diamond. Evie deserved it. The best. The subtle blue hue of the stone was just apparent, simply set in nine carat gold. Nothing fancy, but classy, a precious jewel for Evie's long slim fingers. She would wear it well. Stan puffed up his chest.

`We did it then, we did it.' Doc raised his glass. `Bloody easy. Shame we didn't ask for more. Skol, lads, skol.' They toasted themselves.

`Tell you what,' said Frank, `I could murder some food. I suddenly feel really munchy.'

`Thought you'd never ask.' Doc looked delighted, suddenly ravenous for interesting tastes and textures. As one, the lads downed their beers and stood up, moving towards the bigger restaurants, laughing and shouting along the street. Now they were safe, and could risk behaving like real Englishmen abroad.

They chose a restaurant overlooking the canal, Speisegraacht. It was big and busy. A young waiter seated them by the window, at their request. He brought the menu and they ordered extravagantly. A plate of traditional Dutch starters. Steaks, chips and mayonnaise. A bottle of bubbly. Four more beers. The skill of the waiters amazed them, holding full trays on the flat of their hands right up above the crowds. One young woman was carrying about ten glasses on hers, and Stan 's eyes were drawn like magnets to her breasts, which were straining against her silky top.

`Oi.' Doc poked him. `Get 'em back in, behave yourself.'

They laughed, and when the food came, they ate hungrily and noisily, enjoying the pleasures that money could buy. When they got back out to the streets, it was nailed on that now they'd walk up to the red light area. They couldn't believe how much porn was on show, and visited shop after shop, marvelling at the videos and DVDs, revolted by the excesses of sexual practice that were openly displayed, and laughing at some of the gadgets, like

292

the `pocket fanny' they could get to carry around, made of rubber with coarse hair on. Stan may have been sexually frustrated, but thank God he wasn't that desperate. As it neared midnight, the four men turned into the Achterburgwahl, the sound of their feet firm and loud on the wet pavement, the blood in their veins coursing with energy, engorging their blood vessels, ready to lift them like the corks of a champagne bottle. They were rich in every sense, they were free, and they were in the heart of the red light district. They passed a prostitute's window, and stopped, feeling furtive. A black woman, Afro Caribbean looking, wearing nowt but a red feather boa, stood in profile with one leg up on a chair. She was large, beautiful, and intriguing. The lads were entranced, their breathing heavy in the dark night.

`By,' said Frank, `By. I could give her one. I've never been with a black woman.'

Akbar looked at him, pityingly, but the voice that surprised them in the darkness was Doc's. `Well that's 'cos you've lived such a narrow little life, you daft sod. My first ever lover was black, you know, and she was fabulous.' He sounded nostalgic. `There's more to women than them in Middlesbrough, you know Frank. You want to widen your horizons, lad, widen your horizons.'

They moved on. They saw a tall slim redhead in leather panties, looking bored. Her face was lined with weariness, and she seemed too tired to make much effort. Stan laughed.

`Nice legs, but she's got a face a dog wouldn't lick.' Doc gave him a look, then laughed despite himself. They moved on to see two Thai girls caressing each other. They looked far too young to be out at night, let alone in an Amsterdam window. Aroused despite themselves, the men walked on to where three men were entranced at a window, and stood just behind them, feet steady, arms folded. And they were instantly transfixed by the woman within.

Stan looked straight at her eyes at first, and was stunned into an inner silence. His heart raced with shock, fear, and excitement. The woman looked back at him, and they stonewalled. He

293

became aware that someone had gasped, one of the lads. Stan couldn't move his eyes away – she was absolutely gorgeous. He let himself note her whole body, each little piece, the shapely mouth, the elegant neck, the full breasts, the flat stomach, creamy thighs and long fit legs. Then he returned to the eyes. Evie was gorgeous. He had no idea what she was doing in a prostitute's window, and strangely for now it didn't matter, but she was gorgeous and he wanted her – not just sex, but *her* – and in those seconds, that's all he needed to know.

Twenty three
World Turning

Card XXI – The World

The World is the last card in the Fool's Journey. It represents those moments that you have in life when things and people work in unison, that moment when everything makes sense, and the realisation that all things have happened for a reason, and now join up in wholeness.

Or in Evie's case, the realisation that she has her heart's desire, to be seen as just as important and beautiful as a Birmingham Roller pigeon, to be appreciated in every way, and to feel a connection to dear old Stan. What happens next when you see the World in a tarot reading always depends on the situation, but in this moment, it feels just great.

So now here I am, and I have to say that I've got a bit of thrill out of it, but I can see already how it could be boring doing this forever. I like the outfit; it makes me feel good. I like my body, and I think it's fair to say that my attire is rather tasteful for all that it's revealing. I have taken off my gown, and I am of course in underwear, made of high quality black satin. I have chosen a basque, which ends just below my nipples. My breasts are pushed up and emphasised, though not so squeezed that they've lost their softness. The basque is tightly laced all down the front, and I want my audience to imagine its undoing so that my breasts become released and available. Its material ends above my pubis, and I've chosen pants which are high cut at the side and thonged at the back. The rich satin material lends subtlety to this, so that the thong can only be discerned when I move, through crossing my legs or arranging myself between the sofa and the footstool. My stockings are sheer and pale, deliberately chosen to contrast with the basque and which, in my opinion, suggest a hint of innocence alongside the blatancy. I'm wearing my black ankle strap wedged leather shoes. It's a typical tart's outfit but with class, and I love it.

It's a busy night outside, and three men are now looking in at me. I look straight back and shift slightly, opening my legs just a little and then crossing them tight and high to reveal the side of my buttock. I feel delightfully exposed yet in control. They have caught the tantalising ultimate glimpse, and they are interested. For a moment, so am I. One of them, the one in the middle, is attractive in a young Robert Redford sort of a way, and I imagine that his hands are sexy. Dangerous. I smile bountifully, and rise from my chair. I bend over to pick up my gown, which is made in oriental silk of deep mulberry. My rear view is designed and delivered for their pleasure, and I linger a moment, my G-string covering nothing, serving only to emphasise the cleft between my buttocks. I am powerful, very powerful, and am surprised that I feel aroused. I need to go from the window, to protect myself, for such power could make me very vulnerable. I don't yet know how far I will go, whether to pretend to be busy with someone else out back, or to really get busy with the trio. I buy time. I turn and stretch, and begin to drape the gown around my shoulders. I look towards the men. They are riveted, and one of them has his mouth open. More men appear behind them, looking over shoulders at my performance. There are four of them. Suddenly my eyes are locked with two others; even in the darkness, I can see their greenness, and the simultaneous lust and shock betrayed therein. I guess that I mirror the physiology. The man with the eyes is Stan.

I can't think immediately, but I do know that I'm wondering what to do. Frank, Akbar and Doc are there beside him, and for a second I'm tempted to wave, `oh, hello', as I might if I'd met them in the street in Middlesbrough. But I'm not on the 'Boro Road now; I'm masquerading as a prostitute in Amsterdam, with sod all clothes on. I'm entertaining seven men, and promising sex. The antique replica clock on the wall chimes once. I hold Stan's gaze. I can see the dilation of his pupils, even in the dark. Anything can happen now.

His eyes are beginning to rove over me, first down and then up. An outsider might imagine that he is giving me a quick once over. I, however, suddenly know different. I feel every vibration as his eyes touch first my shoulders, then my breasts, and I know that he is slowly undoing the laces of my basque. He is lingering now on the colour of my skin, the texture of my belly, and he is spellbound. Only when he is fully acquainted with each detail does he allow himself to travel to my pubis, catching the glimpse of soft hair, and savouring the possibilities that lie beneath it. My blood is rushing through my body with the movement of his eyes, and I am engorged with desire. He is caressing my thighs now, deliberately and sensually. He is sweeping softly to my ankles, and I feel his hot breath as it bathes the arches of my feet and comes to rest upon my toes.

In the upward movement of his eyes, I can feel the beating of Stan 's heart. He is aware of every detail of my plumage, every movement, every colour. He knows how to read the minutiae of my wantonness. He is noting every tiny change that I make, the

297

speed of my breath, the suffusion of blood to my skin. I am a little beauty, and he is thrilled. Our eyes re-engage. In my peripheral vision I see that the first group of men are motioning to each other, they are planning to move on. Akbar is saying something to Frank and Doc, and Stan begins to move his hand in a gesture to silence them. They have their hands in their pockets and their feet planted firmly on the ground. I exhale in a small flutter, as the lads admire Stan's stock. I hear a second chime of midnight somewhere in the background.

I don't know what is going to happen in the next minute or even the next second. I notice that the light of the moon is behind the men outside. There is, as Jack Donaldson had predicted, a little lunacy in the air. The chimes still resonate in the air around me. One thing I am sure of is that for the first time in years, Stan has seen me, the real Evie Cutler, both outside and in, and I have registered his interest. The next move will be his.

For the first time in a long time, I am optimistic.

By the same author

An Algarve Affair

Izzie Childs is turning fifty, wondering what happened to feminism, finding herself caught up in the conundrum of being both a smart post-feminist woman, and a little more obsessed than she'd like to be on issues of fat, looks and wrinkles. When she finds herself in Portugal for a month, ensconced in familiar and unfamiliar relationships and holding a twenty-first century version of Abigail's party, Izzie realises that despite a life of counselling and self-awareness, she is deep in mid-life crisis.

In this, the first of a trilogy, Izzie chronicles the inside story on the aging process, and begins to consider a future in which she integrates this with her feminist ideals of the past.

"Izzie's personal journey over a month in the Algarve is funny, charming and filled with insight. A wise, warm and intelligent story about growing up and growing older." Cassandra Parkin, author of *New World Fairy Tales* and *Lighter Shades of Grey*

You may also be interested by...

You may have noticed that Stan's chapters are opened with quotes from one of the hobby's greatest works of literature, *Winners with Spinners*. The author, Graham Dexter, also makes a cameo appearance at the Old Cocks Invitation Fly. His two most recent books are available on Kindle now!

50 Questions Answered for the Less Experienced Roller Flier is the perfect introduction to Birmingham Roller pigeons, now that you know something about those who are in the hobby.

50 Questions Answered for the More Experienced Roller Flier showcases the depths of 50 years' experience as a Rollerman and tackles some of the more in-depth questions that Birmingham Roller fliers might have.